PUBLIC–PRIVATE PARTNERSHIP MONITOR
BANGLADESH

DECEMBER 2022

ASIAN DEVELOPMENT BANK

Notes:
In this publication, "$" refers to United States dollars.
ADB recognizes "China" as the People's Republic of China; "Hong Kong" as Hong Kong, China; and "Korea" as the Republic of Korea.

On the cover: Efficient transport is essential to achieve higher levels of economic growth needed for sustainable poverty reduction. The Railway Sector Investment Program aims to improve the performance of the railway sector in Bangladesh. The distribution grids at Sirajganj Power Plant in northern Bangladesh as part of the Sustainable Power Sector Development Project funded by ADB to generate and distribute electricity to Dhaka and its surrounding areas. Students of class two attended a course at the Akhborpur Government Primary School in Mowlovibazar and Ragib Prodhan takes part in the welding training at the UCEP school under the Skills for Employment Investment Program (SEIP) in Chittagong (photos by M. R. Hasan and Abir Abdullah).

Cover design by Claudette Rodrigo.

Contents

Tables, Figures, and Box

Tables

Figures

Box

Foreword

We are pleased to present the *Public–Private Partnership Monitor—Bangladesh*, a detailed review of the current state of public–private partnership (PPP) enabling environment in selected countries in Asia and the Pacific.

Availability of adequate infrastructure is a measure of a country's ability to sustain its economic growth. For economies across Asia and the Pacific, provision of basic infrastructure services, including water, health, energy, transportation, and communications is an important public sector activity. As demand for infrastructure has increased faster than government budgets, the public sector has increasingly considered partnership with the private sector as an alternate modality for financing infrastructure.

The Asian Development Bank (ADB) estimates that Asia and the Pacific must spend $1.7 trillion a year on infrastructure until 2030 to maintain growth, meet social needs, and respond to the effects of climate change. That amount is expected to go up. The traditional sources of finance for infrastructure—the government's budgetary allocations—have not been enough to meet the demand. Prior to the coronavirus disease (COVID-19) pandemic, ADB estimated an annual infrastructure gap of $204 billion to be filled through private sector investment. That amount is also now expected to increase.

For the private sector, investment in infrastructure, whether through PPPs or otherwise, represents an investment avenue competing with various other investment options available. In order to compete, and to crowd in private capital into infrastructure, governments need to provide a conducive environment to adequately establish and protect the rights of the private sector, and the necessary support to ensure every asset brought to market provides returns that are commensurate with the risks.

The PPP Monitor provides the investor community with business intelligence on the enabling environment, policies, priority sectors, and deals to facilitate informed investment decisions. For ADB developing member countries (DMCs), the PPP Monitor serves as a diagnostic tool to identify gaps in their legal, regulatory, and institutional framework. ADB and other international development agencies can also benefit from the PPP Monitor as it could be useful in initiating dialogues to assess a country's readiness to tap PPPs as a means to develop and sustain its infrastructure.

Building on the success of the previous editions of the PPP Monitor, the new PPP Monitor is now being brought online to widen its reach. More countries will be continually added in the PPP Monitor, and it is expected to become a primary knowledge base for assessing a country's PPP environment for the government and the business community. The PPP Monitor features an interactive online version, which allows users to compare and contrast the key PPP parameters and features across the DMCs. The online version of the PPP Monitor may be accessed at http://www.pppmonitor.adb.org.

The PPP Monitor has been upgraded to provide a "one stop" information source, derived from a consolidation of (i) the previous PPP Monitor; (ii) leading PPP databases of multilateral development banks, such as the World Bank and the International Finance Corporation, and organizations like the Economist Intelligence Unit (Infrascope) and the Global Infrastructure Hub (InfraCompass); (iii) reports of a country's PPP unit; (iv) a country's legal framework; and (v) consultations with leading technical experts and legal firms as well as financial institutions.

The PPP Monitor includes more than 500 qualitative and quantitative indicators to profile the national PPP environment, the sector-specific PPP landscape (for eight identified infrastructure sectors), and the PPP landscape for local government projects. The COVID-19 pandemic has pushed social infrastructure into the forefront of policy and planning; hence, where possible, this PPP Monitor takes a bigger focus on social and municipal aspects like health, education, and affordable housing.

The PPP market in most of ADB DMCs is still at an emerging or developing stage, and continuous regulatory reforms and institutional strengthening are required to facilitate further private sector investment in infrastructure and to create a sustainable pipeline of bankable projects. Through the PPP Monitor, ADB continues to provide support for DMCs in addressing various infrastructure and PPP-related challenges, in developing sustainable infrastructure projects, and in delivering efficient and effective public services through PPPs. ADB also helps DMCs improve their investment climates, formulate sound market regulations, and build robust legal and institutional frameworks to encourage private sector participation in infrastructure through PPPs.

We hope that this PPP Monitor will pave the way for continued dialogue between the public and private sectors and stimulate the adoption of PPPs in the Asia and Pacific region.

F. Cleo Kawawaki
Head, Office of Public–Private Partnership
Asian Development Bank

Acknowledgments

The *Public–Private Partnership Monitor: Bangladesh* was prepared by the Asian Development Bank (ADB) Office of Public–Private Partnership (OPPP), in close coordination with the Bangladesh Resident Mission.

This effort has been led by Sanjay Grover, public–private partnership (PPP) specialist in the PPP Thematic Group Secretariat, who developed, refined, and streamlined the analytical framework for capturing the national, subnational, and sector PPP-related landscape that has been utilized in this document.

F. Cleo Kawawaki, head of OPPP, and Adrian Torres, chief of the PPP Thematic Group, have provided helpful guidance and unfailing support during the development of this PPP Monitor.

The PPP Monitor uses data published by the governments of ADB's developing member countries—on their official websites and in reports, publications, laws, and regulations—as well as data published by other multilateral development agencies and included in industry publications and databases such as those of the World Bank, Organisation for Economic Co-operation and Development, World Economic Forum, International Monetary Fund, Inframation Group, IJGlobal, Economist Intelligence Unit (Infrascope Index), Global Infrastructure Hub, TheGlobalEconomy.com, Bloomberg, S&P Global, Trading Economics, and the PPP Knowledge Lab.

ADB has partnered with CRISIL Infrastructure Advisory and Panapps Inc. CRISIL Infrastructure Advisory, led by Abhijeet Giri, shared its expertise and provided inputs in developing the PPP Monitor for Bangladesh, while Panapps Inc. has published this report online.

Nerinda P. Villones, and Carmelia Godoy have very capably led the management and coordination with the numerous contributors to this report. The contributions and review by Helen Steward, Amer A. Chowdhury, Mukta Malhotra, and Aura Vincencio Abon from OPPP; and by the Bangladesh PPP Authority—led by Ms. Sultana Afroz, secretary and CEO; Abdul Bashar, director general; Najmus Sayadat, director; and Anwar Hossain, director—were instrumental in the quality control of this document.

Several others provided help and support: Cyrel San Gabriel edited the report, Asiatype Inc. performed the typesetting, Joy Quitazol-Gonzalez proofread the page proofs, and Claudette Rodrigo designed the cover. April-Marie Gallega and Ayun Sundari of the Knowledge Support Division of ADB's Department of Communications provided guidance and assistance in the publication process.

Definition of Terms

Term	Definition
Public–private partnership (PPP)	Contractual arrangement between public (national, state, provincial, or local) and private entities through which the skills, assets, and/or financial resources of each of the public and private sectors are allocated in a complementary manner, thereby sharing the risks and rewards, to seek to provide optimal service delivery and good value to citizens. In a PPP, the public sector retains the ultimate responsibility for service delivery, although the private sector provides the service for an extended time. Within the Asian Development Bank operations, all contracts such as performance-based contracts (management and service contracts), lease–operate–transfer, build–own–operate–transfer, design–build–finance–operate, variants, and concessions are considered as various forms of PPP. Excluded are • contracts involving turnkey design and construction as part of public procurement (engineering, procurement, and construction contracts); • simple service contracts that are not linked to performance standards (those that are more aligned with outsourcing to private contractor staff to operate public assets); • construction contracts with extended warranties and/or maintenance provisions of, for example, up to 5 years post completion (wherein performance risk-sharing is minimal as the assets are new and need only basic maintenance); and • all privatization and divestures.
Affermage or lease contracts	Under a lease contract, the private sector developer is responsible for the service in its entirety and undertakes obligations relating to quality and service standards. Except for new and replacement investments, which remain the responsibility of the government contracting agency, the operator provides the service at his expense and risk. The duration of the leasing contract is typically 10 years and may be renewed up to 20 years. Responsibility for service provision is transferred from the public sector to the private sector, and the financial risk for operations and maintenance is borne entirely by the private sector operator. In particular, the operator is responsible for losses and for unpaid consumers' debts. Leases do not involve any sale of assets to the private sector.
Availability- or performance-based payments	Method of investment recovery in PPP projects, when payments to the private party are made by the government contracting agency over the lifetime of a PPP contract in return for making infrastructure or services available for use at acceptable and contractually agreed performance standards.
Best and final offer (BAFO)	An incentive mechanism provided by the government contracting agency to the private sector developer initiating a PPP project through the unsolicited proposal route (USP proponent) to be automatically shortlisted for the final bidding round and provide its best and final offer to match the other bidders' best offer.
Build–lease–transfer	A PPP type whereby a private sector developer is authorized to finance and construct an infrastructure or development facility, and upon its completion hands it over to the government contracting agency on a lease arrangement for a fixed period, after which ownership of the facility is automatically transferred to the government contracting agency.

continued on next page

continued from previous page

Term	Definition
Build–own–operate	A PPP type whereby a private sector developer is authorized to finance, construct, own, operate, and maintain an infrastructure or development facility from which the private sector developer is allowed to recover its total investment, operating and maintenance costs plus a reasonable return thereon by collecting tolls, fees, rentals, or other charges from facility users. Under this PPP type, the private sector developer, who owns the assets of the facility may assign its operations and maintenance to a facility operator.
Build–operate–transfer (BOT)	BOT and similar arrangements are a specialized concession in which a private firm or consortium finances and develops a new infrastructure project or a major component according to performance standards set by the government. Under the BOT arrangements, the private sector developer provides the capital required to build a new facility. Importantly, the private operator now owns the assets for a period set by contract—sufficient to give the developer time to recover investment costs through user charges.
Build–transfer	A PPP type under which the private sector developer undertakes the financing and construction of a given infrastructure or development facility and, after its completion, hands it over to the government contracting agency, which pays the private sector developer, on an agreed schedule, its total investments expended on the project, plus a reasonable rate of return thereon. This arrangement may be employed in the construction of any infrastructure or development project, including critical facilities that, for security or strategic reasons, must be operated directly by the government contracting agency.
Commercial close	Indicates the signing of the PPP contract between the government contracting agency and the identified private sector developer. Usually occurs after the terms and conditions of the draft PPP contract are negotiated and agreed between the government contracting agency and the identified private sector developer.
Competitive bidding	A process under which the bidders submit information detailing their qualifications and detailed technical and financial proposals, which are evaluated according to defined criteria—often in a multistage process—to select a preferred bidder. Competitive bidding may also include competitive negotiations and license schemes.
Concession	A PPP type which makes the concessionaire (established by the selected private sector developer) responsible for the full delivery of services in a specified area, including operation, maintenance, collection, management, and construction and rehabilitation of the system. Importantly, the private sector developer is responsible for all capital investment. Although the concessionaire is responsible for providing the assets, such assets are publicly owned even during the concession period. The public sector is responsible for establishing performance standards and ensuring that the concessionaire meets them. In essence, the public sector's role shifts from being the service provider to regulating the price and quality of service.
Currency conversion swap fee	A premium that is paid by the borrower to settle a swap, in which the parties sell currencies to each other subject to an agreement to repurchase the same currency in the same amount, at the same exchange rate, and on a fixed date in the future.
Direct agreement	An agreement normally made between the concessionaire (established by the private sector developer), the government contracting agency, and the lenders. The agreement usually gives the lenders step-in rights to take over the operation of the key PPP contracts.
Direct negotiations	A type of PPP procurement under which the PPP contract is awarded on the basis of a direct agreement with a private sector developer without going through the competitive bidding process.
Dispute resolution	A process to resolve any dispute between the government contracting agency and the private sector developer as agreed in the PPP contract. The possible dispute resolution mechanisms in a PPP contract could include resolution through • discussion between both parties, • dispute resolution board, • expert determination, • mediation or conciliation, or • arbitration.

continued on next page

continued from previous page

Term	Definition
Environmental impact assessment	A process of evaluating the likely environmental impacts of a proposed project or development, taking into account interrelated socioeconomic, cultural, and human health impacts, both beneficial and adverse.
Feed-in tariff	A policy mechanism designed to accelerate investment in renewable energy technologies by offering long-term purchase agreements for the sale of renewable energy electricity.
Financial close	An event whereby (i) a legally binding commitment of equity holders and/or debt financiers exists to provide or mobilize funding for the full cost of the project, and (ii) the conditions for funding have been met and the first tranche of funding is mobilized. If this information is not available, construction start date is used as an estimated financial closure date.
Financial equilibrium	A mechanism in a PPP agreement for dealing with changes, when changes in specified conditions and circumstances trigger compensating changes to the terms of the agreement. Some civil law jurisdictions emphasize economic or financial equilibrium provisions that entitle a partner to changes in the key financial terms of the contract to compensate for certain types of exogenous events that may otherwise impact returns. The partner is protected as the economic balance of the contract must be maintained and adequate compensation paid for damages suffered. Unexpected changes that merit financial equilibrium may arise from force majeure (major disasters or civil disturbances), government action, and unforeseen changes in economic conditions.
Force majeure	An event that is reasonably beyond the control of the affected party, as a result of which such party's performance of its obligations under the PPP contract is prevented or rendered impossible. Force majeure events may include • war, civil war, armed conflict or terrorism; • nuclear, chemical, or biological contamination, unless the source or the cause of the contamination is the result of the actions of or breach by the concessionaire or its subcontractors; • pressure waves caused by devices travelling at supersonic speeds, which directly causes either party (the "Affected Party") to be unable to comply with all or a material part of its obligations under the contract; or • any other similar events that are beyond the reasonable control of the affected party, and prevent or render impossible the performance by such party of its obligations under the PPP contract.
Government contracting agency	The ministry, department, or agency that enters into a PPP contract with the private sector and is responsible for ensuring that the relevant public assets or services are provided.
Government guarantee	Agreements under which the government consents to bear some or all risks of a PPP project. It is a secondary obligation, which legally binds the government to take on an obligation if a specified event occurs. A government guarantee constitutes a contingent liability, for which there is uncertainty as to whether the government may be required to make payments, and if so, how much and when it will be required to pay. In practice, government guarantees are used when debt providers are unwilling to lend to a private party in a PPP because of concerns over credit risk and potential loan losses. Government guarantees can also be used to benefit equity investors in a PPP company when they require protection against the investment risks they bear.
Government pay (Offtake)	Represents the payment made by the government contracting agency to the concessionaire (established by the private sector developer) for the infrastructure assets provided and services delivered through a PPP project. These payments could be • usage-based—for example, shadow tolls or output-based subsidies; • based on availability—that is, conditional on the availability of an asset or service to the specified quality; and • up-front subsidies based on achieving certain agreed milestones.

continued on next page

continued from previous page

Term	Definition
Gross-cost contract	A type of PPP contract arrangement in the railway sector under which all revenues (from fares and other sources) are transferred to the government contracting agency, and the risks absorbed by the developer are confined to those associated with the cost of operations.
Hybrid arrangement	A method of investment recovery in PPP projects when payments to the private party are made as a combination of user charges and availability payments over the lifetime of a PPP contract, in return for making infrastructure or services available for use at acceptable and contractually agreed performance standards.
Independent power producer (IPP) scheme	A scheme whereby a producer of electrical energy, which is not a public utility, makes electric energy available for sale to utilities or the general public. A scheme whereby a producer of electrical energy, which is a private entity, owns and/or operates facilities to generate electricity and then sells it to a utility, central government buyer, or end users. The IPP invests in generation technologies and recovers its cost from the sale of the electricity.
Institutional arbitration	An arbitration process in which a specialized institution intervenes and takes on the role of administering the arbitration process between the government contracting agency and the private sector developer for a PPP project-related dispute. This institution would have its own set of rules, which would provide a framework for the arbitration, and its own form of administration to assist in the process.
Interest rate swap fee	A premium paid by the borrower for a hedging contract to convert a floating interest rate into a fixed rate. The two parties agree to exchange interest rate payments based on a notional principal amount, with typically one paying a fixed rate and the other generally paying a floating rate.
Joint venture	An alternative to full privatization in which the infrastructure is co-owned and operated by the public sector and private operators. Under a joint venture, the public and private sector partners can either form a new company or assume joint ownership of an existing company through a sale of shares to one or several private investors. The company may also be listed on the stock exchange.
Lender's step-in rights	Lender's rights in project-financed arrangements to "step in" to the project company's position in the contract to take control of the infrastructure project where the project company is not performing.
Management contract	A PPP type which expands the services to be contracted out to include some or all of the management and operation of the public service (i.e., utility, hospital, port authority). Although the ultimate obligation for service provision remains in the public sector, daily management control and authority are assigned to the private partner or contractor. In most cases, the private partner provides working capital but no financing for investment.
Material adverse government action	An action by the government that directly and materially affects the private party of a PPP project in performing its obligations under the relevant PPP contract, and which would reasonably be expected to result in a material adverse effect.
Net-cost contract	A type of PPP contract arrangement in the railway sector under which all revenues (from fares and other sources) are retained by the developer, and traffic and revenue risks are absorbed either fully or as per a contractually agreed portion.
Nominal interest rate	The nominal interest rate is the interest rate applicable to a borrowing before taking inflation adjustment into account. In certain cases, nominal interest rate also refers to the advertised or stated interest rate on a borrowing, without taking into account any fees or compounding of interest. Nominal interest rate = Real interest rate + Inflation rate
Nonrecourse or limited recourse project financing	The financing of the development or exploitation of a right, natural resource, or other assets where the bulk of the financing is to be provided by way of debt, and is to be repaid principally out of the assets being financed and their revenues.

continued on next page

continued from previous page

Term	Definition
Output-based aid (OBA)	Refers to development aid strategies that link the delivery of public services in developing countries to targeted performance-related subsidies. OBA provides a way in which international financial institutions can directly structure their financing to benefit poor people, even when the service provider is a private company. OBA is the use of explicit, performance-based subsidies funded by the donor agencies to complement or replace user fees. It involves the contracting out of basic service provision to a third party—such as private companies, nongovernment organizations, community-based organizations, and even public service providers—with subsidy payment tied to the delivery of specified outputs. This means that targeted and valuable subsidies to disadvantaged populations are funded through donor funds. The private partner, meanwhile, can only recover this funding by achieving specific performance outcomes.
Project bond financing	An alternative source of financing infrastructure project by placing bonds.
Project development	Indicates the stage of the PPP project life cycle including PPP project identification, preparation, structuring, and procurement up to commercial close between the government contracting agency and the private sector developer.
Project development fund (PDF)	A fund dedicated to reimbursing the cost of feasibility studies, transaction advisors, and other costs of project development to encourage contracting agencies to use high-quality transaction advisors and best practices. PDFs provide the specialized resources needed to conduct studies, to design and structure a PPP, and then to procure the PPP.
Real interest rate	The real interest rate is the interest rate applicable to a borrowing that takes inflation rate into account. Real interest rate = Nominal interest rate – Inflation rate
Regulatory framework	A framework encompassing all laws, regulations, policies, binding guidelines or instructions, other legal texts of general application, judicial decisions, and administrative rulings governing or setting precedent in connection with PPPs. In this context, the term "policies" refers to other government-issued documents, which are binding on all stakeholders, are enforced in a manner similar to laws and regulations, and provide detailed instructions for the implementation of PPPs.
Rehabilitate–operate–transfer	A PPP type whereby an existing facility is handed over to the private sector developer to refurbish, operate, and maintain for a franchise period, at the expiry of which the legal title to the facility is turned over to the government contracting agency.
Risk allocation matrix	Matrix indicating the allocation of the consequences of each risk to one of the parties in the PPP contract, or agreeing to deal with the risk through a specified mechanism, which may involve sharing the risk.
Service contract	A PPP type under which the government contracting agency hires a private company or entity to carry out one or more specified tasks or services for a period, typically 1–3 years. The government contracting agency remains the primary provider of the infrastructure service and contracts out only portions of its operation to the private partner. The private partner must perform the service at the agreed cost and must typically meet performance standards set by the government contracting agency. Government contracting agencies generally use competitive bidding procedures to award service contracts, which tend to work well given the limited period and narrowly defined nature of these contracts.
Social impact assessment	Includes the processes of analyzing, monitoring, and managing the intended and unintended social consequences—both positive and negative—of planned interventions (policies, programs, plans, projects) and any social change processes invoked by those interventions. Its primary purpose is to bring about a more sustainable and equitable biophysical and human environment.
Social infrastructure	Covers social services, including hospitals, schools and universities, prisons, housing, and courts.

continued on next page

xvi   Definition of Terms

continued from previous page

Term	Definition
State-owned enterprise	A company or enterprise owned by the government or in which the government has a controlling stake.
Swiss challenge	A process in public procurement when a government contracting agency that has received an unsolicited bid for a project publishes details of the bid and invites third parties to match or exceed it.
Tax holiday	A government incentive program that offers tax reduction or elimination to projects and/ or businesses. In the context of a PPP project, tax holidays are provided to exempt the concessionaire from making any tax payments during the initial demand ramp-up period to make the project financially viable.
Unsolicited bid	A proposal made by a private party to undertake a PPP project. It is submitted at the initiative of the private party, rather than in response to a request from the government contracting agency.
User charges	A method of investment recovery in PPP projects when payments to the private party are fully derived from tariffs paid by users or offtakers over the lifetime of a PPP contract, in return for making infrastructure or services available for use at acceptable and contractually agreed performance standards.
Viability gap funding	A scheme wherein projects with low financial viability are given grants (or other financial support from the government) up to a stipulated percentage of the project cost, making them financially viable as PPPs.

Abbreviations

ADB	–	Asian Development Bank
ADP	–	Annual Development Program
BEPZA	–	Bangladesh Export Processing Zones Authority
BIDA	–	Bangladesh Investment Development Authority
BPDB	–	Bangladesh Power Development Board
CAAB	–	Civil Aviation Authority of Bangladesh
CCEA	–	Cabinet Committee on Economic Affairs
DPHE	–	Department of Public Health and Engineering
FY	–	fiscal year
G2G	–	government-to-government
GDP	–	gross domestic product
GW	–	gigawatt
ICT	–	information and communication technology
IFB	–	invitation for bids
IFC	–	International Finance Corporation
IPP	–	independent power producer
kV	–	kilovolt
LGD	–	Local Government Division
MLD	–	million liters per day
MRTB	–	Ministry of Road Transport and Bridges
MW	–	megawatt
NGO	–	nongovernment organization
PPA	–	power purchase agreement
PPP	–	public–private partnership
PPPTAF	–	PPP Technical Assistance Fund
PSMP	–	Power System Master Plan

RAJUK	—	Rajdhani Unnayan Kartripakkha
RFP	—	request for proposal
Tk	—	taka
UNCTAD	—	United Nations Conference on Trade and Development
VGF	—	viability gap funding
WASA	—	Water Supply and Sewerage Authority
WSS	—	water supply and sanitation

Currency Equivalents

(As of 31 March 2022)

Currency Unit	–	Bangladesh taka
Tk1.00	=	$0.012
$1.00	=	Tk84.80

Guide to Understanding the Public–Private Partnership Monitor

The *Public–Private Partnership Monitor* (PPP Monitor), a flagship publication of the Asian Development Bank (ADB), profiles the current state of the PPP enabling environment in ADB's developing member countries (DMCs) in Asia and the Pacific. The PPP Monitor features, for the first time, a data-driven, interactive online version, which allows users to compare and contrast the key PPP parameters and features across the featured DMCs. While the featured countries are a small sample, more countries will be continually added in the PPP Monitor, which is expected to become a knowledge base for assessing a country's PPP environment for the government and the business community. The new PPP Monitor builds on the success of the first and second editions of the PPP Monitor.

The PPP Monitor provides a snapshot of the overall PPP landscape in the country. This downloadable guide also assesses more than 500 qualitative and quantitative indicators that have been structured per topic—the national PPP landscape, the sector-specific PPP landscape (for eight identified infrastructure sectors and a separate section for other sectors), and the PPP landscape for local government projects. The PPP Monitor also captures the critical macroeconomic and infrastructure sector indicators (including the *Ease of Doing Business* scores) from globally accepted sources.

Each of the topics and associated subtopics presented below are characterized by qualitative and quantitative indicators. Qualitative indicators take the form of a question to which "Yes," "No," "Not Applicable," or "Unavailable" answers can be given. Quantitative indicators are represented in the form of numbers, ratios, investment value, and duration.

For each of the developing member countries covered, the information and data are organized along the following topic clusters:

Overview

Topic	Subtopics
Overview	• Overview of the public–private partnership (PPP) legal and regulatory framework • Number of PPP projects reaching financial close from 1990 to end of 2019 across sectors • Total investment made in PPPs from 1990 to 2019 across sectors • Features of past PPP projects including the number of PPPs procured through various modes • Number of PPP projects under preparation and procurement • Number of PPP projects supported by government • Payment mechanism for PPPs • Foreign sponsor participation in PPPs from 1990 to 2019 • Major sponsors active in the infrastructure sector in the country • Challenges associated with the PPP landscape in the country

National Public–Private Partnership Landscape Indicators

To profile the national PPP landscape, the indicators are grouped into three major categories: national PPP enabling framework, government support for PPP projects, and maturity of the PPP market.

Topic	Subtopics
National public–private partnership (PPP) legal and regulatory framework	Details on the legal and regulatory framework applicable to PPPs and its evolution since the introduction of PPPs in the country Details on the other supporting laws and regulations governing PPPs in the country
PPP types	Details on the PPP types allowed to be used as per PPP legal and regulatory framework. In case the PPP legal and regulatory framework does not specify the PPP types, this section provides the details on the specific PPP types, which have been adopted for various PPP projects at various stages of the PPP life cycle.
Eligible sectors	Details on various infrastructure sectors for which projects could be procured through the PPP route as per the PPP legal and regulatory framework
PPP institutional framework	Details on the PPP institutional framework including the availability of a PPP Unit, the functions of the PPP Unit, the principal public entities associated with PPPs and their respective functions, and the details of the public entities responsible for PPP project identification, appraisal, approval, oversight, and monitoring
Entities responsible for PPP project identification, approval, and oversight	
Entities responsible for PPP project monitoring	
PPP process	Details on the various stages of the PPP process including PPP project identification, preparation, structuring, procurement, and management, as per the PPP legal and regulatory framework in the country
PPP standard operating procedures, tool kits, templates, and model bid documents	Details on the standard operating procedures, and standard templates or model bidding documents available for PPPs (if any) Details on the key clauses in a PPP agreement based on the review of select PPP agreements already executed, and/ or the review of the PPP legal and regulatory framework
Lender's security rights	Rights of lenders including the charge of project assets
Termination and compensation	Definition on whether the private player is eligible for compensation in case of PPP project termination due to various reasons
Unsolicited PPP proposals	Details on possibility of submission of unsolicited PPP proposals, and their treatment, including potential advantages provided to the unsolicited PPP proposal proponent at the PPP procurement stage
Foreign investor participation restrictions	Definition on whether there are any statutory restrictions on foreign equity investments and ownership in PPP projects
Dispute resolution	Definition of the dispute resolution process and the mechanisms available in the country
Environmental and social issues	Details on whether the legal and regulatory framework governing PPPs stipulates a mechanism for managing the environmental and social impact of a PPP project, including the potential environmental and social issues, which could be caused by a PPP project

continued on next page

continued from previous page

Topic	Subtopics
Land rights	Definition of the various mechanisms through which landownership and/or land use rights could be provided to the private partner in respect of the project site for a PPP project
	Details on land records and registration, which could be provided to the private partner
Government financial support for PPP projects	Details on the various mechanisms of government financial support available to make PPP projects financially viable
	Salient features of government financial support mechanisms available
Project development funding support	Details on the various sources through which funding could be availed for the development activities (preparation, structuring, and procurement) of a PPP project
	Details on stages of the PPP project development during which such funding could be availed and utilized, including payments to transaction advisors
PPP project statistics	Details on the key PPP statistics in the country such as the availability of (i) a PPP database showing distribution of PPP projects across sectors and across various stages of the PPP life cycle, and (ii) a national PPP project pipeline and its alignment with the National Infrastructure Plan for the country
Sources of PPP financing	Details on the sources of financing for PPP projects in the country
	Details on typical key financing terms for various sources of financing, banks active in project finance for the last 24 months, active PPP project sponsors in the country for the last 24 months, availability of derivatives market, and availability of credit rating agencies in the country

Sector-Specific Public–Private Partnership Landscape Indicators

To profile the sector-specific PPP landscape, the indicators are grouped into five major categories: (i) sector-specific PPP contracting agencies, (ii) sector laws and regulations, (iii) sector master plan (including sector-specific PPP pipeline), (iv) features of the past PPP projects in the sector, and (v) sector-specific challenges for PPPs. The sectors, which do not appear consistently across the featured countries, are covered under the 'Other Sectors' category in the sector-specific PPP landscape.

Topic	Subtopics
Contracting agencies in the sector	Details on which government agencies could act as the contracting agencies for a public–private partnership (PPP) project
Sector laws and regulations	Details on the applicable sector laws and regulations for PPP projects, including the sector regulators and their respective functions.
Foreign investment restrictions in the sector	Details on the maximum allowed foreign equity investment in greenfield PPP projects in the sector
Standard contracts in the sector	Specification on whether standard contracts are available for PPP projects in the sector

continued on next page

continued from previous page

Topic	Subtopics
Sector master plan	Details on the master plan and/or road map adopted for infrastructure development in the sector by the national government and the corresponding line ministry
	Details on the pipeline of PPP projects for the sector aligned with this sector master plan and/or road map
	Details on the PPP projects under preparation and procurement in the sector
Features of past PPP projects	Features of the past PPP projects based on supporting indicators in terms of the number and value (where applicable) of PPP projects for each supporting indicator
Tariffs applicable to the sector	Details on the indicative tariffs applicable in the sector based on the examples of select PPP or other projects operational in the sector
Typical risk allocation for PPP projects in the sector	Details on the typical risk allocation between the government contracting agency and the private partner based on examples of select PPP projects that have achieved commercial close
Financing details for PPP projects in the sector	Typical financing details based on past PPP projects on the lines of the supporting indicators
Challenges associated with PPPs in the sector	Details on the PPP-related and sector-specific challenges faced by PPP projects in the sector
Typical sector-specific infrastructure indicators for the country	Details on select sector-specific infrastructure indicators for the country

Local Government Public–Private Partnership Landscape

To profile the PPP landscape for local government projects, the indicators are grouped into seven major categories: (i) local governance system, (ii) infrastructure development plans for local governments, (iii) sectors in which local governments can implement PPPs, (iv) revenue sources for local governments, (v) borrowings by local governments, (vi) budgetary allocation to local governments, and (vii) credit rating of local governments.

Topic	Subtopics
Key indicators related to local governments in the country	Details on the local governments using select key indicators on (i) the number and levels of local governments, (ii) the typical expenditure profile and heads, (iii) the typical revenue profile and heads, (iv) the typical debt profile and heads, and (v) grants and transfers from the higher levels of government
Local governance system	Details on the local governance system in the country, including the various levels of local governments; their roles, responsibilities, and functions; and the devolution of powers from the higher levels of government to the various levels of local governments
Infrastructure development plan for local governments	Details on the infrastructure development plans prepared by the local governments based on their capital investment projects in the pipeline, and the coverage of such infrastructure development plans
PPP enabling framework for local governments	Details on the PPP enabling framework applicable to local government PPP projects, including PPP legal and regulatory framework, PPP policy framework, and PPP institutional framework

continued on next page

continued from previous page

Topic	Subtopics
Eligible sectors for PPPs for local governments	Details on the eligible sectors in which PPPs could be undertaken by the local government as government contracting agency
Revenues for local governments	Details on the typical sources of revenue for local governments
Borrowings by local governments	Details on the typical sources of debt financing available for local governments, the purpose for which borrowed funds could be used, the terms of such borrowings, and the borrowing exposure of select local governments
Budgetary allocation to local governments	Details on the budgetary allocations and transfers to the local governments from the higher levels of government
Credit rating of local governments	Details on the precedence of local governments being rated by credit rating agencies in the country, and the details of credit ratings obtained by select local governments in the past
Case study on a local government PPP	A case of a PPP project undertaken by a local government in the past covering details on project background, project assets, PPP structure for the project, risk allocation among the parties for the project, project finance and project revenue details, and key learnings from the PPP project

Critical Macroeconomic and Infrastructure Sector Indicators

This section captures the critical macroeconomic and infrastructure sector indicators (including the *Ease of Doing Business* scores) from globally accepted sources.

Topic	Subtopics
Critical macroeconomic and infrastructure sector indicators	Details of the select key macroeconomic and infrastructure indicators for the country
Ease of Doing Business	Details on the various *Ease of Doing Business* parameters for the country based on the World Bank's *Ease of Doing Business* publication

Time Periods

The research was carried out in 2020 with the aim of reflecting the status as of the end of 2019. Therefore, some indicator data may have changed between the said period and the publication date of this report.

In country-level and sector-level sections, quantitative data in relation to the number of projects reflect the cumulative number of projects over the periods 1990–2017, 1990–2018, and 1990–2019. Otherwise, the data represent the status at each individual year.

I. Overview

Bangladesh has developed its foundation for public–private partnerships (PPPs) in a structured manner. A policy and strategy for PPP was introduced in 2010, which improved the regulation of PPP projects and established an office to promote PPPs. However, the Office for PPP has no statutory authority. Subsequently, a PPP Act was enacted in 2015, aiming to facilitate development of core sector public infrastructure and services. Following the PPP Act, the institutional set-up improved as the Office for PPP became the PPP Authority under the Office of the Prime Minister, with responsibilities including appointing advisors, developing and approving PPP contracts, and supervising the progress of PPP projects. A new PPP unit was established under the Ministry of Finance, and it approves government funding to a PPP.[1] The development of PPPs in Bangladesh is reflected further by the Economist Intelligence Unit Infrascope Index, which gives scores to countries across various regions. Among the 19 countries evaluated, Bangladesh scored an overall rank of 7th for PPPs, with strong showings in institutional structure and market maturity.

After the enactment of the PPP Act in 2015, the government has taken further measures to strengthen the regulatory framework and institutional set-up in the country. As part of the same, it published the *Procurement Guidelines for PPP Projects 2016*, followed by the *Procurement Guidelines for PPP Projects 2018*, the currently applicable guidelines setting out the process, time scales, and institutional roles and responsibilities for delivering each of the phases required in selecting a private partner. The country also has in place clear guidelines and rules related to project screening, technical assistance financing, viability gap funding (VGF), and handling unsolicited proposals—all of which are discussed further in this report. Owing to the well-developed institutional structure and regulatory framework, Bangladesh has been able to successfully close several PPP transactions.

In general economic outlook, Bangladesh has set the gross domestic product (GDP) growth target at 8.2% for fiscal year (FY) 2021. Infrastructure has been a priority area for the government. The proposed outlay for the Annual Development Program (ADP) for FY2021 stands at taka (Tk)2,051.45 billion ($24.19 billion), which is 6.5% of GDP in FY2021 and 36.1% of the total public expenditure/annual budget. The top five sectors—transport; physical planning, water supply, and housing; power; education and religious affairs; and science and information and communication technology—have received 70.5% of total ADP allocation, 0.4% higher than the ADP for FY2020. Within that allocation, the ADP for FY2021 earmarked the highest share, 24.6% (for 298 projects), to the transport sector (roads, railways, bridges, and others related to transport). That was followed by the physical planning, water supply, and housing sector with 12.6% (for 270 projects); and power with 12.1% (for 88 projects). Sixty-one projects were included in a separate PPP list in ADP for FY2021 (compared with 62 in FY2020), which were mainly in transport (82%) and physical planning (18%) sector projects.[2]

---

[1]   Asian Development Bank (ADB). 2019. *Public–Private Partnership Monitor.* Second Edition. Manila. https://www.adb.org/sites/default/files/publication/509426/ppp-monitor-second-edition.pdf.

[2]   Center for Policy Dialogue. 2020. *An Analysis of the National Budget for FY2020–21.* Dhaka. https://cpd.org.bd/wp-content/uploads/2020/06/CPD-Budget-Analysis-FY2021.pdf.

The PPP investment targets in the Seventh Five-Year Plan (2016–2020)[3] are as follows:

- 1.8% of GDP per year,
- Tk3.9 billion per annum,
- 0.8% power sector,
- 1% transport infrastructure, and
- 30% of infrastructure ADP must be PPPs.

From 1990 to 2019, a total of 69 PPP projects across various sectors were implemented. The energy sector has seen widespread interest in PPPs in Bangladesh. Except for one project in the airport sector that was awarded and canceled, the PPPs have largely been successful. Of the projects awarded in information and communication technology (ICT) sector, two were rated as distressed assets as of June 2020. Figure 1 presents the projects that achieved financial closure in 1990 to 2019.

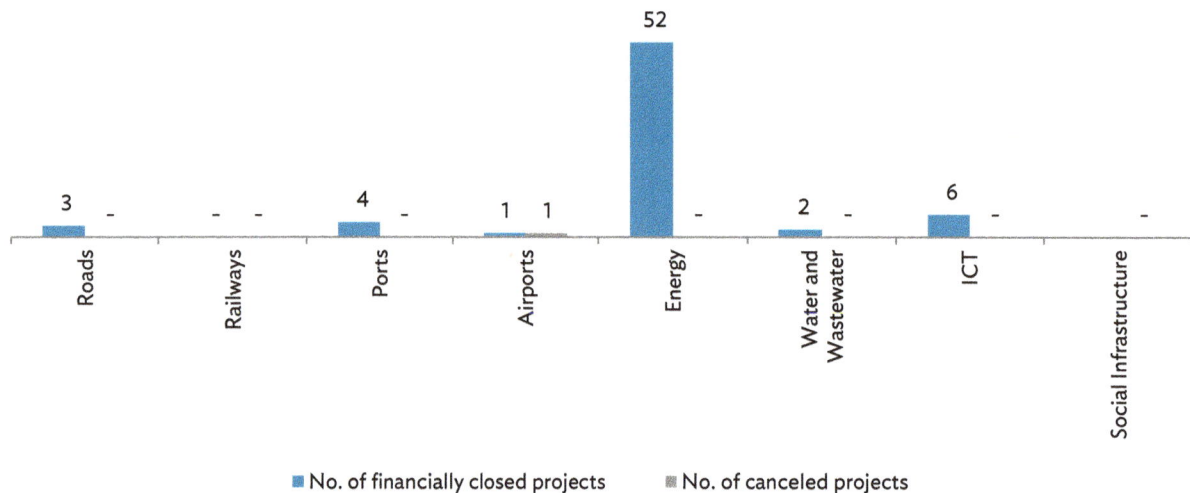

Figure 1: Public–Private Partnership Projects That Achieved Financial Closure, 1990–2019

ICT = information and communication technology.
Notes: Total projects include projects that are active, canceled, distressed, and concluded. The hyphen symbol (-) indicates there are no projects in the sector, or data are not available or not applicable, according to the database.
Source: World Bank. Infrastructure Finance, PPPs and Guarantees. Country Snapshots. Bangladesh. https://ppi.worldbank.org/en/snapshots/country/bangladesh (accessed 2 July 2020).

Figure 2 presents the status of PPP projects across each sector in Bangladesh that were awarded to private players.

In all, PPP projects have attracted investments of $6.74 billion (Tk571.57 billion), 76% of which was contributed by the energy sector. The ports sector also attracted over 12% of PPP investments. The water and wastewater sector (6%), roads sector (4%), and ICT (2%) have accounted for the remaining 12% in investments. Owing to the nature of the sector, ports attracted the highest average investment. In 2018, a project was awarded with $327 million (Tk27.73 billion) for a water treatment plant, leading to a high average project size in the water and wastewater sector as observed in Figure 3, making it the second-largest sector by average project size. Figure 3 shows the total investment in each sector from 1990 through 2019, and the average size of a PPP project in each of these sectors.

---

[3]   It is noted that since the date of the review, a subsequent plan has been published.

Figure 2: Status of Public–Private Partnership Projects across Sectors

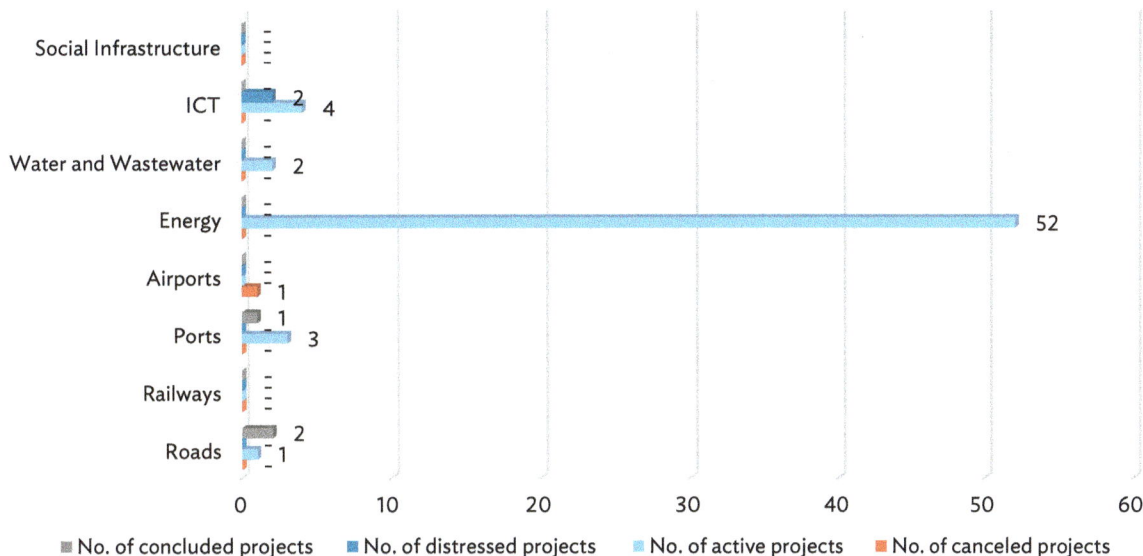

ICT = information and communication technology.
Notes: Total projects include projects that are active, canceled, distressed, and concluded. The hyphen symbol (-) indicates there are no projects in the sector, or data are not available or not applicable, according to the database.
Source: World Bank. Infrastructure Finance, PPPs and Guarantees. Country Snapshots. Bangladesh. https://ppi.worldbank.org/en/snapshots/country/bangladesh (accessed 2 July 2020).

Figure 3: Investment in Public–Private Partnership Projects by Sector, 1990–2019
($ million)

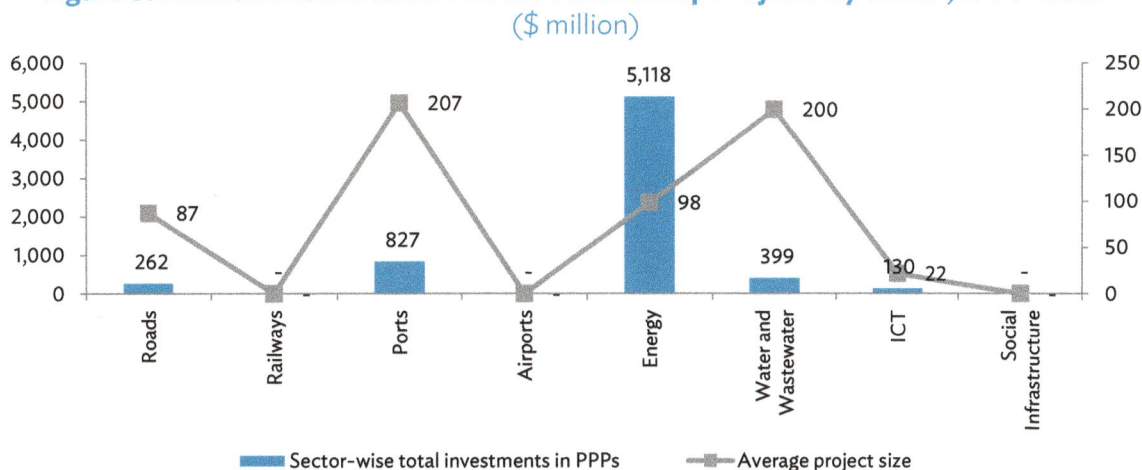

ICT = information and communication technology, PPP = public–private partnership.
Notes: Total projects include projects that are active, canceled, distressed, and concluded. The hyphen symbol (-) indicates there are no projects in the sector, or data are not available or not applicable, according to the database.
Source: World Bank. Infrastructure Finance, PPPs and Guarantees. Country Snapshots. Bangladesh. https://ppi.worldbank.org/en/snapshots/country/bangladesh (accessed 2 July 2020).

The top 10 private sponsors actively engaged in the infrastructure/PPP sector in Bangladesh are listed in Table 1. Together, they have been awarded 25 projects totaling $4.1 billion, or 62% of the total investment value in the country.

Table 1: Top Private Sector Investors for Public–Private Partnership Projects in Bangladesh

Private Sponsor	Country of Origin	Total Investment		Number of PPP Projects
		$ million	Tk billion	
Summit Corporation Limited	Bangladesh	1,191	101.00	9
Orion Group	Bangladesh	705	59.79	3
General Electric	United States	459	38.92	3
Marubeni Corp.	Japan	370	31.38	1
SembCorp Industries	Singapore	293	24.85	1
Long King	PRC	289	24.51	1
Al Jomaih Holding Co.	Saudi Arabia	269	22.81	3
1Malaysia Development Behard	Malaysia	266	22.56	2
SUEZ	France	164	13.91	1
Veolia Environnement	France	164	13.91	1

PPP = public–private partnership, PRC = People's Republic of China, Tk = taka.
Source: World Bank. Infrastructure Finance, PPPs and Guarantees. Country Snapshots. Bangladesh. https://ppi.worldbank.org/en/snapshots/country/bangladesh (accessed 2 July 2020).

From 1990 to 2019, 18 PPP projects were procured through direct appointment, 29 through unsolicited bids, and 25 through a competitive bidding process (including competitive bidding and license scheme) in Bangladesh across various infrastructure sectors.

Figure 4 shows the various modes through which PPP projects were procured from 1990 through 2019.

Figure 4: Various Modes of Procuring Public–Private Partnership Projects, 1990–2019

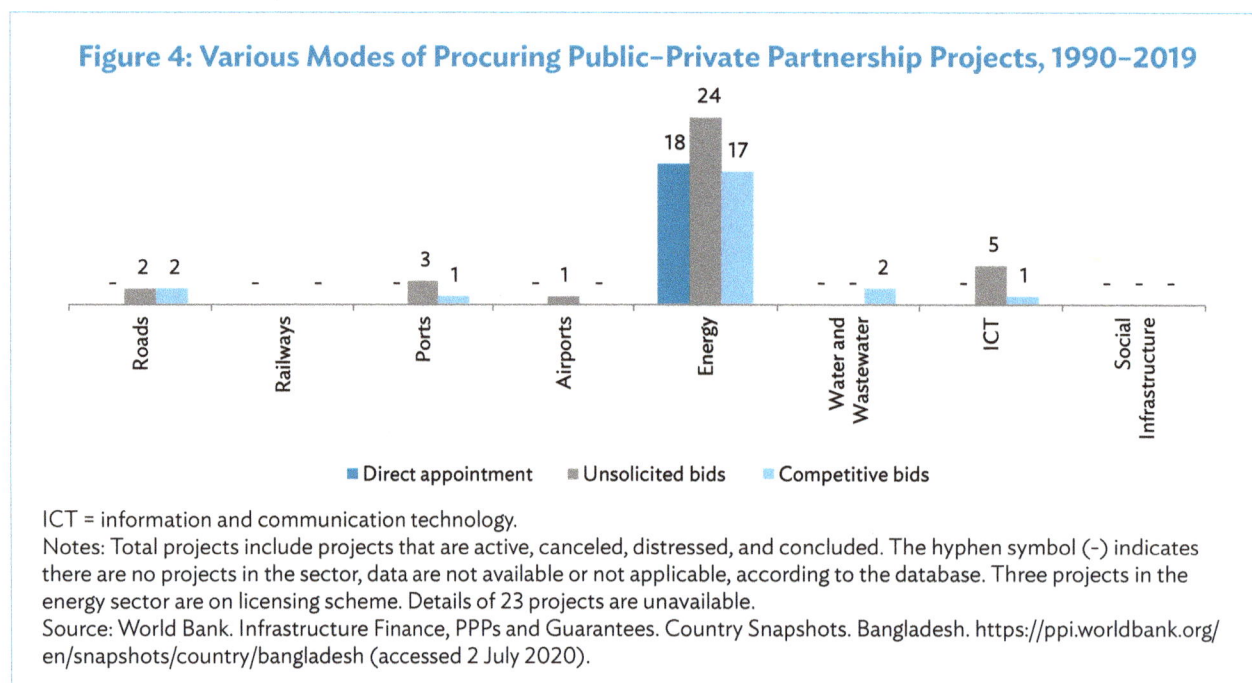

ICT = information and communication technology.
Notes: Total projects include projects that are active, canceled, distressed, and concluded. The hyphen symbol (–) indicates there are no projects in the sector, data are not available or not applicable, according to the database. Three projects in the energy sector are on licensing scheme. Details of 23 projects are unavailable.
Source: World Bank. Infrastructure Finance, PPPs and Guarantees. Country Snapshots. Bangladesh. https://ppi.worldbank.org/en/snapshots/country/bangladesh (accessed 2 July 2020).

Based on the information published by the PPP Authority, there were 58 projects under various stages of preparation and procurement as of mid-June 2020. While the top sectors traditionally evaluated for PPPs accounted for 28 projects under preparation and 8 projects under procurement, the PPP Authority in Bangladesh has also evaluated sectors such as tourism and economic zones, and nontraditional sectors such as industry for PPPs.

Figure 5 shows PPP projects under preparation and procurement as of 2019.

Figure 5: Public–Private Partnership Projects under Preparation and Procurement, 2019

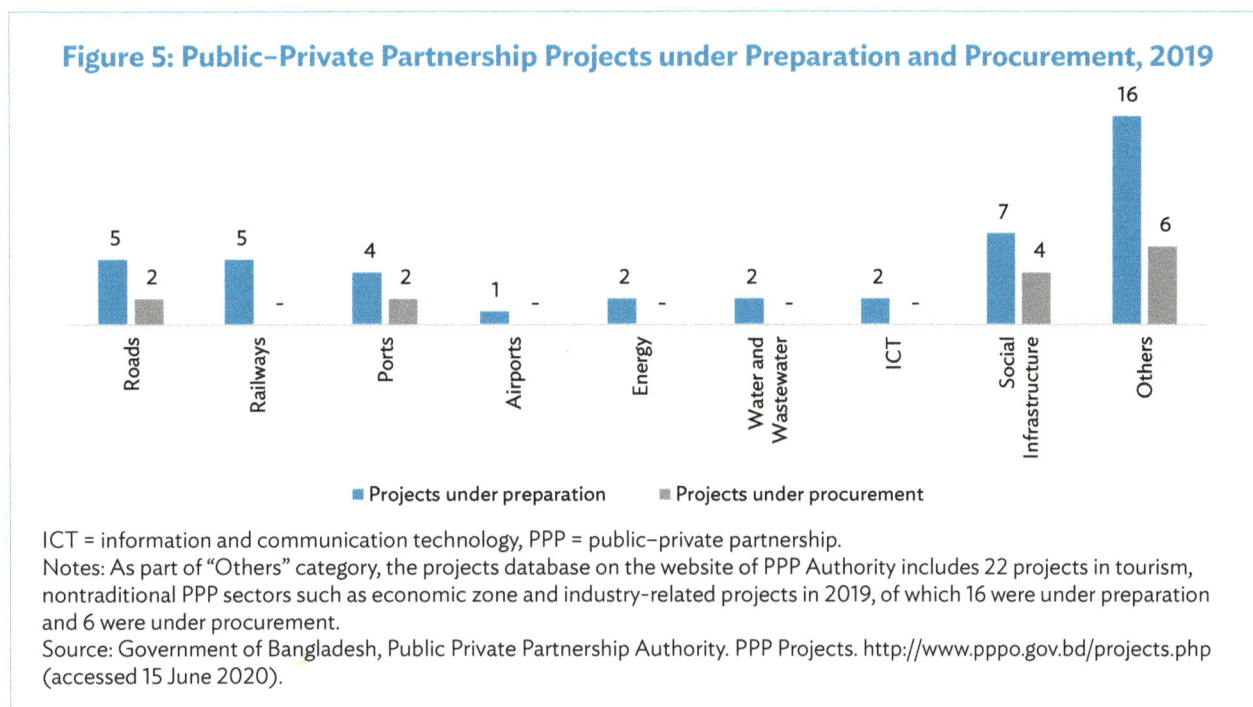

ICT = information and communication technology, PPP = public–private partnership.
Notes: As part of "Others" category, the projects database on the website of PPP Authority includes 22 projects in tourism, nontraditional PPP sectors such as economic zone and industry-related projects in 2019, of which 16 were under preparation and 6 were under procurement.
Source: Government of Bangladesh, Public Private Partnership Authority. PPP Projects. http://www.pppo.gov.bd/projects.php (accessed 15 June 2020).

From 1990 to 2019, 23 PPP projects received government guarantee, of which 22 projects were in the energy sector (nearly 42% of the projects awarded in the sector). Based on the available data, only two projects received VGF by way of capital subsidy from the government.

Figure 6 shows the PPP projects receiving government support in 1990–2019.

Figure 6: Public–Private Partnership Projects with Government Support, 1990–2019

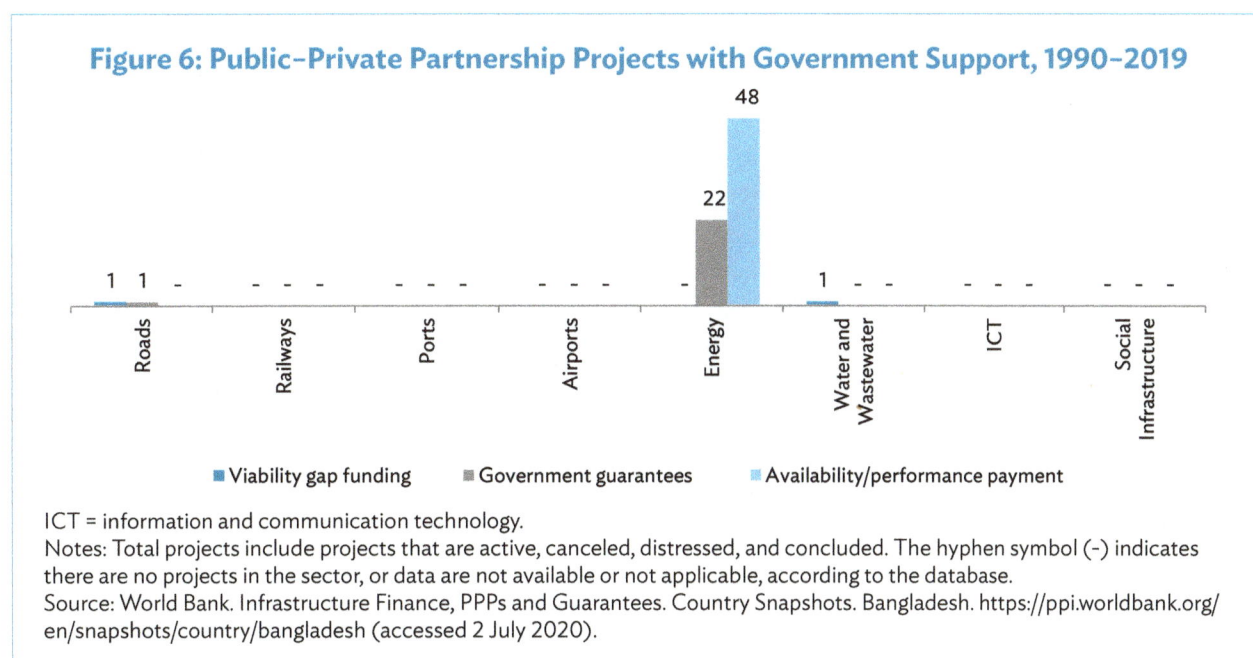

ICT = information and communication technology.
Notes: Total projects include projects that are active, canceled, distressed, and concluded. The hyphen symbol (-) indicates there are no projects in the sector, or data are not available or not applicable, according to the database.
Source: World Bank. Infrastructure Finance, PPPs and Guarantees. Country Snapshots. Bangladesh. https://ppi.worldbank.org/en/snapshots/country/bangladesh (accessed 2 July 2020).

From 1990 to 2019, only energy sector projects were awarded based on the availability of payment mechanism, with 100% of the projects awarded by way of power purchase agreement (PPA) or guaranteed payments based on availability. Figure 7 shows the payment mechanism of the PPP projects in 1990–2019.

Figure 7: Payment Mechanism for Public–Private Partnership Projects, 1990–2019

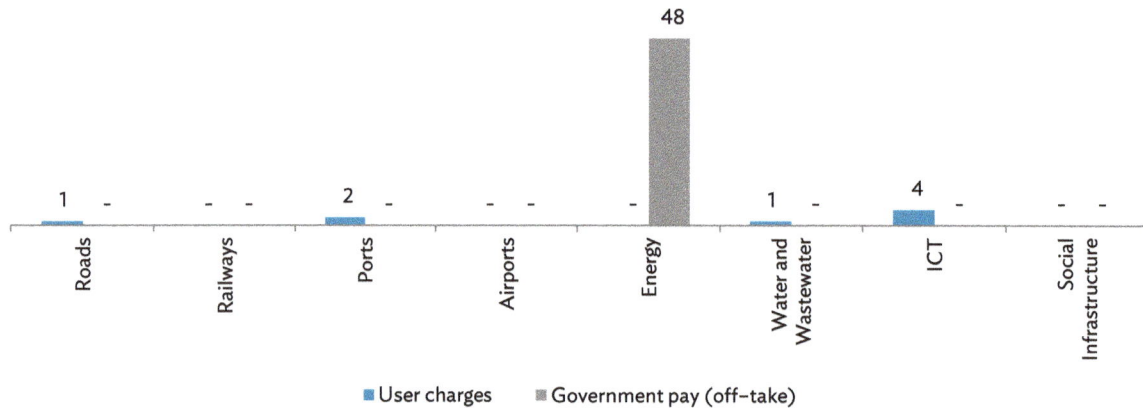

ICT = information and communication technology.
Notes: Total projects include those that are active, canceled, distressed, and concluded. The hyphen symbol (-) indicates there are no projects in the sector, or data are not available or not applicable, according to the database.
Source: World Bank. Infrastructure Finance, PPPs and Guarantees. Country Snapshots. Bangladesh. https://ppi.worldbank.org/en/snapshots/country/bangladesh (accessed 2 July 2020).

From 1990 through 2019, 32 PPP projects in Bangladesh had attracted foreign sponsor participation, of which 28 are currently active while the others are either canceled or lapsed. Projects were distributed across various infrastructure sectors including roads, railways, ports, airports, energy, water and wastewater, ICT, and social infrastructure, as shown in Figure 8.

Figure 8: Foreign Sponsor Participation in Public–Private Partnership Projects, 1990–2019

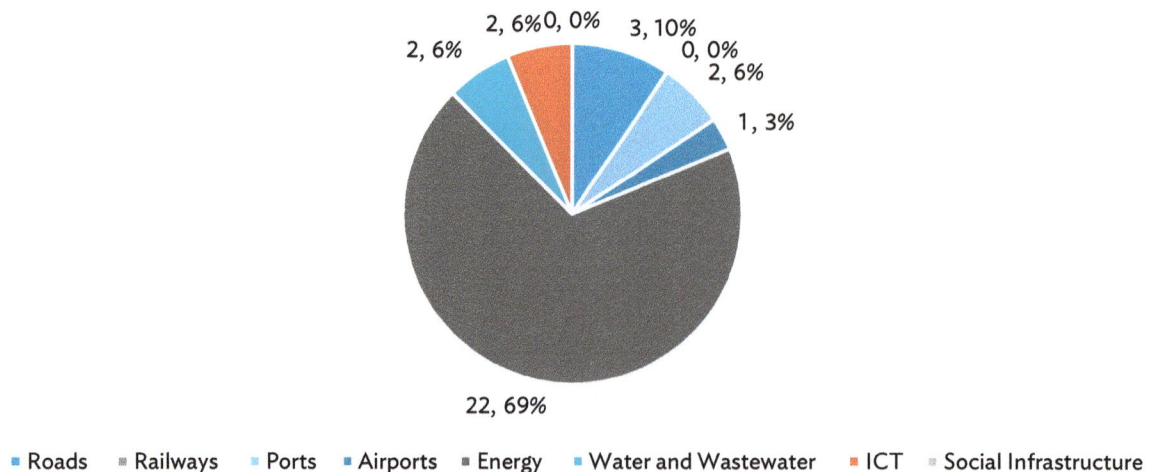

ICT = information and communication technology.
Note: Total projects include those that are active, canceled, distressed, and concluded.
Source: World Bank. Infrastructure Finance, PPPs and Guarantees. Country Snapshots. Bangladesh. https://ppi.worldbank.org/en/snapshots/country/bangladesh (accessed 2 July 2020).

Though the PPP market in Bangladesh is relatively mature, there have been various challenges to PPP implementation.

Bangladesh has a strong emerging regulatory framework, as indicated earlier. However, there are still many other steps needed to make PPPs more acceptable. Developing sector-level frameworks and model documents or standard bidding documents is crucial in bringing added transparency and clarity, with the hope that more in the private sector will bid for projects. A related goal in attracting more private sector interest is creating robust regulatory mechanisms through independent sector regulators and tariff policies for PPP projects.

The lack of long-term financing is a major impediment for PPPs in Bangladesh. While a few specialized institutions have been developed, there is still a major gap in overall financing requirements of the country, which leads to heavy dependence on foreign or development funding routes.

The dated laws in many sectors and commonly applicable regulations related to land acquisition will need amendments and rights for development by the private sector, stronger arbitration mechanisms, and tougher contractual frameworks.

Another challenge of PPPs is the limited capacity of contracting authorities and experience in handling the PPP projects. While initiatives of the PPP Authority—including issuance of guidelines and manuals and undertaking capacity development programs—have led to improved understanding of PPPs, further steps are necessary.

Finally, while the regulatory framework has been put in place, the country may also seek to develop standard bidding documents and model agreements for various sectors in which PPPs are encouraged.

II. National Public–Private Partnership Landscape

Bangladesh has been ahead of many of its Asian peers and has evolved with a strong public–private partnership (PPP) regulatory structure that supports private sector investments in infrastructure. It has also created an empowered institutional structure, working directly under the Prime Minister's Office to drive facilitation of PPPs. A policy and strategy for PPP was introduced in 2010, followed by the PPP Act in 2015, which aimed to spur development of core sector public infrastructure and services. The PPP Act provided a legal framework for the creation of PPPs by involving private sector participation along with the public sector, attracting local and foreign investments, and establishing a reliable authority for driving PPPs.

The PPP Act defines PPP as

> "Contractual arrangement between the contracting authority *(which may either be the Line Authority or the PPP Authority)* and any private partner pursuant to which the private partner
> - assumes the obligation or responsibility for carrying out any public work or providing any service on behalf of the contracting authority;
> - in exchange for carrying out the public work or providing any service on behalf of the contracting authority, receives consideration for the work or services from public funds; charges, levies, or fees from the users or service recipients; or a consolidated profit through receiving consideration, charges, or fees for the said work or services; and
> - accepts the risk arising from carrying out the work in accordance with the terms and conditions of the aforesaid PPP contractual arrangement or providing any service on behalf of the contracting authority."

The act clearly defines the private sector's obligation to take up a public work, with payments based on annuity, availability payment, or user charges with margin, in line with the risk allocation as defined in a contractual arrangement.

NATIONAL PUBLIC–PRIVATE PARTNERSHIP ENABLING FRAMEWORK

1. Public–Private Partnership Legal and Regulatory Framework

Parameters	
Does the country have a national public–private partnership (PPP) law and PPP regulations?	✓
• Public financial management laws and regulations?	✓
• Sector-specific laws and regulations?	✓
• Procurement laws and regulations?	✓

continued on next page

continued from previous page

Parameters	
• Environmental laws and regulations? • Laws and regulations for social compliance? • Laws and regulations governing land acquisition and ownership?[a] • Taxation laws and regulations? • Employment laws and regulations? • Licensing requirements?	✓ UA ✓ ✓ ✓ ✓
What are the other components of the PPP legal and regulatory framework?	Guidelines and rules related to procurement, financing

✓ = Yes, ✗ = No, NA = Not Available, UA = Unavailable
[a] Bangladesh Journal of Legal Studies. 2019. *Law and Practice for Land Acquisition in Bangladesh*. Dhaka. https://bdjls.org/law-and-practice-for-land-acquisition-in-bangladesh/.

Evolution of the Public–Private Partnership Legal and Regulatory Framework in Bangladesh

A policy framework for PPPs was introduced in Bangladesh in 1996 with the Private Sector Power Generation Policy. This marked the launch of PPP projects in the power sector—the 450-megawatt (MW) Meghnaghat and 360 MW Haripur power projects—which are two early success stories. The policy for encouraging partnerships with the private sector continued with the introduction of the Private Sector Infrastructure Guidelines (PSIG) 2004. The Policy and Strategy for Public–Private Partnership, 2010 (PPP Policy 2010) has been introduced, replacing the PSIG 2004. It updates policies and incorporates best international practice to further boost use of PPPs across multiple sectors and to provide a clear and transparent regulatory and procedural framework.[4] The Government of Bangladesh has enacted the Bangladesh Public Private Partnership Act, 2015 (Act No. XVIII of 2015) after repealing the policy and vision drawn up in 2010 (footnote 4).

Between 2010 and 2015, to ease, facilitate, and standardize the process of PPP project preparation and implementation, the government formulated the Guidelines for Viability Gap Funding for PPP Projects in 2012, the Guidelines for PPP Technical Assistance Financing for PPP Projects in 2012, and the PPP Screening Manual in 2013, which together, have helped advance PPPs in the country (footnote 4).

In 2017, the government provided the Policy for Implementing PPP Projects through Government-to-Government (G2G) Partnership, 2017. In 2018, the government also issued Guidelines for Dealing with Unsolicited Proposals, Rules for Viability Gap Funding for PPP Projects, and Procurement Guidelines for PPP Projects (footnote 4). The PPP Policy 2010 shall be deemed repealed in view of the enactment of the PPP Act 2015, according to Section 47(1) of the act.[5] Further, in case of inconsistency with other laws, the provisions of the PPP Act 2015 shall prevail.

[4] Government of Bangladesh, Public Private Partnership Authority. Government Policy. https://www.pppo.gov.bd/government_policy.php (accessed 15 June 2020).
[5] World Bank Group. 2018. *Procuring Infrastructure Public–Private Partnerships in Bangladesh*. Washington, DC.

Table 2 explains major improvements in PPP Regulatory Framework based on these amendments (footnote 4).

Table 2: Major Improvements in Public–Private Partnership Regulatory Framework

Reference Regulation	Brief Explanation
Public–Private Partnership (PPP) Act, 2015	PPPs in Bangladesh are mainly regulated by the Bangladesh PPP Act, 2015 (Act No. 18 of 2015), which was enacted on 16 September 2015. The objective of the act was "to provide for the legal framework for the creation of PPPs by involving private sector participation along with the public sector and attracting local and foreign investments upon connecting Bangladesh with the global economy to ensure extensive investment in infrastructure in different sectors in order to fulfill the basic needs of the people of Bangladesh and to expedite socioeconomic development in the interest of improvement of their living standard, and for establishment of a reliable Authority in this behalf and the matters ancillary thereto."
Rules for Viability Gap Funding (VGF) for PPP Projects, 2018 replacing Guidelines for VGF for PPP Projects, 2012	The Government of Bangladesh has issued guidelines, published in the *Bangladesh Gazette* on 9 September 2012, for providing VGF to subsidize economically viable and financially unviable projects if they are constrained to charge affordable user tariffs or utility payments. The guidelines had set the criteria for eligibility to receive VGF and the procedure for submission, appraisal, approval, disbursement, and monitoring of the VGF. These guidelines of 2012 were repealed and replaced by the Rules for VGF of 2018. The VGF Rules were effective beginning 17 October 2018. The rules cover various elements including applicability, eligibility, approval process, disbursement, monitoring, and other administrative processes related to VGF.
PPP Screening Manual 2013	The PPP Screening Manual is the operational guideline for screening proposed PPP projects, with the goal to secure in-principle approval to these projects and allow them to proceed to the project development phase. This manual was developed based on the PPP Guidelines 2010, which represent the government's existing policy on PPP projects.
Rules for PPP Technical Assistance Fund (PPPTAF) for PPP Projects, 2018 replacing the Guidelines for PPPTAF for PPP Projects, 2012	Through the Guidelines for PPPTAF for PPP Projects, published in the *Bangladesh Gazette* on 2 July 2012, the government offered technical support to develop infrastructure projects undertaken through PPPs. The guidelines provided procedures to be followed for utilization of the PPPTAF and covered applicability, utilization, approval process, recovery, and monitoring of the Fund. These guidelines were repealed and replaced by the Rules for PPPTAF of 2018. The PPPTAF Rules became effective on 30 October 2018. The PPPTAF Rules define various aspects related to handling of the PPPTAF, including its establishment and management, reporting requirements, sources and applicability, eligibility and approval rules, recovery, monitoring, and accounting rules related to the Fund.
Policy for Implementing PPP Projects through Government-to-Government (G2G) Partnership, 2017	Notified on 7 June 2017 by the PPP Authority, the policy builds on strong bilateral relationships and aims to – develop and upgrade large public infrastructure assets in partnership with other countries, support the growing economy in a sustainable manner, and deliver essential public services; and – provide the framework for engagement and modality in delivering PPP projects to be undertaken through a G2G partnership, whereby implementation will be carried out with the support of other governments and executed through their state-owned or private sector entities.
Guidelines for Dealing with Unsolicited Proposals, 2018	Notified in 2018, the guidelines relate to guidance on dealing with unsolicited proposals received by the contracting agencies/PPP Authority. It covers definitions, process of submission and evaluation, eligibility, approval processes, and ways of handling unsolicited proposals.

continued on next page

Table 2 *continued*

Reference Regulation	Brief Explanation
Procurement Guidelines for PPP Projects, 2018	Notified officially on 1 February 2018, these guidelines set out the process, time frames, and institutional roles and responsibilities for delivering each of the phases required for the selection of a private partner. These guidelines apply where the contracting authority is selecting a private partner for the delivery of its PPP project under the PPP Act framework, unless otherwise notified.

Source: Government of Bangladesh, Public Private Partnership Authority. Government Policy. http://www.pppo.gov.bd/government_policy.php (accessed 15 June 2020).

Public–Private Partnership Institutional Setup in Bangladesh

The PPP Policy 2010 led to establishment of the PPP Office the following year. The impetus in the development of the PPP program began in 2012. The PPP Office had played a crucial role in reinvigorating PPPs in Bangladesh until the formation of the PPP Authority under the PPP Act of 2015. The PPP Authority had significant autonomy in administrative and financial matters and was set up under the Prime Minister's Office. The PPP Authority acted as the central point for promoting the PPP concept and supporting line ministries and agencies in developing PPPs.[6]

A number of other institutions were also created to provide comprehensive support and ensure the success of the PPP program. The PPP Unit was established in the Finance Division to oversee, support, and process the requests for financing for the PPP program. The Bangladesh Infrastructure Finance Fund Ltd. was established to provide lending support to PPP project sponsors (footnote 6).

The PPP Authority had also developed a network of focal points at all relevant line ministries to support the processing of PPP projects, and it started the process of establishing PPP cells at select agencies dealing with multiple PPP projects (footnote 6).

Some of the relevant policies and laws in conducting PPP business in Bangladesh were the following:

- The Income Tax Ordinance, 1984;
- The Foreign Exchange Regulation Act, 1947;
- Foreign Private Investment (promotion and protection) Act, 1980;
- Investment Board Act, 1989;
- Industrial Policy, 1999;
- Arbitration Act, 2001;
- Transfer of Property Act (1882), Registration Act (1908), Land Reforms Board Act (1989), and Acquisition and Requisition of Immovable Property Ordinance (1982);
- The Companies Act, 1994; and
- Environmental Conservation Act, 1995 (and amendment, 2000), and Environmental Conservation Rules, 1997.

---

[6] Government of Bangladesh, Public Private Partnership Authority. *Annual Report 2018–2019.* http://www.pppo.gov.bd/annual_report.php (accessed 15 June 2020) although it is noted that since the date of this review, a subsequent annual report has been published.

2. Types of Public–Private Partnerships

The PPP Law 2015 defines a PPP project as "any public sector project which is undertaken for implementation through public–private partnership." The law has not limited PPPs to any specific type and covers projects that include (i) construction or operation of any new infrastructure or a plan to do both; (ii) a plan to reconstruct any existing infrastructure; (iii) a plan to carry out both activities (i) and (ii); or (iv) delivery of all those goods or services, which are not related to any infrastructure facility. Although specific types of PPP contracts are not expressly defined in a regulatory documentation, the contractual models for PPPs in Bangladesh included in *Your Guide to PPP in Bangladesh* are as follows:

- Joint venture and partial divestiture;
- Concessions, build–operate–transfer, build–own–operate–transfer, build–own–operate, Project Finance Initiative, build–lease–transfer, design–build–finance–operate;
- Leases and affermage; and
- Management and operating contracts.

3. Eligible Sectors for Public–Private Partnerships

Whereas the Policy and Strategy for PPP (2010) defined the specific sectors eligible for PPP, the PPP Law (2015) takes a less prescriptive approach, and instead entitles the relevant contracting authority to enter in a PPP contract for the construction or reconstruction of infrastructure. Infrastructure is very broadly defined as "any new or existing physical or nonphysical infrastructure in the public sector through which public goods or public services or both are created or provided" (footnote 1).

The Policy and Strategy for PPP (2010) states that a project is eligible for PPP if it fulfills the applicability criteria in any economic sector, according to the International Standard Industrial Classification of all Economic Activities, Revision 4, specified by the United Nations. However, it also identifies priority sectors that include those indicated in Table 3.[7]

Table 3: Projects Eligible for Public–Private Partnership Mode of Procurement

Eligible Sectors		
Sector	**Subsectors**	**Asset/Facility Type**
Transport and Logistics	Roads	Highways and expressways including mass transit, bridges, tunnels, flyovers, interchanges, city roads, bus terminals, and commercial car parking (ISIC 42 and 49)
	Railways	Railway systems, rolling stock, equipment, and facilities (ISIC 49)
	Airports	Airports, terminals, and related aviation facilities (ISIC 42 and 51)
	Seaports	Port development (sea, river, and land) including inland container terminals, inland container depots, and other services (ISIC 52) Deep sea port development (ISIC 52)

continued on next page

---

[7]   Government of Bangladesh, Public Private Partnership Authority. 2010. *Policy and Strategy for Public–Private Partnership (PPP), 2010.* Dhaka. http://www.pppo.gov.bd/download/ppp_office/Policy-Strategy-for-PPP-Aug2010.pdf.

Table 3 *continued*

Eligible Sectors		
Sector	**Subsectors**	**Asset/Facility Type**
	Transmission pipelines	
	Multimodal logistics parks	
	Container terminals, dry ports	
Energy	Power generation	Power generation, transmission, and distribution services (ISIC 35)
	Power transmission	
	Power distribution	
	Natural resources	
	Oil and gas	Exploration, production, transmission, and distribution of oil, gas, coal and other mineral resources (ISIC 05-09) Oil refinery and production of LPG (ISIC 19)
	Energy conservation and street lighting	
Water and Sanitation	Water supply	Water supply and distribution, sewerage and drainage, effluent treatment plans (ISIC 36-39)
	Water resources and irrigation	Land reclamation; dredging of rivers, canals, wetlands, and lakes; and other related facilities (ISIC 42)
	Wastewater	
	Solid waste management	Environmental, industrial, and solid waste management projects (ISIC 38–39)
Social Infrastructure	Education	Social infrastructure (e.g., health, education, human resources development, research and development, and cultural facilities) (ISIC 85–88)
	Health care	
	Public housing	
	Government buildings	
	Industrial zones and special economic zones	Economic zones, industrial estates and parks, city and property development, including services to support commercial and noncommercial activities (ISIC 81–82)
	Exhibition and convention centers	
	Sports, arts, and cultural facilities	
	Public markets	
Other Infrastructure Sectors	ICT	Telecommunication systems, networks, and services, including ICT (ISIC 60-63) e-service delivery to citizens (ISIC 85)
	Industry	Production of fertilizer (ISIC 20)

continued on next page

Table 3 *continued*

Eligible Sectors		
Sector	**Subsectors**	**Asset/Facility Type**
	Poverty alleviation	Poverty alleviation projects (ISIC 84) – Pourashava and village water supply (ISIC 36) – Remote Area Power Supply Systems, rural gas supply (ISIC 35) – Rural internet projects (ISIC 61) – River passenger terminals/landing stations (ISIC 52) – Rural health services and hospitals (ISIC 86) – Irrigation and other agricultural services (ISIC 36)
	Tourism	Tourism industry (ISIC 79)

ICT = information and communication technology, ISIC = International Standard Industrial Classification, LPG = liquefied petroleum gas.
Source: Government of Bangladesh, Public Private Partnership Authority. 2010. *Policy and Strategy for Public–Private Partnership, 2010.* Dhaka. http://www.pppo.gov.bd/download/ppp_office/Policy-Strategy-for-PPP-Aug2010.pdf.

In addition to the above, the policy indicates other urban, municipal, and rural projects that the government views as priority areas that would help support economic development. However, considering that the PPP Law provides a broad definition of infrastructure and does not restrict PPPs to any particular sector, the above list may be considered inclusive. Other sectors and projects identified by contracting authorities may also be considered for evaluation. It may further be noted that in Bangladesh, energy sector independent power producers (IPPs) are regulated by separate laws and generally follow a different approval and procurement method.

4. Public–Private Partnership Institutional Framework

Parameter	
Does the country have a national public–private partnership (PPP) unit?	✓
What are the functions of the national PPP unit? • Supports the design and operation of the National PPP Enabling Framework? • Helps develop a national PPP pipeline? • Supports the arrangement of funding for project preparation (budgetary allocations, technical assistance funding from multilateral development agencies, operating a dedicated project preparation/project development fund)? • Offers guidance for project preparation to and coordination with the government agencies responsible for sponsoring the projects? • Makes recommendations to the PPP Committee and/or other approving authorities to provide approvals associated with various stages of the PPP process?	✓ ✓ ✓ ✓ ✓

✓ = Yes, ✗ = No, NA = Not Applicable, UA = Unavailable

The PPP Authority in Bangladesh plays the role of a PPP unit for the country. Clause 9 of the PPP Act of 2015 details the power and functions of the authority, which are wide and overarching in the overall PPP program. Some of those functions are

- promulgating, approving, publishing in the gazettes; and using PPP-related policies, regulations, directions, and guidelines;

- providing the necessary direction to the contracting authority;

- framing technical and best practice requirements, prequalification, and bid documents;

- developing model PPP contracts;

- providing consent, establishing the process, approving a bidder, approving a termination (where applicable), approving model contracts, and appointing advisors for PPP projects; and

- reviewing and monitoring the PPP program.[8]

The key institutions involved in PPPs in Bangladesh are shown in Table 4.

Table 4: Key Agencies and Their Roles in Promoting Public–Private Partnerships

Institution	Role
Cabinet Committee on Economic Affairs	Among other things, this committee provides in-principle approval and final approval for a PPP project for the contracting authority to enter into a contract with the preferred bidder and/or the project company.
PPP Authority	The PPP Authority was initially established as the Office for PPP in September 2010 under the Prime Minister's Office to promote the PPP concept. Under the 2015 PPP Act, the Office for PPP was institutionalized as a statutory authority. Its powers and functions are set out in the PPP Act. They include providing decisions on the financial participation and provision of incentives by the government; framing technical and best practice requirements, prequalification, and bid documents; approving the selected bidder; approving the termination of PPP contracts; and approving model PPP contracts.
Line Ministry/Implementing Agency (or contracting authority)	Responsible for the identification, formulation, prequalification, tendering, contract award, and implementation oversight of PPP projects based on the PPP contract.
MOF PPP Unit	Established in the Finance Division of the MOF, the unit is responsible for overseeing the fiscal viability of PPP projects and sanctioning support funding for their development and financing, including managing the three key funds: the PPPTAF, the viability gap funding, and the Bangladesh Infrastructure Finance Fund.

MOF = Ministry of Finance, PPP = public–private partnership, PPPTAF = Public–Private Partnership Technical Assistance Fund.
Source: Asian Development Bank. 2019. *Public–Private Partnership Monitor.* Second Edition. Manila. https://www.adb.org/sites/default/files/publication/509426/ppp-monitor-second-edition.pdf.

Entities Responsible for Public–Private Partnership Project Identification, Approval, and Oversight

Parameter	
Who is responsible for identifying, preparing, and procuring public–private partnership (PPP) projects?	Line ministries and agencies
Is there a PPP committee for providing approvals at various stages of PPP projects?	The Cabinet Committee on Economic Affairs provides approvals at various stages.
Who are the approving authorities other than the PPP Committee for PPP Projects?	Approving the selected bidder and approving termination of PPP contracts are powers within the PPP Authority.
Does the country have an independent think tank for various PPP planning, budgeting, and policy decisions?	✓ The PPP Authority has this role.
Is there a legislature for PPP program oversight?	✓ The PPP Authority has this role.

✓ = Yes, ✗ = No, NA = Not Applicable, UA = Unavailable

---

8   Government of Bangladesh, Public Private Partnership Authority. 2015. *PPP Act 2015.* Dhaka. http://www.pppo.gov.bd/download/ppp_office/PPP-Law-2015.pdf.

The responsibility for the delivery of PPP projects rests with the line ministries and agencies that have been given the role under the Rules of Business of the Government. Line ministry and agency responsibilities include identification and development of the project, the procurement process, selection of the final bidder, and signing of the PPP contract with a private partner. The PPP Authority's role also extends to supporting line ministries and agencies in those responsibilities (footnote 8).

According to Section 14 of the PPP Act 2015, in-principle and final approvals for a PPP project shall be granted by the Cabinet Committee. Both the PPP Law and the PPP Policy refer to the Cabinet Committee on Economic Affairs (CCEA), the committee established by the government under Clause 18 of the Rules of Business, 1996.

The CCEA functions, according to Section 11.3 of the PPP Policy 2010, include

- providing in-principle approval for medium and large PPP projects, and
- approving a selected bidder for large PPP projects after the request for proposal stage.

The PPP Law also indicates that the contracting authority or, as the case may be, the PPP Authority, may, subject to the approval of the Cabinet Committee, declare any project a national priority project as necessitated to accelerate the socioeconomic development of the country or to mitigate the effects of any major adversity faced by the general public on an urgent basis (footnote 8).

Figure 9 shows the involvement and role of various entities.

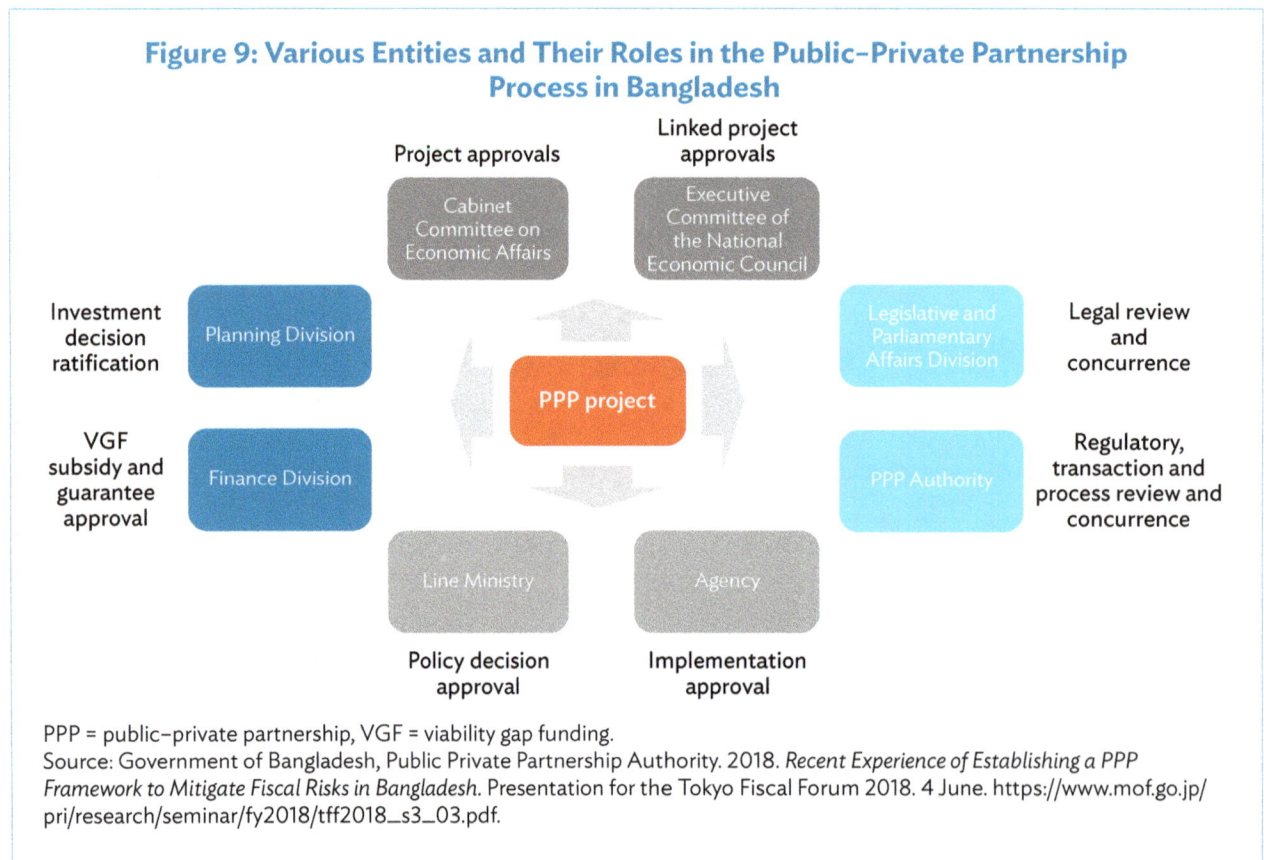

Figure 9: Various Entities and Their Roles in the Public–Private Partnership Process in Bangladesh

PPP = public–private partnership, VGF = viability gap funding.
Source: Government of Bangladesh, Public Private Partnership Authority. 2018. *Recent Experience of Establishing a PPP Framework to Mitigate Fiscal Risks in Bangladesh*. Presentation for the Tokyo Fiscal Forum 2018. 4 June. https://www.mof.go.jp/pri/research/seminar/fy2018/tff2018_s3_03.pdf.

Entities Responsible for Public–Private Partnership Project Monitoring

Parameter	
Is there an entity for monitoring of public–private partnership (PPP) projects after commercial close?	UA
Is there an entity for monitoring and management of fiscal risks and liabilities from PPP projects for the Ministry of Finance (MOF)?	PPP Unit under MOF

✓ = Yes, ✗ = No, NA = Not Applicable, UA = Unavailable

One of the functions of the PPP Authority, according to the PPP Act 2015, is "supervising and coordinating the progress of PPP projects." However, the act does not provide any other framework or details relating to project monitoring or contract management.

The Finance Division of the Ministry of Finance has established the MOF PPP Unit. That unit has responsibility for overseeing the fiscal viability of PPP projects and sanctioning support funding for their development and financing. The MOF PPP Unit has management responsibility for overseeing three key funds—the PPP Technical Assistance Fund, the viability gap funding (VGF), and the Bangladesh Infrastructure Finance Fund.[9]

The PPP Unit works on behalf of the government to monitor budget implications of upcoming PPP projects and to manage any contingent liability exposure the government may deem appropriate to support PPP project financing. In this role, the PPP Unit provides critical support to overall public financial management by giving input to the overall national Medium-Term Budgetary Framework (footnote 9).

5. Public–Private Partnership Process Details

Parameter	
Does the public–private partnership (PPP) legal and regulatory framework provide for a PPP implementation process covering the entire PPP life cycle?	✓
Feasibility Assessment Stage • Technical feasibility? • Socioeconomic feasibility? • Environmental sustainability? • Financial feasibility? • Fiscal affordability assessment? • Legal assessment? • Risk assessment and PPP project structuring? • Value for money assessment? • Market sounding with stakeholders?	✓ ✓ ✓ ✓ ✓a ✓a ✓a ✓a ✓
Is a PPP procurement plan required?	✓
Is there a need to set up a separate PPP procurement committee?	✓
Is competitive bidding the only method for selection of a PPP private developer?	✓
Is the prequalification stage necessary, or does the PPP legal and regulatory framework allow flexibility to skip that?	✗ (single stage bidding is allowed)

continued on next page

---

[9] Government of Bangladesh, Public Private Partnership Authority. MOF PPP Unit. http://www.pppo.gov.bd/mof_ppp_unit.php#:~:text=Public%20 Private%20Partnership%20Authority%20Bangladesh&text=The%20Finance%20Division%20of%20the,for%20their%20development%20 and%20financing.

continued from previous page

Parameter	
Does the PPP legal and regulatory framework provide the option of contract negotiations to the preferred bidder?	✓
Does the PPP legal and regulatory framework allow unsuccessful bidders to challenge the award or submit complaints?	✓
What is the maximum time allowed for unsuccessful bidders to submit a complaint or challenge the award given to the preferred bidder?	5 days
Does the PPP legal and regulatory framework provide for transparency?	✓
Which of the following are required to be published? • Findings from the feasibility assessment? • Procurement notice? • Outcome of stakeholder consultations from market sounding? • Clarifications to prequalification queries? • Prequalification results? • Clarifications to pre-bid queries? • Results for the bid stage and selection of preferred bidder? • Final concession agreement to be entered between the government agency and the preferred bidder? Other PPP project agreements executed between government agency and preferred bidder? • Confidentiality?	✗ ✓ UA ✓ UA ✓ UA ✗ ✓

✓ = Yes, ✗ = No, NA = Not Applicable, UA=Unavailable
ª While these elements are not specifically referred to in the procurement guidelines/PPP Law, they are evaluated as per the process under the PPP Screening Manual and are required.

Section 14 of the Procurement Guidelines for PPP Projects, 2018 on the Feasibility Study of the PPP Project indicates that "To test the overall viability and in order to finalize the scope and commercial structure of the PPP Project, a feasibility study of the PPP Project must be carried out by or on behalf of the Contracting Authority. The scope of the feasibility study may include, but shall not be limited to, the following: technical issues, commercial and financial considerations, environmental factors, social issues, linked projects, and any other issues that may be deemed relevant by the PPP Authority or the contracting authority."[10]

Although not expressly stated in the Procurement Guidelines for PPP Projects (2018), the World Bank Benchmarking of PPP Procurement in Bangladesh mentions that value for money and fiscal affordability assessments are carried out as part of the project development, and the PPP Knowledge Lab makes reference to risk identification and market assessment during preparation of the PPPs.

Section 47 of the Procurement Guidelines provides for negotiations. The Evaluation Committee shall, in order to finalize the PPP contract, negotiate with the preferred bidder in relation to only those terms and conditions, which are identified as capable of being negotiated in the PPP contract. The contracting authority may include other representatives to join the negotiation meetings alongside the Evaluation Committee. It also indicates that negotiations in relation to price and/or rates would only be permitted where it could improve the position of the contracting authority (footnote 10).

10   Government of Bangladesh, Public Private Partnership Authority. 2018. *Procurement Guidelines for PPP Projects*. Dhaka. http://www.pppo.gov.bd/download/ppp_office/Procurement-Guideline-for-PPP-Projects-2018.pdf.

The Procurement Guidelines of 2018 set out the process, timescale, and institutional roles and responsibilities for delivering each of the phases required for selection of a private partner. The guidelines are based on four phases of the project development life cycle: identification phase, development phase, bidding phase, and approval and award phase (footnote 10).

The bidding phase for PPP projects can either be a single-stage bidding process or a two-stage bidding process (footnote 10):

- Single-stage bidding process comprises only an invitation for bid (IFB).
- Two-stage bidding process comprises a request for qualification (RFQ) and a request for proposal (RFP).

Table 5 describes the various stages of a PPP project.

Table 5: Activities from Identification to Award Stage of Public–Private Partnership Projects

Phase	Description
Identification Phase	The identification phase is the first phase in selecting a private partner for the delivery of a PPP project. During this phase, the contracting authority and/or the PPP Authority may identify the project to be delivered on a PPP basis, apply the opinion of the PPP Authority in relation to the project, and seek in-principle approval. Steps in this phase include the following: – The contracting authority (or the PPP Authority) identifies the project to be delivered on a PPP basis preferably from the Government's Annual Development Program. The contracting authority may consult the PPP Authority on the various elements of appropriate project identification. – Where the contracting authority is not an applicable line ministry, such contracting authority will submit the proposal for the identified project (PPP project proposal) for endorsement by its applicable line ministry, which may seek views and feedback from the PPP Authority. After its review, the line ministry may endorse, reject, or seek a resubmission of the proposal from the contracting authority. – Screening of the project proposal by the PPP Authority before submission to the CCEA for in-principle approval. A prefeasibility study may be conducted at this stage. – Line ministry submits the project proposal for the CCEA's in-principle approval after clearance from the PPP Authority. The CCEA provides in-principle approval if found appropriate. Typical timeline for in-principle approval is 2 months.
Development Phase	The development phase is the second phase in selecting a private partner for the delivery of a PPP project. During this phase, the contracting authority, with the support of the PPP Authority and relevant experts, shall determine the feasibility of implementing the project on a PPP basis. Steps in this phase include the following: – Phase to be undertaken only after in-principle approval is accorded. – Contracting authority shall form a project delivery team based on the communication received from the PPP Authority. The project delivery team shall oversee progress and development of the feasibility study and shall ensure that the agreed timelines are met. – The PPP Authority shall establish a project assessment committee for each project.

continued on next page

Table 5 *continued*

Phase	Description
	– Contracting authority shall conduct a feasibility study of the project and submit it to the PPP Authority for review and approval before finalization. Transaction advisors may be appointed for undertaking the feasibility study and for other stages of the project until the project award. Advisors are to be appointed as per the applicable regulations. – The contracting authority may instruct for a registration-of-interest process to be carried out to obtain formalized feedback from the market in relation to the PPP project, subject to the concurrence of the PPP Authority.
Bidding Phase	The bidding phase is the third phase in selecting a private partner for the delivery of a PPP project. During this phase, the contracting authority shall process and approve the applications, proposals, or bids (as applicable) submitted in response to the bid documents (RFQ, RFP, or IFB) issued by the contracting authority to select the private partner who shall implement the project on a PPP basis. Steps in this phase include the following: **Advertising:** – The contracting authority shall advertise all RFQs or IFBs, as applicable based on any guidance or standard templates issued by the PPP Authority or as may be specifically approved by the PPP Authority. The PPP Authority may also issue advertisements in relation to the RFQ or IFB, as applicable. – The PPP Authority may organize other activities, including contacting foreign trade missions in Bangladesh, Bangladeshi trade missions abroad, or using advisors for project promotion activities up to submission of bids. **Online Registration:** Contracting authority may require all interested parties to register online to access the bid documents and other relevant information and to participate in the bidding process. **Data Room Creation and Maintenance:** During the RFQ and IFB stages, only registered entities shall be given access to the Data Room which shall contain the RFQ or IFB (as applicable), any addenda and/or corrigenda to the RFQ or IFB issued by the contracting authority, notice of invitation to the pre-application meeting or pre-bid meeting, and/or any other relevant information for the bidding process. Further, any updates or additional information relating to the PPP project may be uploaded to the Data Room. During the RFP stage, only shortlisted bidders shall be given access to the Data Room. The contracting authority shall apply the type of bidding process for a PPP project based on the instruction of the PPP Authority or any policies, rules, regulations, guidance, guidelines, or notifications issued by the PPP Authority pursuant to the PPP Act. **Stages of Bidding:** – The single-stage bidding process shall be an IFB only. – The two-stage bidding process shall have an RFQ stage and an RFP stage. The RFQ stage of the bidding process shall include prequalification and shortlisting. The maximum number of shortlisted bidders shall be five. These bidders may be invited to submit their technical and financial proposals in two separate sealed envelopes enclosed in an outer single envelope. Alternatively, only financial proposals may be sought at this stage. **Evaluation Criteria and Method for RFQ** – Prequalification may be carried out based on technical and financial capacity of the applicants. – Technical capacity may include examples of the experience of having undertaken projects of a similar nature as defined in the RFQ document. Financial capacity may include examples of experience of having provided and/or raised funds for projects as defined in the RFQ document. In addition, shortlisting may be based on single test or multiple tests. It may specify mandatory compliance requirements.

continued on next page

Table 5 *continued*

Phase	Description
	Evaluation Criteria and Method for RFP or IFB – The evaluation method may either include the quality and cost-based selection method or the cost-based selection method, the decision of which is made by the contracting authority based on concurrence of the PPP Authority. – Tied proposals or tied bids may be dealt by way of inviting best and final offer. **Bidding Documents** – The guidelines provide broad guidance on the IFB, RFQ, and RFP documents indicating the points they should cover. However, there is no reference of any standard documents or model agreements that is available. – The documents prepared by the contracting authority would have to be reviewed by the PPP Authority through project assessment committee, and any feedback received shall be incorporated by that authority. **Timelines:** The guidelines suggest timelines for the bidding process under different models, which may be extended by the contracting authority upon informing the PPP Authority. – The bids submitted in response to the IFB shall be received within a minimum of 42 days from the issuance of the IFB document. – The applications submitted in response to the RFQ shall be received within a minimum of 28 days from the issuance of the RFQ document. – The proposals submitted in response to the RFP shall be received within a minimum of 42 days from the issuance of the RFP document. **Treatment of a Single Application, Proposal, or Bid** – IFB: If only one bid is received, the bidding process shall continue. – RFQ: If only one application is received or only one applicant is shortlisted, the process shall be cancelled and redone, or an IFB shall be attempted. – RFP: If only one proposal is received, the bidding process shall continue. **Opening Committee and Opening Procedure:** The Opening Committee shall be responsible for opening the bids/applications. **Evaluation Committee:** – In evaluating applications, proposals, or bids (as applicable), an evaluation committee shall be formed immediately after the issuance of the RFQ or IFB (as applicable), and in any case no later than the due date. The constitution is recommended by the PPP Authority and must be approved by the line ministry. – The Evaluation Committee shall have either five or seven members. Where the value of the PPP project is Tk8 billion or more, then the Evaluation Committee shall have seven members. **Negotiation:** Upon completion of the evaluation of the proposals or bids (as applicable), the Evaluation Committee may, through the contracting authority, invite the preferred bidder for negotiations.
Approval and Award Phase	The Approval and Award Phase is the fourth and final phase in selecting a private partner for the delivery of a PPP project. During this phase, the PPP contract shall be sent to the CCEA for final approval. The contracting authority, with the support of the PPP Authority, shall issue the letter of award to the preferred bidder. Steps in this phase include the following: – Upon completion of the negotiation, the applicable line ministry shall submit the legally vetted PPP contract to the CCEA for its final approval. – The letter of award shall be issued within 4 weeks following receipt of the CCEA approval.

CCEA = Cabinet Committee on Economic Affairs, IFB = invitation for bids, PPP = public–private partnership, RFP = request for proposal, RFQ = request for qualification.
Source: Government of Bangladesh, Public Private Partnership Authority. 2018. *Procurement Guidelines for PPP Projects*. Dhaka. http://www.pppo.gov.bd/download/ppp_office/Procurement-Guideline-for-PPP-Projects-2018.pdf.

Figure 10 shows the process for PPP project development.

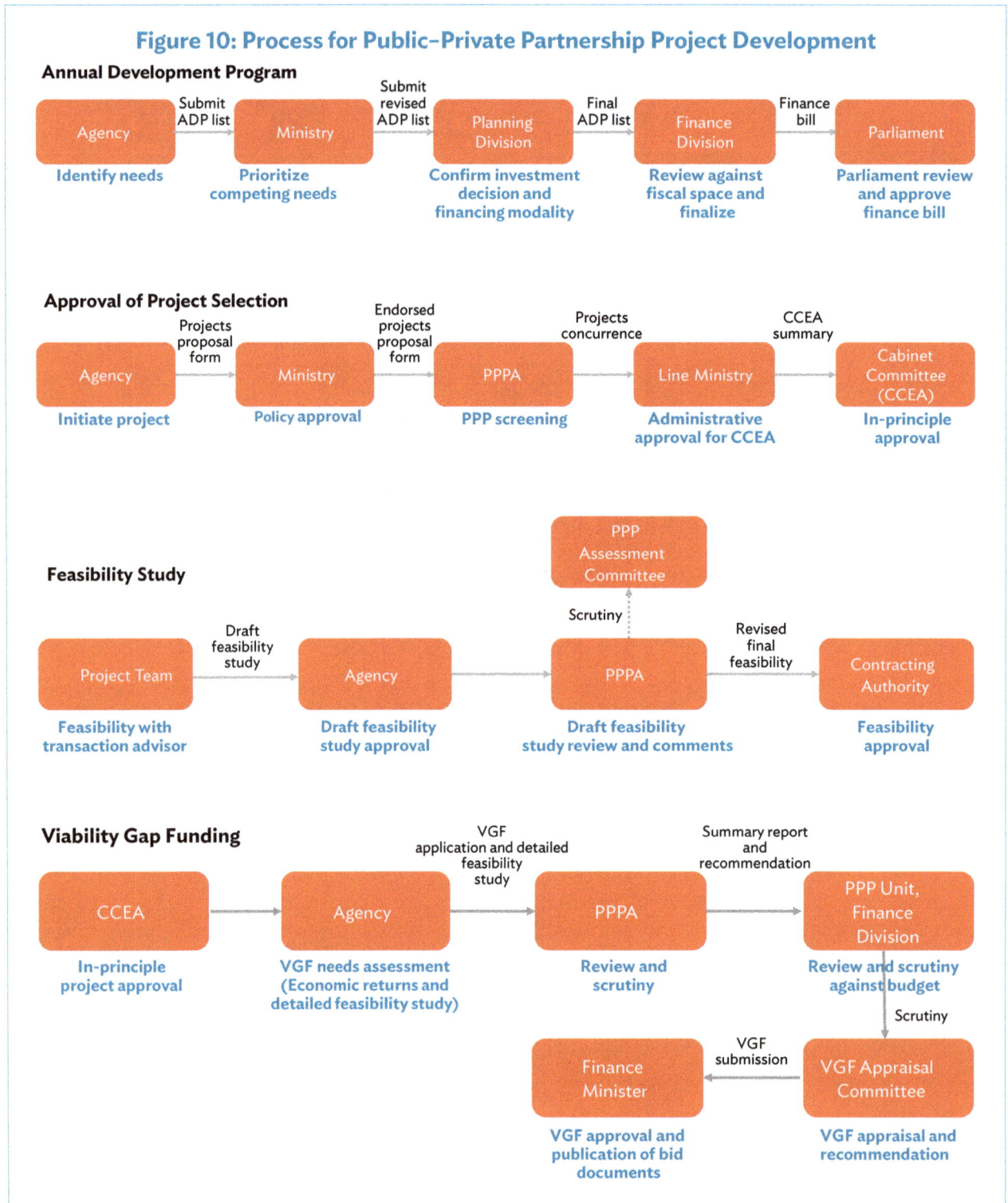

Figure 10: Process for Public–Private Partnership Project Development

continued on next page

Figure 10 *continued*

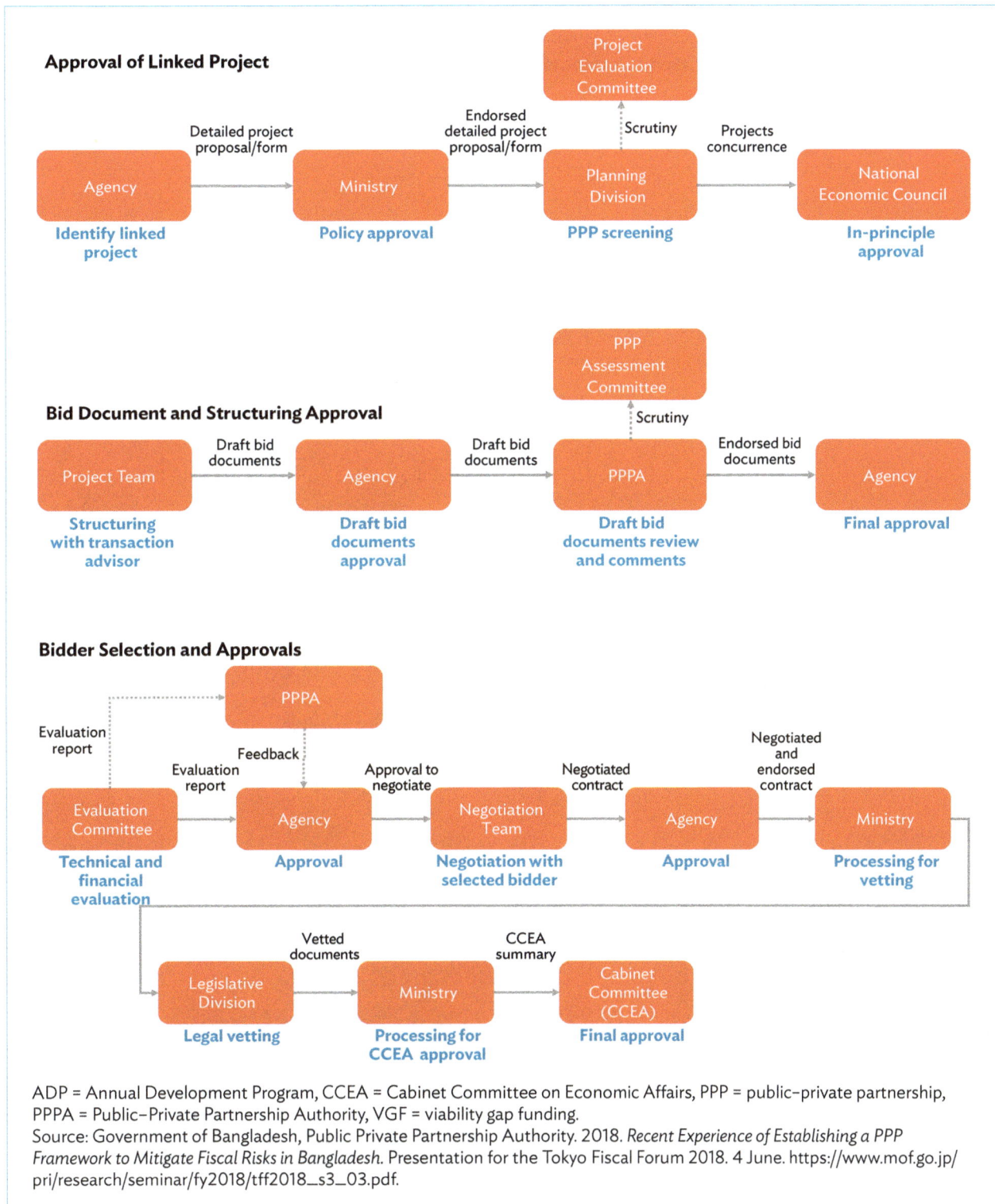

Approval of Linked Project

Agency — Detailed project proposal/form → Ministry — Endorsed detailed project proposal/form → Planning Division ⇡ Scrutiny (Project Evaluation Committee) — Projects concurrence → National Economic Council

Identify linked project — **Policy approval** — **PPP screening** — **In-principle approval**

Bid Document and Structuring Approval

Project Team — Draft bid documents → Agency — Draft bid documents → PPPA ⇡ Scrutiny (PPP Assessment Committee) — Endorsed bid documents → Agency

Structuring with transaction advisor — **Draft bid documents approval** — **Draft bid documents review and comments** — **Final approval**

Bidder Selection and Approvals

Evaluation Committee — Evaluation report → PPPA — Feedback → Agency — Approval to negotiate → Negotiation Team — Negotiated contract → Agency — Negotiated and endorsed contract → Ministry — → Legislative Division — Vetted documents → Ministry — CCEA summary → Cabinet Committee (CCEA)

Technical and financial evaluation — **Approval** — **Negotiation with selected bidder** — **Approval** — **Processing for vetting** — **Legal vetting** — **Processing for CCEA approval** — **Final approval**

ADP = Annual Development Program, CCEA = Cabinet Committee on Economic Affairs, PPP = public–private partnership, PPPA = Public–Private Partnership Authority, VGF = viability gap funding.
Source: Government of Bangladesh, Public Private Partnership Authority. 2018. *Recent Experience of Establishing a PPP Framework to Mitigate Fiscal Risks in Bangladesh.* Presentation for the Tokyo Fiscal Forum 2018. 4 June. https://www.mof.go.jp/pri/research/seminar/fy2018/tff2018_s3_03.pdf.

According to the Policy for Implementing PPP Projects through Government-to-Government (G2G) Partnership issued in 2017, a decision to implement a PPP project on a G2G partnership basis may be taken at any time before the bidding phase has started, or after the bidding phase if it has not been completed successfully. The PPP Authority may submit an official request to other governments to enter into a G2G framework agreement or memorandum of understanding that may define the main features of the procedure (including modalities of expression of interest from other governments; selection process; process for developing, negotiating, and agreeing the terms and conditions of the PPP contract; and dispute resolution process). The PPP Authority may also take up a proposal from any other government interested in entering into a G2G framework agreement.[11]

6. Public–Private Partnership Standard Operating Procedures, Tool kits, Templates, and Model Bid Documents

Parameter	
Does the country have a public–private partnership (PPP) guidelines/PPP guidance manual?	✓
Does the PPP guidelines/PPP guidance manual adequately cover the process, entities involved, roles and responsibilities of various entities, approvals required at various stages, and the timelines for the various stages of the PPP project life cycle?	✓
What are the templates and checklists available in the PPP guidelines/PPP guidance manual? • Project needs assessment and options analysis checklist? • Project due diligence checklist? • Technical assessment checklist? • Environmental assessment checklist? • PPP procurement plan template?	 ✗ ✗ ✗ ✗ ✗
Does the country have standardized/model bidding documents for PPPs? • Model request for qualification (RFQ) document? • Model request for proposal (RFP) document? • Model PPP/concession agreement? • State support agreement? • Viability gap funding (VGF) agreement? • Guarantee agreement? • Power purchase agreement? • Capacity take-or-pay contract? • Fuel supply agreement? • Transmission and use of system agreement? • Performance-based operations and maintenance contract? • Engineering, procurement, and construction contract?	 ✓ ✓ ✓ UA UA UA ✓ ✗ ✓ ✗ ✗ ✗
Does the country have standardized PPP agreement terms?	✓a
Does the country have standardized/model tool kits to facilitate identification, preparation, procurement, and management of PPP projects? • PPP family indicator? • PPP mode validity indicator? • PPP suitability filter? • PPP screening tool? • Financial viability indicator model? • Economic viability indicator model? • Value-for-money (VFM) indicator tool? • Readiness filter?	 ✗ ✗ ✗ ✓b ✗ ✗ ✗ ✗

continued on next page

11   Government of Bangladesh, Public Private Partnership Authority. 2017. *Policy for Implementing PPP Projects through Government to Government (G2G) Partnership, 2017.* Dhaka. http://www.pppo.gov.bd/download/ppp_office/Policy_G2G_Partnership-2017.pdf.

continued from previous page

Parameter	
Is there a framework for monitoring fiscal risks from PPPs? • Process for assessing fiscal commitments? • Process for approving fiscal commitments? • Process for monitoring fiscal commitments? • Process for reporting fiscal commitments? • Process for budgeting fiscal commitments?	 × × × × ×
Are there fiscal prudence norms/thresholds to limit fiscal exposure to PPPs?	×
Is there a process for assessing and budgeting contingent liabilities from PPPs?	×

✓ = Yes, × = No, NA = Not Applicable, UA=Unavailable
a Clause 26 of the PPP Law provides guidance on terms and conditions of a partnership contract.
b While there are no tools for suitability filters or financial viability, the screening manual covers various elements including suitability of a project for PPP, financial viability, VFM-related aspects, and related elements.

The government adopts the World Bank standard bidding documents for procurement of all projects that are funded by the bank. Further, the PPP Authority website newsletter dated 14 July 2012 confirms that, based on the consultations with various stakeholders, including the line ministries, implementing agencies, and donor agencies, the PPP Authority— considering the comments and insights obtained from the consultation and review process—finalized the Draft PPP Law, Project Screening Manual, Project Development Manual, Tender Process Manual, Environmental and Social Safeguards Framework, and four Model Concession Agreements.[12] However, copies of such agreements could not be accessed on the website of the PPP Authority or other reference material reviewed, and it is therefore unclear if the same are being deployed.

The Sustainable and Renewable Energy Development Authority provides for model contracts for IPPs in Bangladesh.

Key Clauses Related to Public–Private Partnership Agreement

Clause 26 of the PPP Law provides guidance on terms and conditions of a partnership contract. The clause indicates that the PPP contract may provide for any, or all, of the matters indicated in Table 6.

Table 6: Terms and Conditions Related to Public–Private Partnership Projects

Modality of the Project	Term of Contract	Public Goods and Public Services
Technical specifications and compliance standards	Environmental and security requirements	Performance indicators and date of completion
Expenditure recovery mechanism through collecting levy and strategy for its adjustment	Construction and operations bond	Insurance
Acceptance test and method	Rights and obligations of the parties to the public–private partnership (PPP) contract and risk allocation	Modality and amount of government financial participation

continued on next page

---

12   Government of Bangladesh, Public Private Partnership Authority. 2012. *Remarkable Progress Achieved in the Country's PPP Preparation.* http://www.pppo.gov.bd/download/ppp_office/Remarkable-Progress-Achieved-PPP-Preparation.pdf.

Table 6 *continued*

Modality of the Project	Term of Contract	Public Goods and Public Services
Transfer of assets (if any) after the end of the PPP contract	Post transfer confirmation letter and method	Submission of report
Supervision strategy of the contracting authority	Ownership of assets	Immediate steps during disaster
Governing law	Provision for arbitration	Rights over project area and security interest

Source: Government of Bangladesh, Public Private Partnership Authority. 2015. *PPP Law 2015*. Dhaka. http://www.pppo.gov.bd/download/ppp_office/PPP-Law-2015.pdf.

Public–Private Partnership Screening Manual 2013

The PPP Screening Manual is the operational guideline for screening PPP project proposals in order to secure in-principle approval and proceed to the next phase—the project development process. This manual is aimed at providing guidance to the main stakeholders through the following:[13]

- the line ministry or implementing agency proposing the PPP,
- the PPP Authority reviewing and recommending the PPP, and
- the Cabinet Committee for Economic Affairs (CCEA) that is approving the PPP.

The manual also provides clarity and transparency based on which PPP projects will be screened. While the manual has been prepared based on the PPP Policy of 2010, it has not been repealed and continues to be applicable after the PPP Act replaced the PPP Policy. The manual covers various screening conditions for a project: applicability of a PPP, sector coverage, legally permissible, output-driven, sufficient size, financially viable, marketable, bankable, implementable, and endorsement (footnote 13).

Figure 11 provides a snapshot from the manual of the steps for gaining in-principle approval of a PPP project.

---

[13]   Government of Bangladesh, Public Private Partnership Authority. 2013. *PPP Screening Manual*. Dhaka. http://www.pppo.gov.bd/download/ppp_office/PPP-Screening-Manual_Final-Draft_09April2013.pdf.

Figure 11: Steps for Gaining In-Principle Approval for Public–Private Partnership Projects

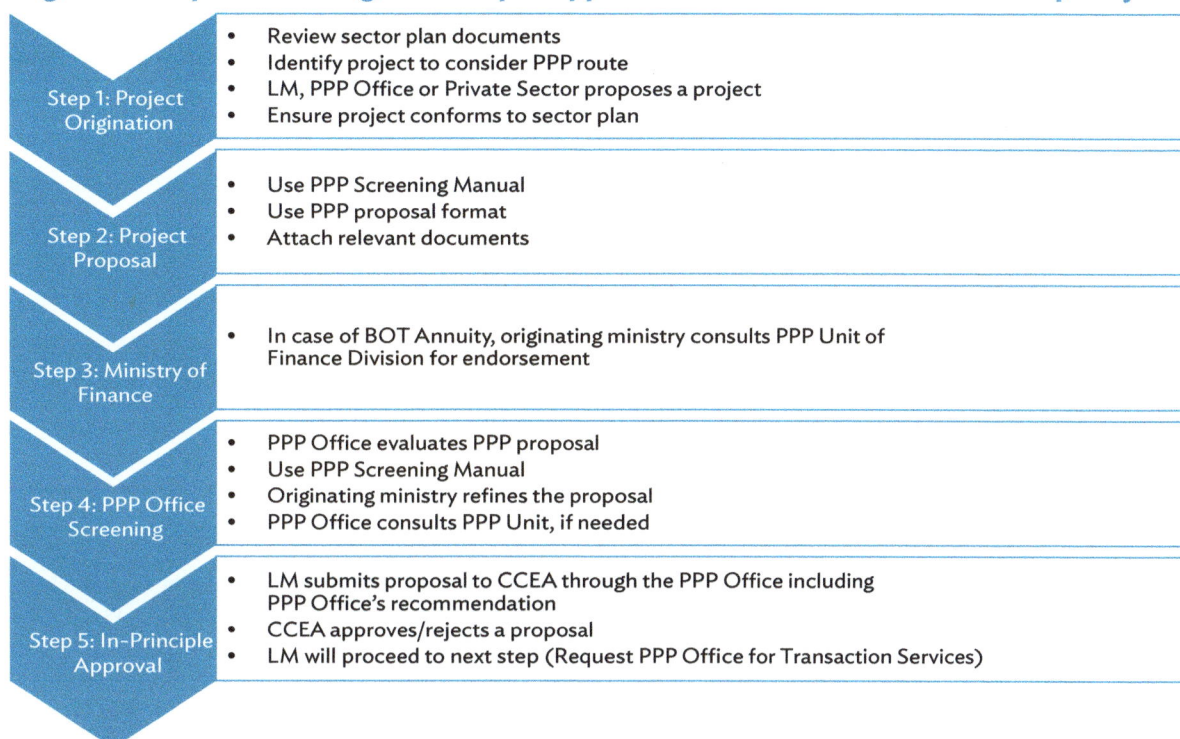

Step 1: Project Origination
- Review sector plan documents
- Identify project to consider PPP route
- LM, PPP Office or Private Sector proposes a project
- Ensure project conforms to sector plan

Step 2: Project Proposal
- Use PPP Screening Manual
- Use PPP proposal format
- Attach relevant documents

Step 3: Ministry of Finance
- In case of BOT Annuity, originating ministry consults PPP Unit of Finance Division for endorsement

Step 4: PPP Office Screening
- PPP Office evaluates PPP proposal
- Use PPP Screening Manual
- Originating ministry refines the proposal
- PPP Office consults PPP Unit, if needed

Step 5: In-Principle Approval
- LM submits proposal to CCEA through the PPP Office including PPP Office's recommendation
- CCEA approves/rejects a proposal
- LM will proceed to next step (Request PPP Office for Transaction Services)

BOT = build-operate-transfer, CCEA = Cabinet Committee on Economic Affairs, LM = line ministry, PPP = public–private partnership.
Source: Government of Bangladesh, Public Private Partnership Authority. 2013. *PPP Screening Manual*. Dhaka. http://www.pppo.gov.bd/download/ppp_office/PPP-Screening-Manual_Final-Draft_09April2013.pdf.

Other Critical Contractual Provisions and Public–Private Partnership Enabling Considerations

Parameter	
Does the law specifically enable lenders the following rights:	
• Security over the project assets?	✓
• Security over the land on which they are built (land use right)?	✓
• Security over the shares of a PPP project company?	✓
Can there be a direct agreement between the government and lenders?	✓
Do lenders get priority in the case of insolvency?	✓
Can lenders be given step-in rights?	✓

✓ = Yes, ✗ = No, NA = Not Applicable, UA = Unavailable
Source: Asian Development Bank. 2019. *Public–Private Partnership Monitor*. Second Edition. Manila. https://www.adb.org/sites/default/files/publication/509426/ppp-monitor-second-edition.pdf.

According to the Bangladesh Bank, the policy framework for foreign investment in Bangladesh is based on the Foreign Private Investment (Promotion and Protection) Act (1980), which ensures legal protection to foreign investment in Bangladesh against nationalization and expropriation. It also guarantees nondiscriminatory treatment between foreign and local investment, and repatriation of proceeds from sales of shares and profit (footnote 1).

It is not possible to give asset security by means of a general security agreement due to the requirement of perfection of security, which involves registration, notification, or recording with separate regulators or parties. An agreement is required in relation to each type of asset, notwithstanding there are different forms of security available such as mortgage over immovable property, hypothecation over present and future book debts, movable properties and plant and machinery, pledge over shares, letters of credit, and corporate or personal guarantees (footnote 1).

Security over shares can be taken by way of pledge of shares, by executing a share pledge agreement. To create a security interest by way of pledge in favor of the lender, the chargors are required to deposit with a third party

- original certificates in respect of the shares; and
- blank share transfer forms executed by each of the chargors, along with verification of the same by the borrower (footnote 1).

Secured creditors have priority over all other creditors and claimants, except floating charge holders as per the Companies Act (1994) and the Bankruptcy Act (1997). The debts are fully payable unless the assets are insufficient to meet them, in which case they are abated in equal proportions (footnote 1).

Parameter	
Does the law specifically enable compensation payment to the private partner in case of early termination due to • Public sector default or termination for reasons of public interest? • Private sector default? • Force majeure?	✓[a] ✓[a] ✓[a]
Does the law enable the concept of economic/financial equilibrium?	✓[a]
Does the law enable compensation payment to the private partner due to • Material adverse government action? • Force majeure? • Change in law?	✓[a] ✓[a] ✓[a]

✓ = Yes, ✗ = No, NA = Not Applicable, UA = Unavailable

[a] The Public–Private Partnership (PPP) Law does not provide for specific guidelines or stipulations related to the above aspects. However, it does not expressly disable the authority from inclusion of terms related to termination and compensation. In general, the regulatory framework does not expressly regulate material adverse government action, force majeure (unforeseen circumstances that prevent someone from fulfilling a contract), or change in law. Chapter 6 of the PPP Act on terms and conditions of partnership contract does not expressly state that the contract shall contain provisions for grounds for termination. However, this is not an exhaustive list, and compensation for such events can be negotiated within the contractual terms agreed between the parties in the PPP agreement.

The Power Purchase Agreement (PPA) for Solar Power Projects expressly provides for events of termination, compensation, force majeure, and default events, and the process and applicability of compensations in each of these events. It does not, however, provide for any recourse for change in law or adverse government actions.

Provisions in Model Contracts

A party to a concession contract is generally excused from performing its obligations when a force majeure event occurs. There are no specific regulations as to force majeure costs. However, under the model contracts, where an indirect political force majeure event occurs after the commercial operation date, and the insurance proceeds recoverable by the project company are insufficient to cover the force majeure costs incurred, the project company can claim a reimbursement from the contracting party equal to 50% of the shortfall.[14]

Under the model contracts, if a direct political force majeure event occurs after a commercial operation date, the project company can claim a reimbursement from the contracting party equal to all the force majeure costs properly and reasonably incurred by the project company in respect of the force majeure event. On termination due to a prolonged force majeure event, the authority generally pays to the contractor 100% of the senior debt termination amount plus equity at par, minus the amount equal to insurance claims admitted and/or paid by the insurance companies (footnote 14).

7. Unsolicited Public–Private Partnership Proposals

Parameter	
Does the public–private partnership legal and regulatory framework allow submission and acceptance of unsolicited proposals?	✓
What are the advantages provided to the project proponent for an unsolicited bid? • Competitive advantage at bid evaluation? • Swiss challenge? • Compensation of the project development costs? • Government support for land acquisition and resettlement cost? • Government support in the form of viability gap funding and guarantees?	 ✓ ✓ [a] ✗ ✓ ✓

✓ = Yes, ✗ = No, NA = Not Applicable, UA = Unavailable
[a] The Guidelines for Unsolicited Proposals (2018) does not explicitly state whether the mode of selection is acceptable or not.

Section 20 of the PPP Act 2015 defines unsolicited proposals as "a written proposal for the implementation of a PPP Project submitted unilaterally by an Original Proponent on its own initiative and not in response to any Formal Government Request," and provides for accepting unsolicited proposals by the contracting authorities. The act further clarifies that the procedure for handling unsolicited proposals shall be in line with the guidelines approved by the Board of Governors of the PPP Authority.[15]

In line with this, the government has published in a gazette the Guidelines for Unsolicited Proposals, 2018, which guides authorities in handling unsolicited proposals. Based on the guidelines, the private sector proponent can submit a concept note—setting out the proposed PPP project scope and its past relevant experience—to the contracting authority for review and consideration, with a copy to the applicable line ministry and the PPP Authority. If a concept note obtains the necessary approvals, then the applicable proponent will be asked to submit its detailed unsolicited proposal. However, the government is not obliged to consider the proposal.[16]

Article 16 of the Guidelines for Unsolicited Proposals indicates the mode of competitive bidding for unsolicited proposals that may include a bonus system as set out in Article 17, or other appropriate methods that may be proposed by the PPP Authority and approved by the approving authority (CCEA). To that extent, the guidelines make options for selection inclusive and do not explicitly discourage other procedures. Therefore, in addition

---

[14] Thomson Reuters, Practical Law. Project Finance in Bangladesh: Overview. https://uk.practicallaw.thomsonreuters.com/Document/I4a320d6517c111e89bf099c0ee06c731/View/FullText.html?transitionType=SearchItem&contextData=(sc.Search).

[15] Government of Bangladesh, Public Private Partnership Authority. 2015. *PPP Law, 2015*. Dhaka. http://www.pppo.gov.bd/download/ppp_office/PPP-Law-2015.pdf.

[16] Government of Bangladesh, Public Private Partnership Authority. 2018. *Guidelines for Unsolicited Proposals, 2018*. Dhaka. http://www.pppo.gov.bd/download/ppp_office/Guidelines-for-Unsolicited-Proposals-2018.pdf.

to competitive advantage in the form of bonus points, the authorities may also adopt other models such as the Swiss challenge (footnote 16).

According to Article 17 of the Guidelines for Unsolicited Proposals (2018), the bonus for the unsolicited bidder would be equivalent to 7% of the evaluation score assessed by the evaluation committee for the proposal or bid submitted by the unsolicited bidder (footnote 16). In previous guidelines (i.e., PPP Unsolicited Procedures, 2014), the Swiss challenge system was also included in the mode of competitive bidding.

Compensation

Article 18 of the guidelines clarifies that all costs related to the unsolicited proposal shall be borne by the project proponent only:

> "All costs and expenses associated with the preparation and submission of the unsolicited proposal or any other costs shall be fully borne by the Original Proponent. The Applicable Line Ministry and/or the Contracting Authority shall not be liable in any manner whatsoever for any such costs and/or expenses incurred by the Original Proponent nor shall they be liable for any losses suffered by the Original Proponent and/or for any actions by the Original Proponent and/or for any consequences thereof" (footnote 16).

It is noted that the Guidelines for Dealing with Unsolicited Proposals (2018) make no specific reference to government support for land acquisition and resettlement costs or viability gap funding (VGF), except that during the project development phase, the contracting authority may seek the PPP Authority's approval to assess the need for VGF and guarantees. However, the Procurement Guidelines for PPP Projects (2018) shall apply to unsolicited proposals subject to incorporation of the requirements of the unsolicited proposal guidelines (footnote 16).

Further, the Rules for Viability Gap Funding for PPP Projects (2018) state that "the VGF shall apply to all kinds of PPP Projects including the national priority PPP projects, and PPP projects taken under the Policy for Implementing PPP Projects through Government-to-Government (G2G) Partnership, 2017."[17]

8. Foreign Investor Participation Restrictions

Parameter	
Is there any restriction for foreign investors on • Land use/ownership rights as opposed to similar rights of local investors? • Currency conversion?	✓ ✓
Public–private partnership projects with foreign sponsor participation (number)	UA

✓ = Yes, ✗ = No, NA = Not Applicable, UA = Unavailable

Foreign Participation

Pursuant to Paragraph 1, Chapter 9 of the Guidelines for Foreign Exchange Transactions (Forex Guidelines), foreign investors are free to make investments in Bangladesh except for a few reserved sectors such as arms and ammunition, nuclear energy or power, security printing, and minting, as mentioned in the Industrial Policy of the Government in force. There is no limitation pertaining to foreign equity participation in nonreserved sectors. An

---

[17]   Government of Bangladesh, Public Private Partnership Authority. 2018. *Rules for Viability Gap Financing for Public–Private Partnership Projects, 2018.* Dhaka. http://www.pppo.gov.bd/download/ppp_office/Rules-for-VGF-for-PPP-Projects-2018.pdf.

entity carrying out a project in a nonreserved sector may, therefore, be set up in collaboration with local investors or may be wholly owned by foreign investors. Therefore, the selected private partner can be a local entity, an entity with 100% foreign ownership, or a foreign-owned local entity (footnote 1).

It is noted that a number of PPPs that have reached financial close were exclusively owned by foreign enterprises, for example, in the transport sector (airports and ports), energy sector (thermal power generation), and social infrastructure sector (health) (footnote 1).

With regard to the use of foreign labor, nationals of all foreign countries, with the exception of Israel, are eligible for work permits in Bangladesh as long as they are age 18 or older. However, according to the Bangladesh Investment Development Authority (BIDA) and the Bangladesh Export Processing Zones Authority (BEPZA) guidelines, expatriate work permits can normally be granted only for posts that require skills and expertise that is not available locally (footnote 1).

The guidelines also specify that the ratio of expatriate to national employees in any company is capped at 1:20 in industrial companies, and 1:5 in commercial offices. According to the Investment Policy Review by the United Nations Conference on Trade and Development (UNCTAD) (2013), the regulatory framework on the issue of work permits lacks transparency and clarity. The laws and regulations that are relevant include the Foreigners Act of 1946, the Foreigners Order of 1951, the Registration of Foreigners Act of 1939, the Bangladesh Control of Entry Act of 1952, and guidelines from BIDA and BEPZA. The key trade policy in Bangladesh is covered in the Export Policy 2015–2018, the Import Policy Order 2015–2018, the Imports and Exports (Control) Act of 1950, and some sector policies. According to the Investment Policy Review by UNCTAD (2013), approval of imports of machinery and equipment has to be sought from BIDA. However, exemptions of duties on the import of machinery and spare parts (for a period of 12 years, or up to 10% of the total capital invested) are offered by the government in certain projects, for example, in power generation. Moreover, companies located in the export processing zones benefit from the standard exemptions of import duties (footnote 1).

The Foreign Investment Act of 1980 guarantees the right of repatriation of invested capital, profits, capital gains, post-tax dividends, and approved royalties and fees. Foreign firms can repatriate funds without much difficulty, provided the appropriate documentation is in order. The foreign exchange regulations may restrict repatriation of divestment proceeds to the net asset value, with repatriation of capital and capital gains being subject to strict reporting requirements or authorization by the Central Bank of Bangladesh, the Bangladesh Bank (footnote 1).

Foreign currency borrowing

For private sector borrowing of foreign currency loans, the Bangladesh Bank requires the borrower to obtain permission from BIDA. Borrowers can raise foreign borrowing from internationally recognized sources such as international banks, international capital markets, multilateral financial institutions, export credit agencies, and suppliers of equipment. Foreign borrowing is allowed for project financing only and cannot be used for working capital. In providing approval, BIDA considers the borrower's past conduct and the financial viability and profitability of the project. The following conditions are generally applicable:

- A maximum 70:30 debt-to-equity ratio. For some sectors such as power, a debt-to-equity ratio of up to 80:20 is allowed.

- A standard interest ratio of up to London interbank offered rate (LIBOR) +4%. An all-in cost ceiling is considered in determining interest, which also includes other annualized fees and expenses (footnote 14).

Foreign direct investments into sectors

Bangladesh actively seeks foreign investment, particularly in the agribusiness, garment and textiles, leather and leather goods, light manufacturing, electronics, light engineering, energy and power, information and communication technology (ICT), plastic, health care, medical equipment, pharmaceutical, ship building, and infrastructure sectors.[18]

Foreign and domestic private entities can establish and own, operate, and dispose of interests in most types of business enterprises. Four sectors, however, are reserved for government investment:

- arms, ammunition, and other defense equipment and machinery;
- forest plantation and mechanized extraction within the bounds of reserved forests;
- production of nuclear energy; and
- security printing (footnote 18).

BIDA is the principal authority tasked with supervising and promoting private investment. In addition to BIDA, three other investment promotion agencies—BEPZA, Bangladesh Economic Zones Authority (BEZA), and Bangladesh Hi-Tech Park Authority (BHTPA)—promote domestic and foreign investment. BEPZA promotes investments in export processing zones (footnote 18).

Bangladesh allows private investment in power generation and natural gas exploration, but efforts to allow full foreign participation in petroleum marketing and gas distribution have stalled. Regulations for telecommunication infrastructure currently include provisions for 60% foreign ownership (70% for tower sharing). In addition to the four sectors reserved for government investment, there are 17 controlled sectors that require prior clearance or permission from the respective line ministries or authorities (footnote 18). These are

- deep-sea fishing;
- bank/financial institutions in the private sector;
- insurance companies in the private sector;
- generation, supply, and distribution of power in the private sector;
- exploration, extraction, and supply of natural gas/oil;
- exploration, extraction, and supply of coal;
- exploration, extraction, and supply of other mineral resources;
- large-scale infrastructure projects (e.g., flyover, elevated expressway, monorail, economic zone, inland container depot/container freight station);
- crude oil refinery (recycling/refining of lube oil used as fuel);
- medium and large industries using natural gas/condensate and other minerals as raw material;
- telecommunications service (mobile/cellular and land phone);
- satellite channels;

---

[18]   US Department of State. 2020. 2020 Investment Climate Statements: Bangladesh. https://www.state.gov/reports/2020-investment-climate-statements/bangladesh/.

- cargo/passenger aviation;
- sea-bound ship transport;
- seaports/deep seaports;
- Voice over Internet Protocol (VOIP/IP) telephone; and
- industries using heavy minerals accumulated from sea beaches.

In certain strategic sectors, the Government of Bangladesh has placed unofficial barriers on the ability of foreign companies to divest from the country (footnote 18).

9. Dispute Resolution

Parameter	
Does the country have a dispute resolution tribunal?	✓
Does the country have an institutional arbitration mechanism?	✓
Can a foreign law be chosen to govern public–private partnership (PPP) contracts?	✓
What dispute resolution mechanisms are available for PPP agreements? • Court litigation? • Local arbitration? • International arbitration?	✓ ✓ ✓
Has the country signed the New York Convention on the Recognition and Enforcement of Foreign Arbitral Awards?	✓

✓ = Yes, ✗ = No, NA = Not Applicable, UA = Unavailable

Clause 30 of the PPP Act expressly provides that disputes arising from the application or interpretation of the provision of the PPP agreement would be settled through mutual agreement between the parties or, if the dispute is not settled, a neutral expert mediator shall intervene. If the dispute is still not resolved by the mediator, it would be referred to arbitration. Furthermore, disputes may only be settled as described above irrespective of other acts or enactments, by means of national or international arbitration rules. The seat of arbitration would normally be in Dhaka; however, in special circumstances and by mutual agreement, the seat may be in other countries as well. Remedy from national or international courts cannot be sought before endeavoring to resolve the dispute under the dispute resolution process as set out in the PPP Act, which takes precedence over any other acts or enactments (footnote 1). The PPP Act provides that the decision taken under an arbitration arrangement pursuant to Clause 30 shall be final.

Arbitration. The first law enacted to tackle arbitration issues was the Arbitration Act 1940, well before Bangladesh came into existence as an independent country. That act was eventually repealed with the enactment of the Arbitration Act 2001, which was heavily influenced by the United Nations Commission on International Trade Law (UNCITRAL) Model Law on International Commercial Arbitration (1985). As stated in Section 11 of the Arbitration Act 2001, it is the right of parties to an arbitration tribunal proceeding to determine the number of arbitrators and, if the parties fail to mutually decide upon the number of arbitrators, there will be three.[19]

---

[19] M. H. Habib. 2021. The International Arbitration Review: Bangladesh. *The Law Reviews*. 4 July. https://thelawreviews.co.uk/title/the-international-arbitration-review/bangladesh.

Foreign Law. The Bangladesh courts will uphold a choice of foreign law agreed among the parties while entering into a contract. It was decided in PLD 1964 Dacca 637 that when the intention of the contractual parties as to the law governing the contract is expressed in words, this expressed intention determines the proper law of the contract and, in general, overrides every other presumption (footnote 14).

10. Environmental and Social Issues

Parameter	
Is there a local regulation establishing a process for environmental impact assessment?	✓
Is there a legal mechanism for the private partner to limit environmental liability for what is outside of its control or caused by third parties?	UA
Is there a local regulation establishing a process for social impact assessment?	✓
Is there involuntary land clearance for public–private partnership projects?	✓

✓ = Yes, ✗ = No, NA = Not Applicable, UA = Unavailable

The Environment Conservation Act (1995) establishes the Department of Environment, which enforces the Environmental Clearance Certificate scheme. The scheme makes it compulsory for any industrial project to obtain a permit before operating. The Environmental Conservation Rules of 1997 define the procedures that industrial investors must follow to obtain a certificate (footnote 1).

Procurement Guidelines for PPP Projects, 2018 specify that the feasibility study of a PPP project includes an overview of environmental and social issues that may need to be addressed, and legislation requires an environmental impact assessment to be carried out (PPP Screening Manual, 2013). An environmental impact assessment evaluates the direct and indirect effects of a project on humans, fauna, and flora; soil, water, air, climate, and landscape; and material assets and the cultural heritage (footnote 1).

There is no special regulation regarding land clearance for PPP projects; however, the Government of Bangladesh has the right, for the benefit of the public, to take private ownership of land by compulsory purchase. This practice has been used for a number of projects, including social infrastructure and transportation projects (footnote 1).

11. Land Rights

Parameter	
Which of the following is permitted to the private partner? • Transfer land lease/use/ownership rights to third party? • Use leased/owned land as collateral? • Mortgage leased/owned land?	✓ ✓ UA
Is there a legal mechanism for granting wayleave rights, for example, laying water pipes or fiber cables over land occupied by persons other than the government or the private partner?	UA
Is there a land registry/cadastre with public information on land plots?	✓
Which of the following information on land plots is available to the private partner? • Appraisal of land value? • Landowners?	✓ ✓

continued on next page

continued from previous page

Parameter	
• Land boundaries?	✓
• Utility connections?	✓
• Immovable property on land?	✓
• Plots classification?	✓

✓ = Yes, ✗ = No, NA = Not Applicable, UA = Unavailable
Source: Asian Development Bank. 2019. *Public–Private Partnership Monitor*. Second Edition. Manila. https://www.adb.org/sites/default/files/publication/509426/ppp-monitor-second-edition.pdf.

There is no special regulation regarding land rights under the PPP framework in Bangladesh; therefore, the general law will apply. The 1972 Constitution (last amended in 2014) provides that all citizens shall have the right to hold, acquire, transfer, and dispose a property; however, the 1950 State Acquisition and Tenancy Act sets a 33-acre land ceiling for private landowners (footnote 1).

The International Comparative Legal Guides for Bangladesh states that, in practice, there is a general understanding that foreign entities cannot own land (based on the Land Office refusing to allow registration to any person not holding a Bangladeshi identification) and, as such, land has to be owned by foreigners through incorporating a company in Bangladesh. The International Comparative Legal Guides also notes that, in many cases, land owned by municipal corporations is leased out to interested parties for long tenures, with restrictions in respect of the transfer of a lease to a foreign entity (footnote 1).

According to the Investment Policy Review by UNCTAD (2013), access to land titles and land registration are subject to many laws and regulations, including the Transfer of Property Act of 1882, the Registration Act of 1908, and the Land Reforms Board Act of 1989. These laws and regulations make it complex, long, and costly to administer and find relevant information for a piece of land. The Bangladesh Registration Rules (2014) stipulate that, among other things, land value, owners, boundaries, and immovable property on land should be captured during land registration (footnote 1).

In Bangladesh, real estate may be held as an owner with freehold right, as a lessee with leasehold rights, or as a licensee with mere right to use.[20]

- **Freehold right**. The landlord of the property enjoys absolute right, title, and interest in the property. Freehold right may be acquired by way of inheritance, gift, will, or purchase. Landlords can deal with the property in the way they desire.

- **Leasehold right**. A person enjoying freehold rights may lease the property along with certain rights, as per agreed terms and conditions, and for a stipulated period, against some consideration to another person to use the property strictly as per the agreed terms and for a specified purpose only.

- **License**. A license is a right to do or continue to do, in or upon the immovable property of the landlord, something which would, in the absence of such right, be unlawful, and such right does not amount to an easement or an interest in the property. A mere license does not create an interest in property to which it relates.

20   DFDL. 2018. *Investment Guide Bangladesh, 2018*. Dhaka. https://www.dfdl.com/resources/publications/investment-guides/bangladesh-investment-guide-2018/.

Foreign persons or entities are not allowed to own real property in Bangladesh. However, certain structures allow foreigners to have ownership rights to real property. Foreigners may incorporate a local company with 100% foreign ownership and have that foreign-owned local company own property. Foreigners can establish joint-venture companies in Bangladesh that can own real property or shares of a local company that owns real property. Foreigners may also lease land in certain specialized areas, such as export processing zones (footnote 20).

GOVERNMENT SUPPORT FOR PUBLIC–PRIVATE PARTNERSHIP PROJECTS

Direct government support for PPP projects in Bangladesh comes primarily by way of project preparation funds and viability gap funding. The country has developed a framework and rules for efficient execution and utilization of the funds.

Overview of Government Support Facilities

Parameter	
Project Funding Support	
Is there a dedicated government financial support mechanism for public–private partnership (PPP) projects?	✓
What are the instruments of government financial support available under this government financial support mechanism?	
• Capital grant?	✓
• Operations grant?	✓
• Annuity/availability payments?	✓
• Guarantees to cover	
– Currency inconvertibility and transfer risk?	✕
– Foreign exchange risk?	✕
– War and civil disturbance risk?	✕
– Breach of contract risk?	✕
– Regulatory risk?	✕
– Expropriation risk?	✕
– Government payment obligation risk?	✓
– Credit risk?	✕
– Minimum demand/revenue risk?	✕
– Risk of making annuity/availability payments in a timely manner?	✕
What are the caps/ceilings for the government financial support under each of the above-mentioned government financial support instruments?	40% of the estimated capital cost for capital grant; 40% of estimated project cost for annuity.
Is there a minimum PPP project size (investment) for a PPP project to be eligible for receiving government financial support?	✕

continued on next page

continued from previous page

Parameter	
Are there minimum financial commitment requirements for private developer equity before government support can be drawn?	✗ The rules indicate a pro-rata disbursement based on equity contribution, but no specific minimum limits.
Is government financial support required, usually the bid parameter for PPP projects?	✓[a]
Are unsolicited PPP proposals eligible to receive government financial support?	✓
Are there standard operating procedures for providing government financial support to PPP projects? • Appraisal and approval process? • Budgeting process? • Disbursement process? • Monitoring process? • Accounting, auditing, and reporting process?	 ✓ ✓ ✓ ✓ ✓
Who are the signatories to the Government Financial Support Agreement?	PPP Unit of Finance Division; lead financial institution and project company/ special-purpose vehicle
Who is responsible for monitoring the performance of PPP projects with government financial support? • Independent engineer? • Government agency? • Ministry of Finance?	Contracting authority and lead financial institution
What are the other forms of government support available for PPP projects? • Land acquisition funding support? • Funding support for resettlement and rehabilitation of affected parties?[b] • Tax holidays/exemptions? • Real estate development rights? • Advertising and marketing rights? • Interest rate/cost of debt subventions? • Other subsidies and subventions?	 UA ✓ ✓ UA UA UA UA
Can other forms of government support be availed over and above the government financial support, through various instruments listed above?	✓

✓ = Yes, ✗ = No, NA = Not Applicable, UA = Unavailable

[a] Rule No. 5, subpoint (i) of the Rules for Viability Gap Funding for PPP Projects (2018) states that "The viability gap funding (VGF) amount shall be set by the Government or the Preferred Bidder's offer and in both cases the bid parameter shall be in accordance with the PPP Act and Power Generation Policy, 2018." Also, subpoint (j) states that "Where the VGF is based on Preferred Bidder's offer, the VGF shall form a key component of the financial evaluation criteria alongside other technical evaluation criteria." However, both the Procurement Guidelines 2018 and the PPP Law are silent on specific selection/bid parameters for projects that make use of VGF-related proposals.

[b] Asian Development Bank. 2019. *Public–Private Partnership Monitor.* Second Edition. Manila. https://www.adb.org/sites/default/files/publication/509426/ppp-monitor-second-edition.pdf.

Clause 16 of the PPP Law clarifies details about the financial participation of the government in PPP projects, and states that "the government may provide financing against the following activities of PPP projects, such as

- technical assistance financing,
- viability gap financing,
- financing against equity and loan,
- financing against linked component, and
- financing against such other activities as may be determined by the PPP Authority."

Thereby, the options and forms in which the government could support PPPs have been kept open-ended and based on recommendations made by the PPP Authority.

Viability Gap Funding

As indicated above, Clause 16 specifies that the government could extend its support by way of viability gap funding (VGF). The operationalization of the VGF was initially driven by the Guidelines for VGF for PPP Projects, 2012, which were repealed and replaced by the Rules for VGF for PPP Projects, 2018. The latter defines various rules toward operationalizing the VGF. The rules provide that the VGF could be applicable to any kind of PPP projects, including unsolicited proposals, in the following form:

- capital grant, in which case the maximum support would be up to 40% of the total estimated capital cost of the project; or
- annuity, in which case the maximum support would be up to 40% of the total estimated project cost; or
- combination of both, in which case the maximum support would be up to 40% of the total estimated project cost (footnote 17).

From the eligibility perspective, the rules prescribe certain prerequisites, including the following:

- The PPP project shall be a project taken up under the PPP Act and shall provide a public service against predetermined tariff or user charge.
- The project meets the threshold economic rate of return (ERR), as specified by the PPP Unit, Finance Division from time to time.
- The project should have detailed feasibility study prepared, including computation of ERR (footnote 17).

Based on the project company's request for disbursement received by the PPP Unit of the Finance Division through the contracting authority, the PPP Unit shall review the request and disburse the VGF to the project company through the lead financial institution, as per agreed terms. Point 10 of the rules also specifies that the "Contracting Authority shall be responsible for regular monitoring and periodic evaluation of the PPP Project compliance with agreed milestones and performance levels" and further indicates that "the Lead Financial Institution shall also be responsible for regular monitoring and periodic evaluation of the PPP Project compliance with agreed milestones and performance levels..., and it shall also send a quarterly progress report to the Contracting Authority, PPP Authority, and PPP Unit of the Finance Division" (footnote 17).

Although the VGF has not been utilized yet in the country, agreements have been reached for the VGF to support the road projects indicated below:

- Dhaka Elevated Expressway,
- Upgrading of Dhaka Bypass to 4-Lane (Madanpur–Debogram–Bhulta–Joydevpur),
- Flyover from Shantinagar to Mawa Road via 4th (New) Bridge over Buriganga River, and
- Dhaka-Chittagong Access Controlled Highway.

Land Acquisition and Resettlement

The government support for PPP projects may also take the form of acquisition or requisition of land, resettlement of populations, or the provision of utilities. Examples where the government was responsible for land acquisition are the Bibiyana 300–450 MW Gas-Fired Combined Cycle Power Project and the Dhaka Elevated Expressway PPP Project. According to the World Bank Benchmarking of PPP Procurement in Bangladesh, the procuring authority spends an average of 270 calendar days for obtaining permits, land, and/or right-of-way required under the regulatory framework. The applicable law in this regard is the Acquisition and Requisition of Immovable Property Act, 2017 (footnote 1).

Government Guarantees and Tax Subsidies

PPP regulations are silent on the provision of government guarantees. In practice, a number of energy generation projects received payment guarantees under PPAs; however, in other sectors, guarantees have not been provided. The government is offering fiscal incentives to PPP investors, such as reduced import tax on capital goods and various tax holidays, with the aim of reducing the cost of implementing the project and enhancing its viability. The government has also provided tax exemptions for foreign technicians on capital gains and royalty fees, and on the income of a project company in relation to the implementation of PPP projects in certain sectors (including highways, bridges, and ports). Value-added tax exemptions are also available in relation to certain services provided for PPP projects, and the incentives may vary based on the project location (footnote 1).

Parameter	
Project Development Funding	
What are the various sources of funds for public–private partnership (PPP) project preparation? • Budgetary allocations? • Dedicated project preparation/Project Development Fund? • Technical assistance from multilateral/bilateral and donor agencies? • Recovery of project preparation funding from the preferred bidder?	✓ ✓ ✓ ✓
At what stage of the PPP project can the project preparation/development funding be availed by the government agency? • Prefeasibility stage? • Detailed feasibility stage? • Transaction stage?	✗ ✓ ✓
Is there a threshold size (investment) for a PPP project to avail project development funding?	✗
Is there a list of project preparation/project development activities toward which the project development funding can be utilized?	✓
Can the project development funding be utilized to appoint transaction advisors for PPP projects?	✓

continued on next page

continued from previous page

Parameter	
Is there a specific process to be followed by government agencies to appoint transaction advisors?	✓
What are the payment mechanisms for making payments to transaction advisors? • Time-sheet based? • Milestone-based?	 ✓ ✓
Are there standard agreements and documents pertaining to project development funding?	UA
Who are the signatories to the project development funding agreements?	PPP Authority and line agency/ministry

✓ = Yes, ✗ = No, NA = Not Applicable, UA = Unavailable

According to procurement guidelines issued by the government, the contracting authority or the PPP Authority should adhere to the process provided in the Public Procurement Act, 2006 and the Public Procurement Rules, 2008, including any amendments to them, in order to appoint the transaction advisor(s) and/or consultant(s) until the applicable policies, rules, regulations, guidance, guidelines, or notifications for appointment of transaction advisor(s) and/or consultants under the PPP Act are promulgated.

Public–Private Partnership Technical Assistance Fund

Clause 16 of the PPP Law specifies that the government could extend its support by way of technical assistance financing. The operationalization of the Public–Private Partnership Technical Assistance Fund (PPPTAF) was initially based on the Guidelines for PPPTAF, 2012, which were repealed and replaced by the Rules for PPPTAF 2018. The latter defines various rules toward operationalizing the technical assistance fund. The fund is administered and managed by the PPP Authority, and fund utilization is reported semiannually to the PPP Unit, Finance Division.

The PPPTAF had an initial government contribution of Tk2 billion and is replenished by way of

- recovery from the successful bidders;
- budgetary support, if required, by the Ministry of Finance; and
- grants from national and international financial institutions or development partners, subject to government approval.[21]

Rule 6 of the Rules for PPPTAF describes the activities eligible for utilizing the fund, such as

- development of individual PPP projects, including detailed feasibility and procurement;
- capacity-building activities;
- promotional activities for PPP programs and projects;
- development of regulations, policies, and other related activities for PPP; and
- development of sector-based programs for PPP (footnote 21).

21   Government of Bangladesh, Public Private Partnership Authority. 2018. *Rules for Public–Private Partnership Technical Assistance Financing, 2018.* Dhaka. http://www.pppo.gov.bd/download/ppp_office/Rules-for-PPPTAF-2018.pdf.

One of the prerequisites for PPP projects to use the PPPTAF is the CCEA's in-principle approval, which indicates that the PPPTAF cannot be utilized for prefeasibility studies. The fund can be used for appointing consultants by the PPP Authority, if such appointment is made on a competitive bidding basis, as per the Public Procurement Act, 2006, and rules made thereunder. Fund utilization is based on the proposal submitted by the contracting authority, reviewed by the PPP Authority, and approved by an interministerial committee based on recommendations of the PPP Authority (footnote 21).

The Public Procurement Rules, 2008 of Bangladesh provide guidelines and standard documents for selection of consultants that include both lump-sum contracts and time-based contracts, signifying that both modes are allowed in Bangladesh.

MATURITY OF THE PUBLIC–PRIVATE PARTNERSHIP MARKET

Parameter	
Public–Private Partnership (PPP) Project Statistics	
Is there a national PPP database for the country?	✕
Is the distribution of PPP projects across infrastructure sectors available?	NA
Is the distribution of PPP projects across various stages of the PPP life cycle available? – Prefeasibility preliminary assessment stage? – Full feasibility assessment stage? – Transaction stage? – Commercial close? – Financial close?	NA NA NA NA NA

✓ = Yes, ✕ = No, NA = Not Applicable, UA = Unavailable

There is no comprehensive database of the projects that could be accessed for the overall PPP projects.

Parameter	
Does the country publish a national public–private partnership (PPP) project pipeline?	✓
At what frequency is the national PPP project pipeline published?	UA
Is the national PPP project pipeline based on the national infrastructure plan for the country?	✕

✓ = Yes, ✕ = No, NA = Not Applicable, UA = Unavailable

The PPP Law and Guidelines for procurement specify that the "Contracting Authority and/or the PPP Authority may identify a Project to be delivered on a PPP basis from the list of Projects set out in the Government's Annual Development Program or may identify a Project that is not listed in the ADP," indicating that the projects taken up on PPP need not necessarily be part of the country's annual development program but should be justified on a need basis for necessary approvals from the PPP Authority and the CCEA.

The PPP Authority prepares and maintains a PPP project pipeline that is published in its annual report and available on the PPP Authority's website. The pipeline provides the name and status of the project, along with a short profile of the project for investors. The status of the project reflects at which stage the project currently is and is categorized as follows:[22]

22   Government of Bangladesh, Public Private Partnership Authority. PPP Projects. http://www.pppo.gov.bd/projects.php.

- Preparation Stage
  - (i)   CCEA approved (in principle)
  - (ii)   Project development stage – Advisor appointment to be initiated
  - (iii)   Project development stage – Advisor appointment
  - (iv)   Project development stage – Detailed feasibility study ongoing
  - (v)   Project development stage – Detailed feasibility study completed
- Procurement Stage
  - (i)   Procurement stage – CCEA final approval to be obtained
  - (ii)   Procurement stage – Invitation for bids (IFB) to be issued
  - (iii)   Procurement stage – IFB evaluation ongoing
  - (iv)   Procurement stage – Evaluation completed
  - (v)   Procurement stage – Legal vetting ongoing
  - (vi)   Procurement stage – Request for proposal (RFP) to be issued
  - (vii) Procurement stage – RFP issued
  - (viii) Procurement stage – RFP evaluation ongoing
  - (ix)   Procurement stage – Negotiation completed
  - (x)   Procurement stage – No bid received
  - (xi)   Procurement stage – Tender unsuccessful
  - (xii) Procurement stage – Retender to be started
- Award Stage
  - (i)   Award stage – Contract to be signed
  - (ii)   Award stage – Contract signed
- Post-Award Stage
  - (i)   Construction stage
  - (ii)   Operational stage

The Bangladesh Economic Review 2019 lists 56 projects in 13 sectors, worth $23.8 billion, that have been approved for implementation through PPP.[23]

In addition, many independent power producers (IPPs), considered to be a form of PPP, are listed in the renewable energy master database of the Sustainable and Renewable Energy Development Authority.

---

[23]   Ministry of Finance, Finance Division. 2019. *Bangladesh Economic Review 2019*. Dhaka. https://mof.portal.gov.bd/sites/default/files/files/mof.portal.gov.bd/page/e8bc0eaa_463d_4cf9_b3be_26ab70a32a47/Banglades%20Economic%20Review%202019%20Eng.zip.

Parameter	Yes / No
Sources of Public–Private Partnership (PPP) Financing	
Who are the typical entities financing PPP projects in the country?	
– Private developers?	✓
– Construction contractors?	UA
– Institutional/financial/private equity investors?	UA
– Pension funds?	UA
– Insurance companies?	UA
– Banks?	✓
– Nonbank financial companies/financial institutions?	✓
– Donor agencies?	✓
– Government agencies and state-owned enterprises?	✓
What is the distribution of financing among these entities financing PPP projects?	UA
Does the country have a history of issuing bonds by infrastructure projects?	✗
How many infrastructure projects/private developers for infrastructure projects have raised funding through bond issuances?	NA
What is the value of funding raised through capital markets by PPPs?	NA
Does the country have a matured derivatives market to hedge certain risks associated with PPPs?	✗
Does the country have a National Development Bank?	✓
Does the country have credit rating agencies to rate infrastructure projects?	✓
Typically, what are the credit ratings achieved/received by infrastructure projects?	UA
Is there a threshold credit rating for infrastructure PPPs below which institutional investors, pension funds, and insurance companies would not invest in infrastructure PPPs?	UA
What is the typical funding model for infrastructure PPPs—corporate finance or project finance?	Both
Are there regulatory limits/restrictions for maximum exposure banks can take to infrastructure projects?	UA

✓ = Yes, ✗ = No, NA = Not Applicable, UA = Unavailable

Table 7 shows the vehicles and options available in Bangladesh to support PPP projects financially.

Table 7: Financing Options for Infrastructure Projects in Bangladesh

Unit	Role
Bangladesh Infrastructure Finance Fund Limited (BIFFL)	To encourage the private sector to invest in public–private partnership (PPP) projects, the BIFFL, a nonbanking financial institution, was incorporated by the Ministry of Finance in 2011. The objective is to provide long-term financing in local currency to infrastructure projects that meet the BIFFL's investment criteria. The BIFFL seeks to attract investment from both institutional and retail investors (including nonresident Bangladeshis and overseas foreign workers) to provide an alternative savings/investment vehicle in the Bangladesh market. The BIFFL is managed independently, following objective investment criteria, and is targeted to provide a variety of capital products to PPP projects, including long-term debt, short-term construction capital, and equity (future). In August 2020, the Asian Development Bank approved a $50 million loan to the Government of Bangladesh to fund PPP infrastructure projects in the country. The project will support government efforts in strengthening the BIFFL's institutional capacity to develop PPP infrastructure projects.

continued on next page

Table 7 *continued*

Unit	Role
Infrastructure Development Company Limited (IDCOL)	The IDCOL, established in 1997 by the Government of Bangladesh as a nonbank financial institution, plays a major role in bridging the financing gap for developing medium- to large-scale infrastructure and renewable energy projects in Bangladesh. The company now stands as the market leader in private sector energy and infrastructure financing in Bangladesh. The IDCOL offers a full range of financing solutions to viable private-sector-owned infrastructure projects, including long-term local and foreign currency loans, working capital loans, debt and equity arrangement, debt restructuring, takeover financing, and financial advisory and agency services. The IDCOL has expanded its infrastructure financing window, bringing in social and tourism infrastructure as well as infrastructure-backward linkage industries under the broad definition of infrastructure. The IDCOL also provides concessionary financing support to projects with significant positive contributions toward environmental conservation and pollution control.
Investment Promotion and Financial Facility (IPFF)	The IPFF aims to finance private infrastructure projects based on PPP. Private investors can approach the participating financial institutions (PFIs) to access funds allocated under the IPFF program. The first round of international investment position (IIP) had World Bank's International Development Association (IDA) credit of $307 million, with the Government of Bangladesh cofinancing $60 million. The implementing agency was the Bangladesh Bank, operating through 19 PFIs. The IPFF II Project (July 2017–June 2022), a follow-on project of the IPFF, has been taken up by the Government of Bangladesh (with the financial support of the World Bank) to create a sustainable platform for long-term financing in infrastructure and further strengthen the capacity of the private sector in filling the substantial infrastructure gap in Bangladesh. The main objective of the project is to increase long-term financing for infrastructure and to build capacity of local financial institutions for promoting private-sector-led infrastructure financing in Bangladesh. The estimated cost of the IPFF II Project is $416.7 million ($356.7 million from the IDA and $60.0 million from the Government of Bangladesh). The eligible sectors for financing under the IPFF II Project include power; port development; environmental, industrial, and solid waste management; highways and expressways; airports; water supply and distribution; industrial estates and parks; social sector; and information technology. The technical assistance component is being utilized in procuring consultants and building capacity of key stakeholders, such as the PPP Authority and the BIFFL. Component 1 of the IPFF II was a long-term infrastructure financing component, while Component 2 was technical assistance. Component 1 was provided to PFIs for further on-lending and investment support of long-term infrastructure investments by private sector investors and an investment sponsor. In addition to conventional debt, Component 1 was envisaged to include innovative debt instruments such as promoter/sponsor loans, mezzanine financing, takeout financing facilities, and specialized project/infrastructure bonds. In addition, equity and credit guarantees and credit enhancement were piloted through the BIFFL.

Sources: Asian Development Bank. 2020. *Bangladesh: Strengthening Bangladesh Infrastructure Finance Fund Limited Project.* Manila. https://www.adb.org/projects/51311-001/main; Bangladesh Bank. Bangladesh. https://www.bb.org.bd/aboutus/dept/dept_details.php; Bangladesh Infrastructure Finance Fund Limited. About BIFFL. https://biffl.org.bd/; and IDCOL. Bangladesh. https://idcol.org/home/about.

Table 8 shows the features of key infrastructure financing sources in Bangladesh.

Table 8: Key Infrastructure Financing Sources in Bangladesh

Item	Non/Limited Recourse Loan	Non/Limited Recourse Local Currency Loan	Project Financing, Local Public Sector Banks	Interest Rate Swaps	Currency Swaps	Project Financing through Project Bond Issuance
Maximum tenor, in years	5–7	6–8	5–10	15	<5	UA
Up-front arrangement fee, bps	UA	100–200				UA
Floor rate	LIBOR	Central Bank Lending Rate				UA
Margin rate, bps	UA	UA				UA
Percentage of foreign debt out of total debt for project financing			<30%			UA
Percentage of project bonds out of total debt for project financing						
Typical debt-to-equity ratio			75:25			
Timeline to financial close (month)			>12			
Minimum DSCR covenant levels, x			>1.5x			
Nominal interest rates						
Real interest rates						
Security package		-				

bps = basis points, DSCR = debt service coverage ratio, LIBOR = London interbank offered rate, UA = unavailable.
Source: Asian Development Bank. 2019. *Public–Private Partnership Monitor*. Second Edition. Manila. https://www.adb.org/sites/default/files/publication/509426/ppp-monitor-second-edition.pdf.

Table 9 shows the most active banks in project finance in Bangladesh over the past 24 months.

Table 9: Active Banks in Project Finance in Bangladesh in 24 Months Preceding December 2019

Bank	Total Project Financing		Transaction
	$ million	Tk billion	
Bank of China	590.16	50.05	1
Export-Import Bank of China (China Exim Bank)	590.16	50.05	1
China Construction Bank	590.16	50.05	1
Exim Bank of China	461.00	39.09	1

continued on next page

Table 9 *continued*

| Bank | Total Project Financing | | Transaction |
	$ million	Tk billion	
Industrial and Commercial Bank of China	400.00	33.92	1
Sumitomo Mitsui Banking Corporation	219.00	18.57	3
Clifford Capital	173.00	14.67	2
Infrastructure Development Company, Limited	80.87	6.86	1

Source: Inframation Group. Country Factbook—Bangladesh. https://www.inframationnews.com/country-factbook/3747026/bangladesh.thtml (accessed 7 July 2020).

Equity sponsors also play an important role in the development of projects. Table 10 shows the most active project sponsors over the last 24 months.

Table 10: Active Project Sponsors in Bangladesh in 24 Months Preceding December 2019

| Name | Total Project Financing | | Transaction |
	$ million	Tk billion	
S. Alam Group	2,459.00	208.53	1
SEPCO Electric Power Construction Corporation III	2,459.00	208.53	1
HTG Development Group	2,459.00	208.53	1
Italian–Thai Development	1,133.37	96.11	1
Summit Power Limited (Bangladesh)	207.00	17.55	1
Mitsubishi Corporation	139.00	11.79	1
Summit Corporation Limited	139.00	11.79	1
Symbior Solar	80.87	6.86	1
Paragon Group	80.87	6.86	1

Source: Inframation Group. Country Factbook— Bangladesh. https://www.inframationnews.com/country-factbook/3747026/bangladesh.thtml (accessed 7 July 2020).

Credit Rating Agencies in Bangladesh

There were eight credit rating agencies registered in Bangladesh in early 2020, as indicated in Table 11.[24]

Table 11: Credit Rating Agencies in Bangladesh

Rating Company	Subsidiary/Technical Partner of	Date of Issuance of Registration Certificate
Credit Rating Information and Services Ltd.	Rating Agency Malaysia Berhad	28/08/2002
Credit Rating Agency of Bangladesh Ltd.	ICRA Limited of India	24/02/2004
Emerging Credit Rating Ltd.	Malaysian Rating Corporation Berhad	22/06/2010

continued on next page

24   Bangladesh Securities and Exchange Commission. List of Credit Rating Agencies. https://www.sec.gov.bd/home/cragency (accessed 24 June 2020).

Table 11 *continued*

Rating Company	Subsidiary/Technical Partner of	Date of Issuance of Registration Certificate
National Credit Rating Ltd.	The Pakistan Credit Rating Agency Ltd.	22/06/2010
ARGUS Credit Rating Services Ltd.	DP Information Group, Singapore	21/07/2011
WASO Credit Rating Company (BD) Limited	Financial Intelligence Services Ltd.	15/02/2012
Alpha Credit Rating Limited	Istanbul International Rating Services Inc.	20/02/2012
The Bangladesh Rating Agency Limited	Dun & Bradstreet South Asia Middle East Ltd.	07/03/2012

Note: Dates expressed in dd/mm/yyyy format.
Source: Bangladesh Securities and Exchange Commission. List of Credit Rating Agencies. https://www.sec.gov.bd/home/cragency (accessed 24 June 2020).

The credit rating agencies are regulated by the Bangladesh Securities and Exchange Commission. According to the annual financial stability report of 2018 published by the Central Bank of Bangladesh (the Bangladesh Bank), "Most of the corporate entities/exposures obtained the similar credit rating in 2018 in comparison to the rating of 2017. The percentage of upward migration of credit ratings was greater than downward migration in 2018" reflecting the "resilience of the financial system with respect to corporate solvency."[25]

---

[25]   Bangladesh Bank. 2018. *Financial Stability Report 2018*. Issue 9. Dhaka. https://www.bb.org.bd/pub/puball.php (accessed 20 July 2020).

III. Sector-Specific Public–Private Partnership Landscape

A. ROADS

Parameter	Value	Unit
Length of the total road network	2,39,226	kilometer
Quality of road infrastructure	3.2	1 (low) – 7 (high)

Sources: The Global Economy. Compare Countries. https://www.theglobaleconomy.com/compare-countries/; and Trading Economics. Bangladesh—Road Total Network. https://tradingeconomics.com/bangladesh/roads-total-network-km-wb-data.html.

1. Contracting Agencies in the Roads Sector

The Ministry of Road Transport and Bridges (MRTB) oversees this sector. In Bangladesh, roads and bridges are two different subjects with two different departments—the Road Transport and Highways Division, and the Bridges Division. Each is responsible for implementing their respective projects. The Roads and Highways Department is the contracting authority for implementing road and highway public–private partnership (PPP) projects. The Bridges Division implements PPP bridge and flyover projects (footnote 1).

2. Roads Sector Laws and Regulations

The roads sector still does not have an independent regulator to perform checks on service standard, performance, safety, and tariff. The controlling and regulating roles are carried out by each subdivision within the MRTB (footnote 1). Table 12 indicates the key institutions in the roads sector in Bangladesh.

Table 12: Key Institutions in the Roads Sector in Bangladesh

Agency	Function
Roads and Highways Department (RHD)	The RHD was created in 1962 when the old Construction and Building organization was split into two bodies, the other being the Public Works Department. The RHD is responsible for the construction and maintenance of major road and bridge network in Bangladesh. Since the department has been established, the size of the major road network in Bangladesh has grown from 2,500 kilometers to the present network of 22,096 kilometers.
Bangladesh Bridge Authority, Bridges Division	The Bridges Division plays a significant role in the socioeconomic development of Bangladesh. This division was created in March 2008 to deal with all matters relating to planning, implementation, monitoring, and evaluation of construction of bridges that are at least 1,500 meters in length, toll roads, flyovers, expressways, causeways, and link roads. It also seeks to secure funds for projects from both external and internal sources.

Sources: Bangladesh Bridge Authority. BBA at a Glance. http://www.bba.gov.bd/site/page/d27d493c-4aa1-4ce1-a932-452ec2a5665b/-; and Government of Bangladesh, Roads and Highways Department. Overview of RHD. https://rhd.portal.gov.bd/site/page/b34dca5c-5352-4fd2-9533-715058f45951/-.

Regulations in the roads sector include

- Highway Act, 2001;
- Road Maintenance Fund Board, 2013;
- Bangladesh Bridge Authority Act, 2017;
- Road Transport Law, 2018;
- Bangladesh Road Transport Authority Law, 2017;
- Dhaka Transport Coordination Authority (Amendment) Act, 2012;
- The Toll Act, 1851;
- Padma Multipurpose Bridge Project (Land Acquisition) Act, 2009;
- Jamuna Bridge Authority Ordinance, 1975; and
- Dhaka Elevated Expressway Project (Land Acquisition) Act, 2011.

2.1 Foreign Investment Restrictions in the Roads Sector

Parameter	2017	2018	2019
Maximum allowed foreign ownership of equity in greenfield projects	100%	100%	100%

There are no limitations to foreign investments except for certain restricted sectors. The above may be reviewed against the restrictions and limitations held by the government, as explained in Chapter II Section 8.

2.2 Standard Contracts in the Roads Sector

Type of Contract	Availability
Public–private partnership/concession agreement	✕
Performance-based operations and maintenance contract	✕
Engineering, procurement, and construction contract	✕

✓ = Yes, ✕ = No, NA = Not Applicable, UA = Unavailable
Source: Asian Development Bank. 2019. *Public–Private Partnership Monitor*. Second Edition. Manila. https://www.adb.org/sites/default/files/publication/509426/ppp-monitor-second-edition.pdf.

3. Roads Sector Master Plan

The Road Master Plan for 2009–2029 outlines maintaining road and bridge assets and improving connectivity, along with developing strategic road networks, as impetus for meeting economic and traffic growth targets. Bangladesh has sought technical assistance from the Asian Development Bank (ADB) to update the Road Master Plan by fourth quarter of 2019. The projects identified under the Road Master Plan (2009–2029) include the following:[26]

- 37 capital programs and projects, with an estimated total cost of $5.1 billion; and
- recurrent expenditure programs, including traffic management, periodic maintenance, and road safety measures for these projects, with a cost estimated at $3.5 billion.

---

[26] Private Infrastructure Development Group, GuarantCo, and Technical Assistance Facility. 2019. *Study of Bangladesh Bond Market*. Dhaka. https://guarantco.com/gco/wp-content/uploads/2019/Documents/news/Study-of-Bangladesh-Bond-Market.pdf.

There are several projects planned by the MRTB in Bangladesh being taken up by both the Road Transport and Highways Division and the Bridges Division. A list of megaprojects that are being taken up by the Ministry under each division are indicated below:[27]

- Payra Bridge on Payra River (Lebukhali Bridge) Construction Project,
- Greater Dhaka Sustainable Urban Transport Project,
- Dhaka Mass Rapid Transit Development Project (Metrorail),
- Upgradation of Joydebpur–Chandra–Tangail–Elenga Road (N-4) 4-Lane Highway,
- Kanchpur, Meghna and Gomti 2nd Bridge Construction and Bridge Rehabilitation Project,
- Western Bangladesh Bridge Improvement Project,
- Cross-Border Road Network Improvement Project (Bangladesh),
- Sasek Link Road-2: Elenga–Hatikumrul–Rangpur Highway 4-Lane Upgradation, and
- Completion of unfinished work of a four-lane development project from Jatrabari intersection of Dhaka–Khulna (N-6) highway (including Ikuria–Babubazar link road) to Mawa and with five lanes for vehicles in Panchchar–Bhanga section.

The projects that are at planning stage being taken up by the Bangladesh Bridge Authority are shown in Table 13.

Table 13: Projects of the Bangladesh Bridge Authority under Planning Stage

No.	Name of Project	Estimated Cost		Status
		($ million)	(Tk billion)	
1	Construction of Dhaka–Ashulia Elevated Expressway	1,300.00	110.24	A memorandum of understanding has been signed with the China National Machinery Import and Export Corporation (based in the People's Republic of China) to implement the project on government-to-government basis. Negotiation on commercial proposal is progressing.
2	Feasibility study for the construction of Subway in Dhaka City	30.25	2.57	Expression of interest invited for appointment of consultant. Proposals received and evaluation progressing.
3	Feasibility study for the construction of Dhaka Chittagong Elevated Expressway	10.12	0.86	Expression of interest invited for appointment of consultant. Proposals received and evaluation progressing.
4	Construction of Dhaka East West Elevated Expressway	1,050.00	89.04	CCEA In-principle approved and Technical Feasibility complete
5	Construction of bridge on Labukhali Dumki–Boga–Dashmina–Amragachi road over the river Galachipa	74.00	6.28	Feasibility study completed and preliminary development project proforma/proposal (PDPP) has been approved

continued on next page

---

27   Ministry of Road Transport and Bridges, Road Transport and Highways Division. Megaprojects. http://103.48.18.161/mega_project.php (accessed 11 August 2020).

Table 13 *continued*

No.	Name of Project	Estimated Cost ($ million)	Estimated Cost (Tk billion)	Status
6	Construction of bridge on Rahmatpur Babuganj–Muladi–Hizla road over the river Arialkhan	73.00	6.19	Feasibility study completed and PDPP has been approved
7	Construction of bridge on Kochua–Betagi Patuakhali–Lohalia–Kalaya road over the river Payra	104.00	8.82	Feasibility study completed and PDPP has been approved
8	Construction of bridge on Patuakhali Amtoli–Barguna–Kakchira road over the river Payra	156.00	13.23	Appointment of consultant for conducting feasibility study being processed
9	Construction of bridge on Bakergonj–Baufal road over the river Karkhana	125.00	10.60	Appointment of consultant for conducting feasibility study being processed
10	Construction of bridge on Barisal–Bhola road over the river Kalabadar and Tetulia	3,000.00	254.41	Appointment of consultant for conducting feasibility study being processed

Source: Bangladesh Bridge Authority Projects. http://www.bba.gov.bd/ (accessed 3 August 2020).

The website of the Bangladesh Bridge Authority publishes on a regular basis a list of projects that are at various stages of development: ongoing projects, projects in pipeline, completed projects, and feasibility study reports.[28] The Road Transport and Highways Division also publishes on its website a list of projects classified into megaprojects, foreign-aided projects, fast-track projects, and approved projects.[29]

The PPP Authority lists the projects specifically taken up on a PPP basis. As per the PPP Authority's list of projects updated up to March 2020, there are seven projects in the roads sector, of which five are under preparation and two under procurement. A list of projects is provided in Table 14.

Table 14: Projects under Preparation and Procurement as per the Public–Private Partnership Authority

Project Name	Status
Construction of Outer Ring Road	Technical feasibility complete and Transaction advisor mobilized
2nd Padma Multipurpose Bridge at Paturia–Goalundo	CCEA approved (in principle)
Improvement of Chattogram–Cox's Bazar Highway on PPP Basis	Project development stage – Detailed feasibility study ongoing
Gabtoli–Nabinagar PPP Road	Technical feasibility complete, VGF approval from Finance Division under process
Dhaka–Chittagong Access Controlled Highway	Project development stage – Detailed feasibility study ongoing

CCEA = Cabinet Committee on Economic Affairs, PPP = public–private partnership, RFP = request for proposal.
Source: Government of Bangladesh, Public Private Partnership Authority. PPP Projects. http://www.pppo.gov.bd/projects.php (accessed 15 June 2020).

---

[28] Bangladesh Bridge Authority. Projects. http://www.bba.gov.bd/.
[29] Ministry of Road Transport and Bridges, Road Transport and Highways Division. Projects. https://rthd.portal.gov.bd/.

3.1 Projects under Preparation and Procurement in the Roads Sector

Figure 12 shows the number of projects under preparation and procurement in the roads sector of Bangladesh.

Figure 12: Public–Private Partnership Road Projects under Preparation and Procurement

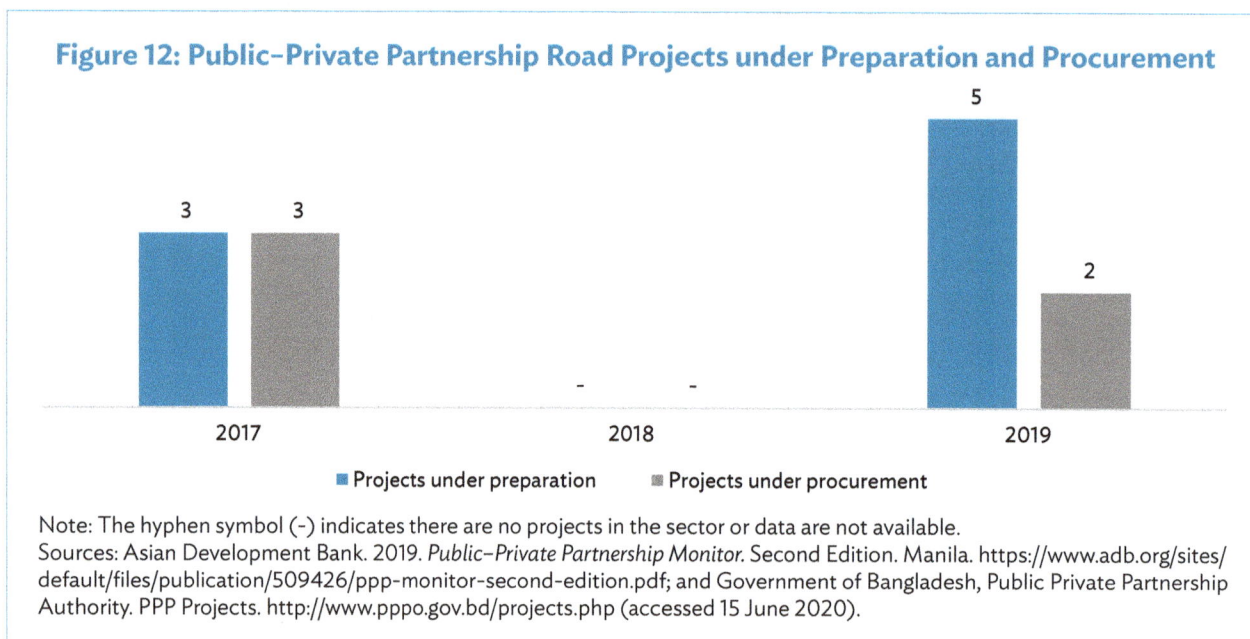

Note: The hyphen symbol (-) indicates there are no projects in the sector or data are not available.
Sources: Asian Development Bank. 2019. *Public–Private Partnership Monitor.* Second Edition. Manila. https://www.adb.org/sites/default/files/publication/509426/ppp-monitor-second-edition.pdf; and Government of Bangladesh, Public Private Partnership Authority. PPP Projects. http://www.pppo.gov.bd/projects.php (accessed 15 June 2020).

4. Features of Past Public–Private Partnership Projects in the Roads Sector

Figure 13 presents the number of PPP projects procured through various modes, including direct appointment, unsolicited bids, and competitive bids in Bangladesh's roads sector.

Figure 14 shows the number of PPP projects that have reached financial closure and the total value of those projects in Bangladesh's roads sector.

The roads sector had two projects (two contracts related to Jamuna Bridge), the first was completed in 2003 and the second in 2009. Currently, there is only one active project—the Dhaka Bypass Expansion—which was awarded in 2019.

Figure 13: Modes of Procurement for Public–Private Partnership Roads

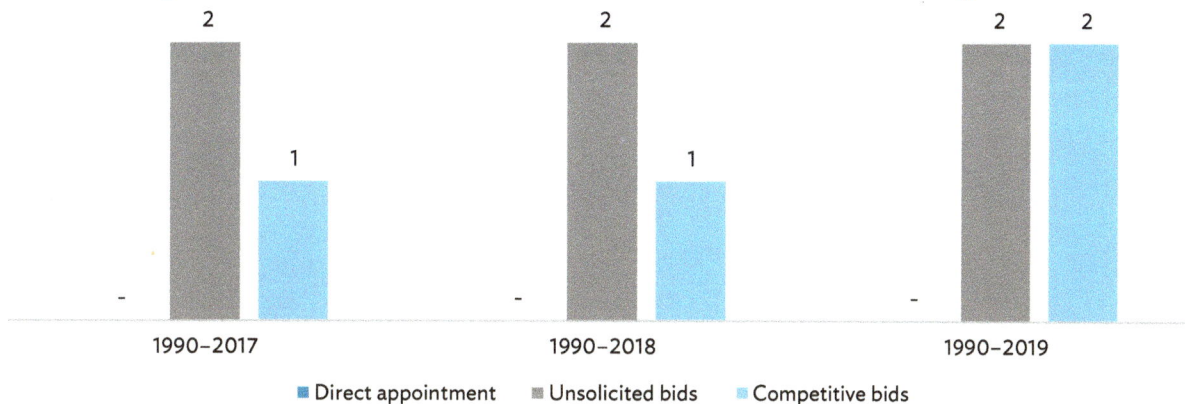

■ Direct appointment   ■ Unsolicited bids   ■ Competitive bids

Notes: Only active and concluded projects are considered in the above graph. The hyphen symbol (-) indicates there are no projects in the sector, or data are not available or not applicable, according to the database.
Source: World Bank. Infrastructure Finance, PPPs and Guarantees. Country Snapshots. Bangladesh. https://ppi.worldbank.org/en/snapshots/country/bangladesh (accessed 2 July 2020).

Figure 14: Public–Private Partnership Road Projects Reaching Financial Closure

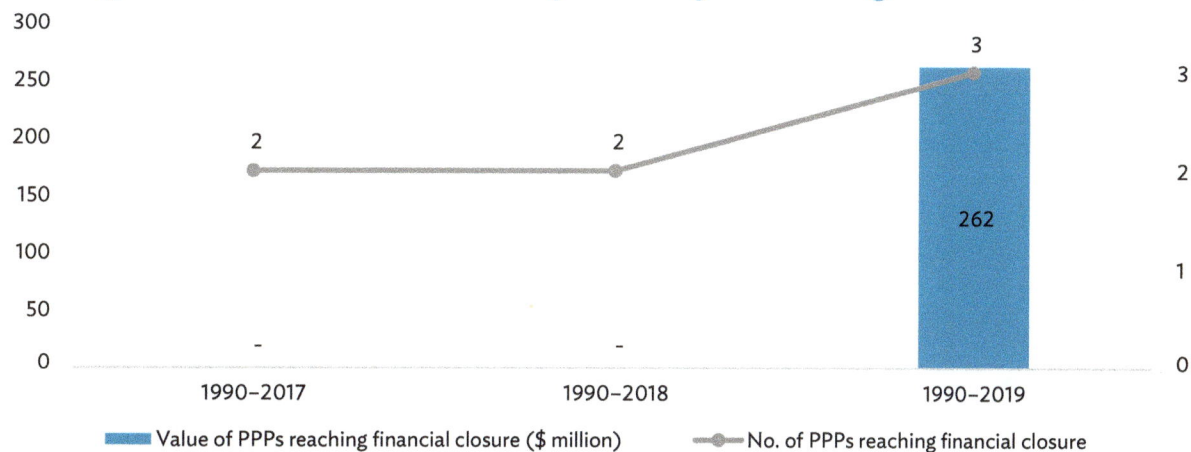

■ Value of PPPs reaching financial closure ($ million)   ●— No. of PPPs reaching financial closure

PPP = public–private partnership.
Notes: Only active and concluded projects are considered in the above graph. The hyphen symbol (-) indicates there are no projects in the sector, or data are not available or not applicable, according to the database. Information on the value of PPP for the two projects up to 2018 are unavailable.
Source: World Bank. Infrastructure Finance, PPPs and Guarantees. Country Snapshots. Bangladesh. https://ppi.worldbank.org/en/snapshots/country/bangladesh (accessed 2 July 2020).

Figure 15 presents the number of PPP projects that have received foreign sponsor participation in Bangladesh's roads sector.

Figure 15: Public–Private Partnership Road Projects with Foreign Sponsor Participation

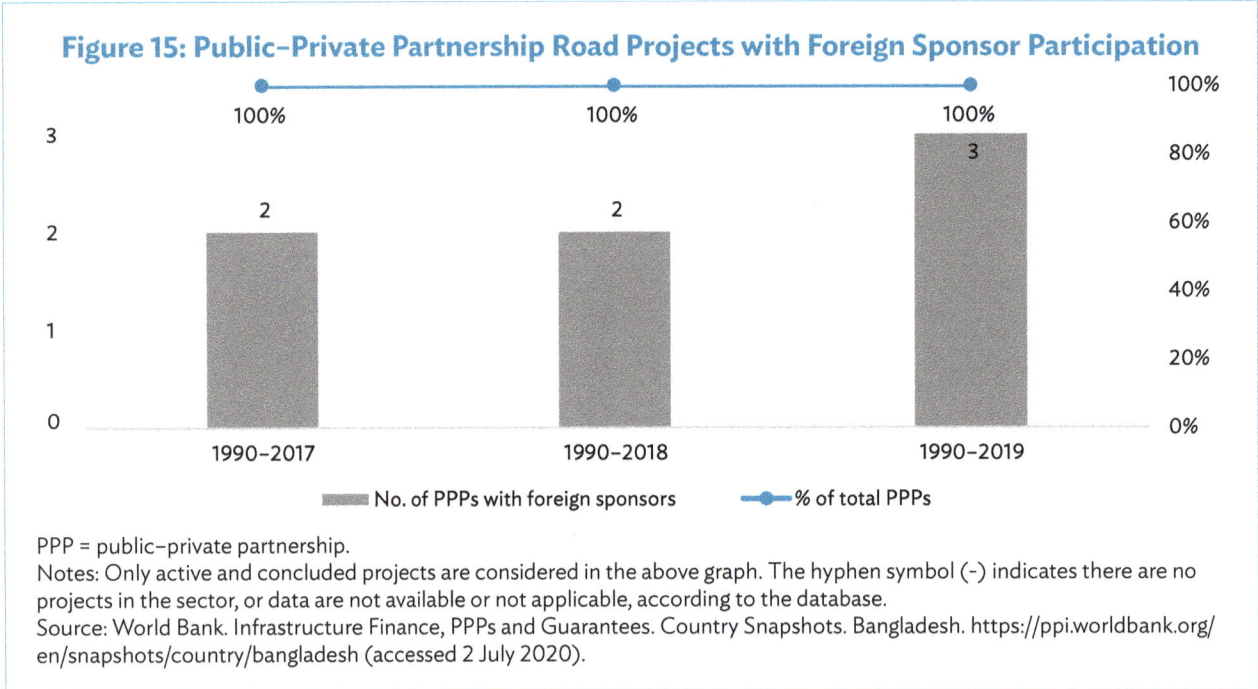

PPP = public–private partnership.
Notes: Only active and concluded projects are considered in the above graph. The hyphen symbol (-) indicates there are no projects in the sector, or data are not available or not applicable, according to the database.
Source: World Bank. Infrastructure Finance, PPPs and Guarantees. Country Snapshots. Bangladesh. https://ppi.worldbank.org/en/snapshots/country/bangladesh (accessed 2 July 2020).

Figure 16 shows the number of PPP projects that have received government support, including viability gap funding, government guarantees, and availability/performance payment in Bangladesh's roads sector.

Figure 16: Government Support to Public–Private Partnership Road Projects

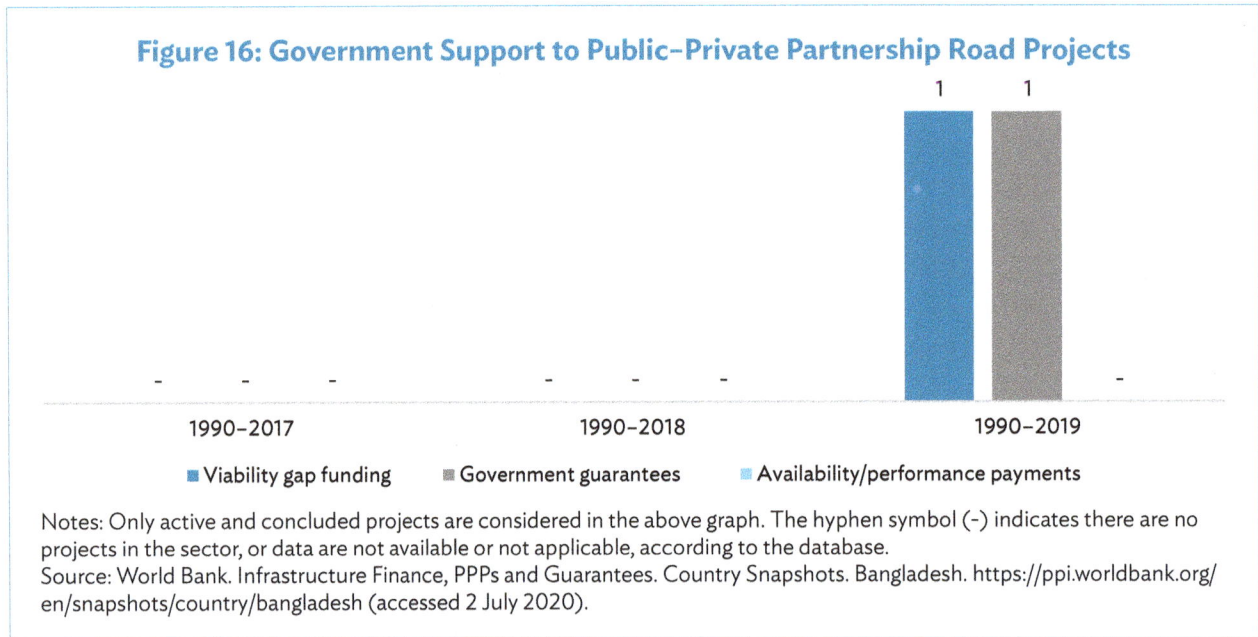

Notes: Only active and concluded projects are considered in the above graph. The hyphen symbol (-) indicates there are no projects in the sector, or data are not available or not applicable, according to the database.
Source: World Bank. Infrastructure Finance, PPPs and Guarantees. Country Snapshots. Bangladesh. https://ppi.worldbank.org/en/snapshots/country/bangladesh (accessed 2 July 2020).

Figure 17 presents the number of PPP projects that have received payment in the form of user charges and government pay (offtake) in Bangladesh's roads sector.

Figure 17: Payment Mechanisms for Public–Private Partnership Road Projects

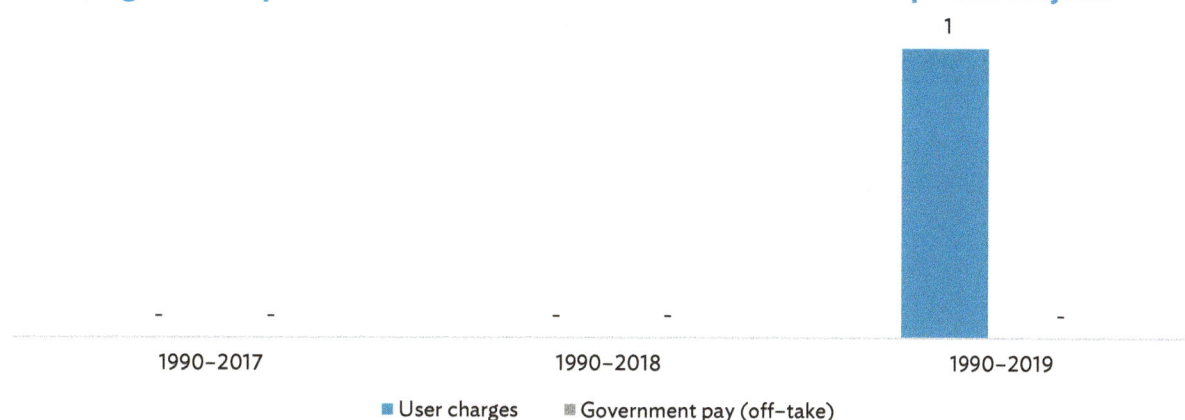

Notes: Only active and concluded projects are considered in the above graph. The hyphen symbol (-) indicates there are no projects in the sector, or data are not available or not applicable, according to the database.
Source: World Bank. Infrastructure Finance, PPPs and Guarantees. Country Snapshots. Bangladesh. https://ppi.worldbank.org/en/snapshots/country/bangladesh (accessed 2 July 2020).

4.1 Tariffs for Public–Private Partnership Road Projects

Private concessionaires have a legal right to collect revenue from road users. Depending on the type of PPP contract and/or concession agreement, they may have to inject a portion of the revenue into system maintenance or return a portion to the grantor or the host government agency (footnote 1).

Fees are charged at the agreed tariff, and fee increment is also on a per-project basis. Tariffs on tolls (tariff setting and indexation) are regulated by the MRTB. The allowable fare increment is normally stated in each concession agreement. Clause 2 of the Tolls Act 1851 gives the government power to establish tolls on roads and bridges and to appoint toll collectors. However, specific regulations related to private sector projects could not be found.[30]

There is a national toll policy enacted by the government, but this excludes application over roads, highways, and bridges developed under PPP projects. Such tolls are to be decided during the project development phase. The form of project is determined with the PPP Screening Manual. Screening Condition No. 6 ascertains whether the private sector operator raises sufficient revenue from the project to recover its costs and generate a sufficient commercial return. The projects must generate adequate revenue to recover life cycle costs and yield sufficient commercial return. The interpretation of this condition is twofold, depending on the type of PPP mode proposed: (i) cost recovery through user charges or (ii) cost recovery through build-operate-transfer annuity (annual payment) (footnote 13).

---

[30]   Ministry of Law, Justice and Parliamentary Affairs, Bangladesh. 1851. *The Tolls Act, 1851.* https://rthd.portal.gov.bd/sites/default/files/files/rthd.portal.gov.bd/law/b777dc03_adef_4c24_8383_38220da8d009/1.%20Toll_Act.pdf.

Examples of current toll rates for PPP road schemes are provided in Table 15.

Table 15: Toll Rates at Bangabandhu Bridge

Category	Rate in Taka (Tk)
Motorcycle	40.00
Car/light vehicle	500.00
Small bus	650.00
Large bus	900.00
Small truck	850.00
Medium truck	1,100.00
Large truck	1,400.00

Source: Bangladesh Bridge Authority. Toll Rate Bangabandhu Bridge (last updated 13 March 2017). www.bba.gov.bd/site/page/4093c137-8d48-46db-a1cb-54aaf5924a5c/- (accessed 3 August 2020).

4.2 Typical Risk Allocation for Public–Private Partnership Road Projects

There are no model contract documents that were available for the roads sector. However, based on the general principles of the sector, there is a typical risk allocation for a toll project based on standard operating procedures for PPP projects (Table 16).

Table 16: Risk Allocations to the Public and Private Sectors for Road Projects, by Risk Type

Risk Type	Private	Public	Shared	Comment
Traffic			✓	
Collection risk	✓			
Competition risk	✓			
Government payment risk	✓			
Environmental and social risks	✓			
Land acquisition risk		✓		
Permits	✓			
Geotechnical risk	✓			
Brownfield risk: inventories, studies, property boundaries, project scope		✓		
Political risk	✓			
Force majeure			✓	
Foreign exchange risk			✓	For one of the road PPP projects, a partial indexation mechanism has been proposed.[a]

PPP = public–private partnership.
[a] Asian Development Bank (ADB) Office of Public–Private Partnership (sourced from ADB Bangladesh Resident Mission).
Source: ADB. 2019. *Public–Private Partnership Monitor*. Second Edition. Manila. https://www.adb.org/sites/default/files/publication/509426/ppp-monitor-second-edition.pdf.

4.3 Financing Details of Public–Private Partnership Projects in the Roads Sector

Parameter	1990–2017	1990–2018	1990–2019
Public–private partnership (PPP) projects with foreign lending participation	1	1	1
PPP projects that received export credit agency/international financing institution support[a]	1	1	1
Typical debt-to-equity ratio	UA	UA	UA
Time for financial close		UA	

✓ = Yes, ✗ = No, NA = Not Applicable, UA = Unavailable
[a] Includes both foreign bank lending and international financial institution support.
Source: World Bank. Infrastructure Finance, PPPs and Guarantees. Country Snapshots. Bangladesh. https://ppi.worldbank.org/en/snapshots/country/bangladesh (accessed 2 July 2020).

5. Challenges in the Roads Sector

- Risks due to uncertainty in ridership or users making the project not bankable (footnote 1).

- Land acquisition delays due to decentralization of the process and objections by local residents, particularly in high-density urban areas (footnote1).

- Lack of uniform tolling policy for PPP projects.

B. RAILWAYS

Parameter	Value	Unit
Length of total railway network	2,835.00	total route, kilometer (km)
Total number of passengers carried	10,040.00	million passenger-km
Total volume of freight carried	1,053.00	million ton-km
Quality of railway infrastructure	3.10	1 (low) – 7 (high)

Sources: The Economist Intelligence Unit. Bangladesh. https://infrascope.eiu.com/; The Global Economy. Railway Passengers—Country Rankings. https://www.theglobaleconomy.com/rankings/railway_passengers/; The Global Economy. Railway Transport of Goods—Country Rankings. https://www.theglobaleconomy.com/rankings/Railway_transport_of_goods/; and The Global Economy. Railroad Infrastructure Quality—Country Rankings. https://www.theglobaleconomy.com/rankings/railroad_quality/.

1. Contracting Agencies in the Railway Sector

The Bangladesh Railway is the contracting authority for rail projects.

2. Railway Sector Laws and Regulations

There are no independent regulators for railways. The Ministry of Railways plays the role of regulator. The Bangladesh Railway is the key institution under the Ministry of Railways. The Department of Railway Inspection, also under the Ministry of Railways, is responsible for maintenance-related railway activities.

Bangladesh Railway

The Bangladesh Railway, a principal transportation agency of the country, is owned and managed by the government.

The railway is bifurcated into two zones, East and West, under the administrative control of two general managers who are accountable to the Bangladesh Railway director general for its day-to-day operation. For policy guidance, a nine-member Bangladesh Railway Authority was formed, with the Minister of Communications as its chairman. The general managers of the two zones are assisted by various specialized departments responsible for operation, maintenance, and financial management. Each zone is divided into two divisions, headed by a divisional railway manager and assisted by divisional officers of departments such as personnel, transportation, commercial, finance, mechanical, way and works, signaling and telecommunication, electrical, medical, and Railway Nirapatta Bahini. Workshop divisions, one in each zone, are in Pahartoli and Syedpur, each headed by a divisional superintendent.[31]

Department of Railway Inspection

The Department of Railway Inspection is under the direct control of the Ministry of Railways. The Government Railway Inspector inspects tracks and other installations of the Bangladesh Railway to make necessary repairs and rectify irregularities to ensure safe and comfortable movement of trains, as per the responsibilities assigned by the Railway Act, 1890 (ACT IX of 1890). The secretary provides inspection reports and recommendations to the Ministry of Railways. Matters that require direct intervention from the Ministry of Railways are referred to the ministry. The government circular that establishes the Railway Department provides that tracks, trains, and major railway stations and installations are to be inspected and any reported train accidents are to be investigated.[32]

2.1 Foreign Investment Restrictions in the Railway Sector

Parameter	2017	2018	2019
Maximum allowed foreign ownership of equity in greenfield projects	100%	100%	100%

The above may be reviewed against the restrictions and limitations held by the government, as explained in Chapter II Section 8.

2.2 Standard Contracts in the Railway Sector

Type of Contract	Availability
Public–private partnership/concession agreement	✕
Performance-based operations and maintenance contract	✕
Engineering, procurement, and construction contract	✕

✓ = Yes, ✕ = No, NA = Not Applicable, UA = Unavailable
Source: Asian Development Bank. 2019. *Public–Private Partnership Monitor*. Second Edition. Manila. https://www.adb.org/sites/default/files/publication/509426/ppp-monitor-second-edition.pdf.

---

[31]   Bangladesh Railway. At a Glance. https://railway.portal.gov.bd/site/page/ce7dd6af-c7c8-4811-86b3-ba871e2e406e/At-a-Glance.
[32]   Ministry of Railways. Organization. https://mor.gov.bd/site/page/e063678a-4897-4e07-b9c8-85b6e956ed27/Department-of-inspections-of-Railway (Circular No. 2-E-2 / Miscellaneous-6 / 69-65 dated 14-11-98 BANG / 26-02-90 Eng).

3. Railway Sector Master Plan

The Bangladesh Railway has released a comprehensive Railway Master Plan, 2016–2045, which was approved in 2018 and issued in 2019. The plan responds to Vision 2021 and Vision 2041 as it includes rehabilitation and improvement of rolling stock and infrastructure, increasing line capacity, increasing the modal share of rail, and further expansion of the rail network to areas currently not served. The master plan provides a phased development and investment plan and a proposed total investment outlook (Table 17).[33]

Table 17: Extracts from the Bangladesh Railway Master Plan, 2016–2045
(Tk billion)

Phase	Period	Total No. of Projects	Government of Bangladesh	Foreign Assistance	Foreign Assistance/ PPP	Foreign Assistance/ Government of Bangladesh	Total Cost
Phase 1	2016–2020	83	66.73	776.13	90.30	544.57	1,478.33
Phase 2	2021–2025	67	114.12	728.12	34.39	320.17	1,196.80
Phase 3	2026–2030	37	80.54	...	16.00	845.07	941.61
Phase 4	2031–2035	23	7.26	...	...	961.59	968.85
Phase 5	2036–2040	14	1.25	94.48	...	730.76	826.49
Phase 6	2041–2045	6	1.25	15.34	...	107.95	124.54
Total		**230**	**271.15**	**1,614.07**	**140.69**	**3,510.11**	**5,536.62**

... = not available, PPP = public–private partnership, Tk = taka.
Source: Bangladesh Railway. Master Plan of Bangladesh Railway. https://railway.portal.gov.bd/site/page/8e5a704d-72e2-4d69-b443-21988229cbbc/Future-Plan.

As per the PPP Authority project pipeline, there are five projects in the railway sector that are at various stages of project preparation (Table 18). Not all projects are directly related to railway infrastructure; however, logistics infrastructure linked to railways or railway stations has been included.

Table 18: Projects under Preparation and Procurement as per the Public–Private Partnership Authority

Project Name	Status
Multimodal hub at Bimanbandar Railway Station	CCEA approved (in principle)
Multimodal hub at Kamalapur Railway Station	CCEA approved (in principle)
Light rapid transit system for Narayanganj City	CCEA approved (in principle)
Detailed design, construction, operation, and maintenance of MRT Line-2	CCEA approved (in principle)
Circular railway line	Project development stage – Detailed feasibility study ongoing

CCEA = Cabinet Committee on Economic Affairs, MRT = mass rapid transit.
Source: Government of Bangladesh, Public Private Partnership Authority. PPP Projects. http://www.pppo.gov.bd/projects.php (accessed 15 June 2020).

---

[33] Bangladesh Railway. Master Plan of Bangladesh Railway. https://railway.portal.gov.bd/site/page/8e5a704d-72e2-4d69-b443-21988229cbbc/Future-Plan.

3.1 Projects under Preparation and Procurement in the Railway Sector

Figure 18 shows the number of projects at the preparation and procurement stage.

Figure 18: Public–Private Partnership Railway Projects under Preparation and Procurement

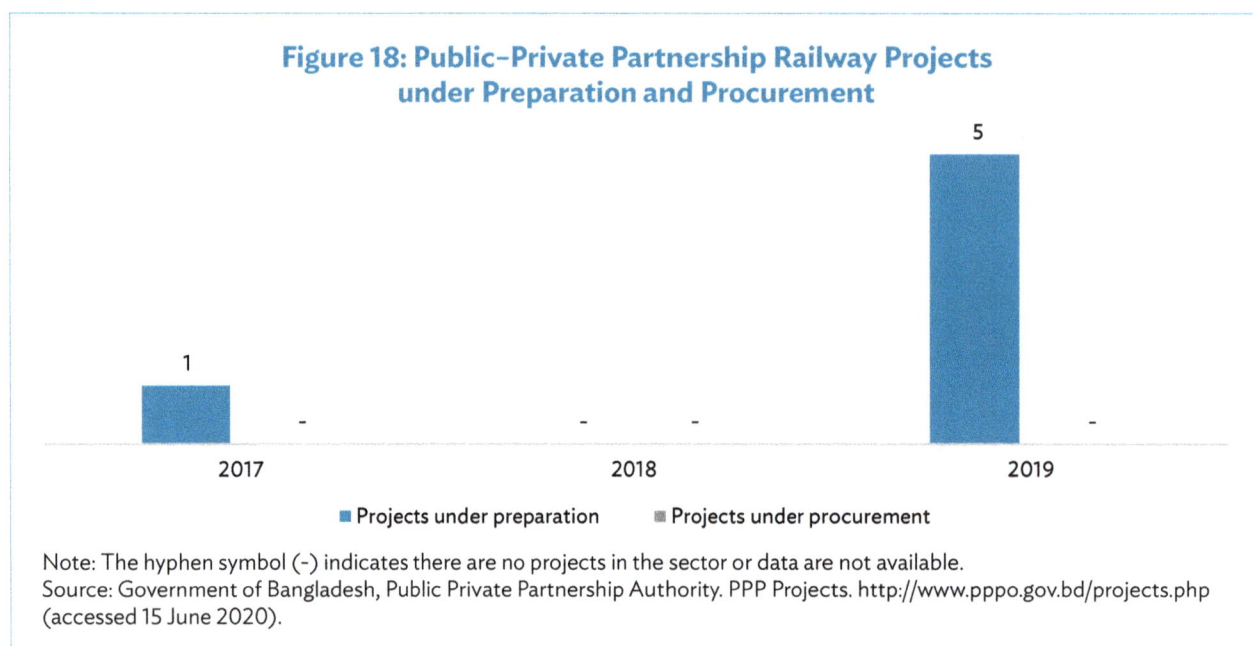

Note: The hyphen symbol (-) indicates there are no projects in the sector or data are not available.
Source: Government of Bangladesh, Public Private Partnership Authority. PPP Projects. http://www.pppo.gov.bd/projects.php (accessed 15 June 2020).

4. Features of Past Public–Private Partnership Projects in the Railway Sector

"The information on features of past PPP projects in Bangladesh's railway sector is not available."

4.1 Tariffs in the Railway Sector

The private party has a legal right to collect revenue from users, whether passenger or freight. The PPP concept for Bangladesh railways is still in an early development stage. There is no set type of PPP contract and/or concession agreement (footnote 1).

4.2 Typical Risk Allocation for Railway Public–Private Partnership Projects

There is no framework that has yet emerged for private participation in railways, and it would be difficult to establish risk allocation for the same.

4.3 Financing Details of Public–Private Partnership Projects in the Railway Sector

Parameter	1990–2017	1990–2018	1990–2019
Public–private partnership (PPP) projects with foreign lending participation	NA	NA	NA
PPP projects that received export credit agency/international financing institution support	NA	NA	NA
Typical debt-to-equity ratio	NA	NA	NA
Time for financial close		NA	

✓ = Yes, ✗ = No, NA = Not Applicable, UA = Unavailable

5. Challenges in the Railway Sector

- Lack of investment. There has been a shift of investment focus from railways to roads over the years. Consequently, there has not been any construction of new railway routes or maintenance of existing routes due to lack of funds for projects (footnote 26).

- Slow implementation. Lack of funding and resources has resulted in slow implementation of projects in the sector. In some cases, even with funding obtained, there have been delays in implementation due to delays in the decision-making process (footnote 26).

- Climate change. Bangladesh experiences heavy rainfall, and the Brahmaputra River that flows through the country is subject to frequent flooding. Hence, the railway sector needs to formulate strategies and raise funds to be able to successfully tackle the effects of such climatic catastrophes (footnote 26).

- Limited private sector capabilities. Most of the railway services are dominated by the public sector except in services such as ticketing, information and communication technology (ICT), and repair services, leading to limited capacities of the private sector in other areas. Opening up opportunities for the private sector in other areas of operations and management may increase the scope for private sector growth and active participation.

C. PORTS

Parameter	Value	Unit
Total number of ports	4	no.
Total container traffic at ports	2,827,000	TEU
Quality of port infrastructure	3.6	1 (low) – 7 (high)
Quality of trade and transport-related infrastructure index	2.5	1=low to 5=high

TEU = twenty-foot equivalent unit.
Sources: The Economist Intelligence Unit. Bangladesh. https://infrascope.eiu.com/; The Global Economy. Port Traffic—Country Rankings. https://www.theglobaleconomy.com/rankings/Port_traffic/; and World Port Source. Ports. http://www.worldportsource.com/countries.php.

1. Contracting Agencies in the Ports Sector

Relevant state-owned port authorities, under the Ministry of Shipping, can enter into a contract upon approval.

2. Ports Sector Laws and Regulations

The Ministry of Shipping is responsible for formulating policies for Bangladesh's maritime sector, which includes ports, inland water transport, national waterways, and ocean shipping (footnote 1).

Most Bangladesh imports and exports are handled through Chittagong Port, which has no private sector operator in its terminal operations. The Chittagong Port Authority, functioning under the control of the Ministry of Shipping, sets and regulates the tariffs for services and facilities offered at Chittagong Port. The Chittagong Port Authority Ordinance (1976) gives full financial and administrative autonomy to the Chittagong Port Authority. Similarly, the Mongla Port Authority imposes and collects various fees at Mongla Port. Tariffs for inland water transport are regulated by the government. The Department of Shipping is responsible for regulating inland water transport in parallel with the Bangladesh Inland Water Transport Authority on main routes, and with the Bangladesh Inland Water Transport Corporation on secondary routes (footnote 1).

The Bangladesh Land Port Authority imposes various tariffs for services and facilities offered at all the landside ports throughout the country (footnote 1).

The key institutions involved in regulating the ports sector are shown in Table 19.

Table 19: Key Institutions in the Ports Sector in Bangladesh

Agency	Function
Ministry of Shipping	The Ministry of Shipping encompasses shipping and ports sectors, which include national waterways, inland water transport, ports, and ocean shipping. It oversees safety and environmental matters and the regulatory aspects of maritime shipping and maritime education. The ministry formulates policies and plans on these subjects and facilitates quick implementation of various projects. The ministry also oversees maintenance and expansion of viable, efficient, and dependable water transportation and communication systems as the cheapest way of economic activities in both rural and urban areas. The ministry implements its policy and decisions and administers allocated business through the following 10 directorates: (i) Directorate General of Shipping (ii) Chittagong Port Authority (iii) Mongla Port Authority (iv) Payra Port Authority (v) Bangladesh Land Port Authority (vi) National Maritime Institute (vii) Bangladesh Inland Water Transport Authority (viii) Bangladesh Inland Water Transport Corporation (ix) Bangladesh Marine Academy (x) Bangladesh Shipping Corporation
Bangladesh Inland Water Transport Authority (BIWTA)	The BIWTA is the planning, development, and regulatory authority for waterways in Bangladesh. The BIWTA has undertaken schemes for development of inland river ports. These ultimately resulted in the creation of five major inland river ports (in Dhaka, Narayanganj, Chandpur, Barisal, and Khulna) at the initial stage. Subsequently, six new inland river ports were created—at Patuakhali (in 1975), Nagarbari (1983), Aricha (1983), Daulatdia (1983), Baghabari (1983), and Narsingdi (1989)—to cater to growing requirements in the inland waterways transport sector. The BIWTA also developed five ferry terminals—at Aricha, Daulatdia, Nagarbari, Mawa, and Char Janajat—to connect the capital city via ferry service with districts on the other side of the Padma and Jamuna rivers. The BIWTA provided facilities in these river ports for public use.
Bangladesh Inland Water Transport Corporation (BIWTC)	Located in Dhaka, the BIWTC is an autonomous, service-oriented government-owned entity that owns and operates river vessels and ships and river ports in Bangladesh. The key activities of the entity include running ferry services, passenger services, cargo services, and ship repair services.
Department of Shipping	The Department of Shipping is an agency under the Ministry of Shipping, Bangladesh. It is the maritime safety administration of Bangladesh responsible for the formulation and implementation of national policies and legislation to ensure the safety of life and ships at sea, development of shipping industry, maritime education and certification, employment and welfare of seafarers, and other shipping-related matters. The department is also responsible for ensuring the compliance of international conventions relating to maritime matters. The Department of Shipping was established in 1976. As a regulatory body, its functions are administered in accordance with two main legal instruments: The Bangladesh Merchant Shipping Ordinance, 1983 and the Inland Shipping Ordinance, 1976. The head office of the department is in Dhaka. The Department of Shipping is the competent authority to regulate the maritime sector in Bangladesh. It is responsible for the enforcement of maritime regulations concerning both Bangladeshi vessels and foreign vessels using Bangladesh ports.

continued on next page

Table 19 *continued*

Agency	Function
Chittagong Port Authority	The Chittagong Port Authority is responsible for the following: (i) management, maintenance, improvement, and development of the Chittagong Port; (ii) provision and maintenance of adequate and efficient port services and facilities in the port and approaches to the port; and (iii) regulation and control of berthing and movement of vessels and navigation within the port.
Bangladesh Shipping Corporation	The Bangladesh Shipping Corporation runs the national fleet, but its presence in the container sector is limited to a joint venture with the Indian and Sri Lankan state shipping companies in operating feeder services to Chittagong and Mongla.

Sources: Asian Development Bank. 2019. *Public–Private Partnership Monitor*. Second Edition. Manila. https://www.adb.org/sites/default/files/publication/509426/ppp-monitor-second-edition.pdf; Bangladesh Inland Water Transport Authority. Background and Creation. http://www.biwta.gov.bd/site/page/fe5ad955-65b9-42d0-89a1-e40195261dae/-; Bangladesh Inland Water Transport Corporation. Activities of BIWTC. http://www.biwtc.gov.bd/site/page/ee1d42bc-a763-4bc1-b4ce-f2dce4a8c1e0/-; Bangladesh Shipping Corporation. History. https://bsc.portal.gov.bd/; Chittagong Port Authority. Functions of CPA. http://www.cpa.gov.bd/site/page/420f02c4-44a2-42bc-8a53-d747921a7a90/-; Government of Bangladesh, Department of Shipping. About Us. http://dos.gov.bd/site/page/e847ba4b-8b44-4fa1-8d6f-4d5a8292f5e2/-; and Ministry of Shipping. Background. https://mos.portal.gov.bd/site/page/3c024802-0fbf-4479-a977-b169d3d3cb9a/Background.

Relevant regulations in the sector are as follows:[34]

- The Ports Act, 1908;
- The Inland Shipping Ordinance, 1976;
- Bangladesh Inland Water Transport Authority Rules of Business, 1959;
- Privately Owned Internal Container Terminal Construction and Operation Manual, 2013;
- Bangladesh Inland Water Transport (Route Permit, Time Table and Fare) Rule, 2019; and
- Draft Bangladesh Merchant Shipping Act, 2020 and Regulations.

2.1 Foreign Investment Restrictions in the Ports Sector

Parameter	2017	2018	2019
Maximum allowed foreign ownership of equity in greenfield projects	100%	100%	100%

The above may be reviewed against the restrictions and limitations held by the government, as explained in Chapter II Section 8.

2.2 Standard Contracts in the Ports Sector

Type of Contract	Availability
Public–private partnership/concession agreement	UA
Performance-based operations and maintenance contract	UA
Engineering, procurement, and construction contract	UA

✓ = Yes, ✗ = No, NA = Not Applicable, UA = Unavailable

[34]   Ministry of Shipping. Acts. https://mos.portal.gov.bd/site/view/law/Acts-&-Ordinance.

3. Ports Sector Master Plan

As per the comments received from the Public–Private Partnership (PPP) Authority, "there is no sector-level master plan for ports in Bangladesh. There is individual plan for each port, e.g., Chittagong Port." For example, the website of the Chittagong Port Authority includes a section on Development Plan that articulates projects conceived at the port level over the short, medium, and long term.

The PPP Authority project pipeline indicates the projects that are under various stages of preparation and procurement, a list of which is provided in Table 20.

Table 20: Projects under Preparation and Procurement in the Ports Sector

Project Name	Status
Construction of Bay Terminal – undertaken on PPP model on the basis of government-to-government	Technical feasibility complete and Transaction advisor mobilized
Payra Port Coal Terminal	Procurement stage – Legal vetting ongoing

PPP = public–private partnership.
Source: Government of Bangladesh, Public Private Partnership Authority. PPP Projects. http://www.pppo.gov.bd/projects.php (accessed 15 June 2020).

3.1 Projects under Preparation and Procurement in the Ports Sector

Figure 19 reflects the number of projects under preparation and procurement in the ports sector in Bangladesh.

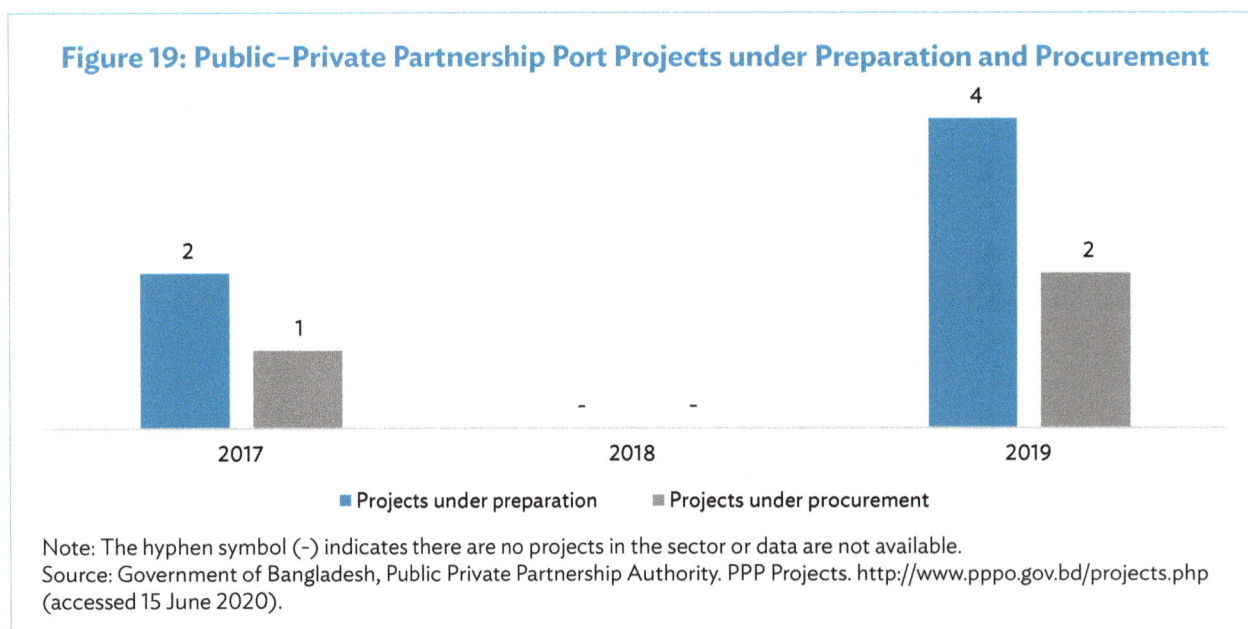

Figure 19: Public–Private Partnership Port Projects under Preparation and Procurement

Note: The hyphen symbol (-) indicates there are no projects in the sector or data are not available.
Source: Government of Bangladesh, Public Private Partnership Authority. PPP Projects. http://www.pppo.gov.bd/projects.php (accessed 15 June 2020).

4. Features of Past Public–Private Partnership Projects in the Ports Sector

Figure 20 shows the number of PPP projects procured through various modes including direct appointment, unsolicited bids, and competitive bids in Bangladesh's ports sector.

Figure 20: Modes of Procurement for Public–Private Partnership Port Projects

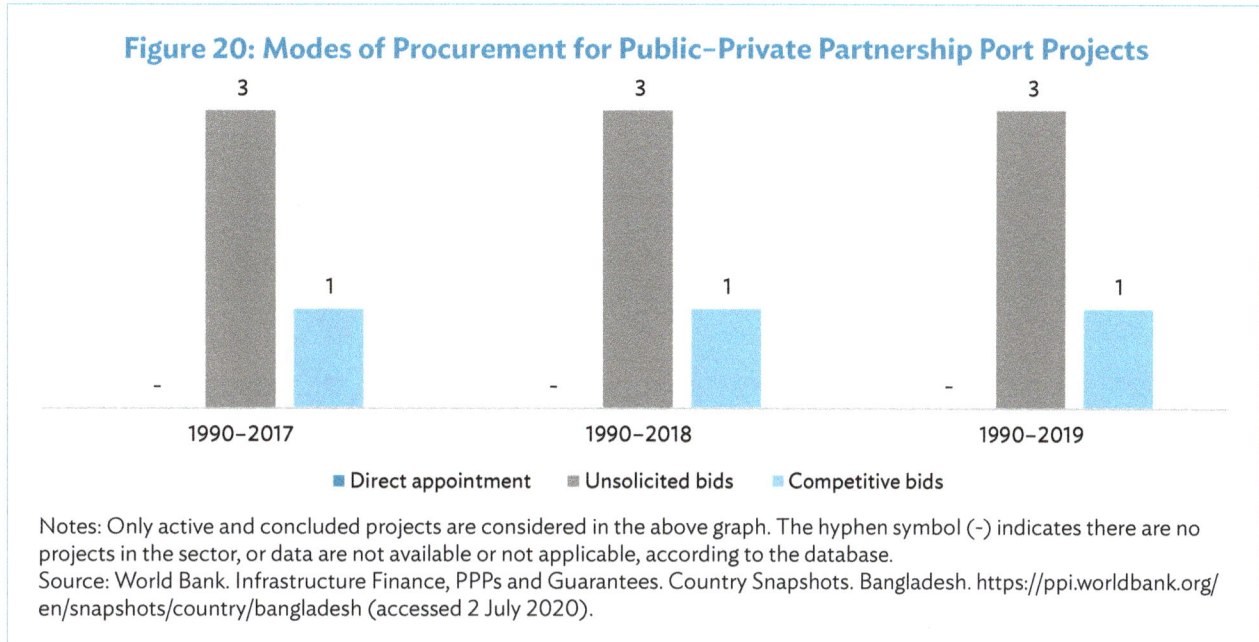

Notes: Only active and concluded projects are considered in the above graph. The hyphen symbol (-) indicates there are no projects in the sector, or data are not available or not applicable, according to the database.
Source: World Bank. Infrastructure Finance, PPPs and Guarantees. Country Snapshots. Bangladesh. https://ppi.worldbank.org/en/snapshots/country/bangladesh (accessed 2 July 2020).

Figure 21 presents the number of PPP projects that have reached financial closure and the total value of those projects in Bangladesh's ports sector.

Figure 21: Public–Private Partnership Port Projects Reaching Financial Closure

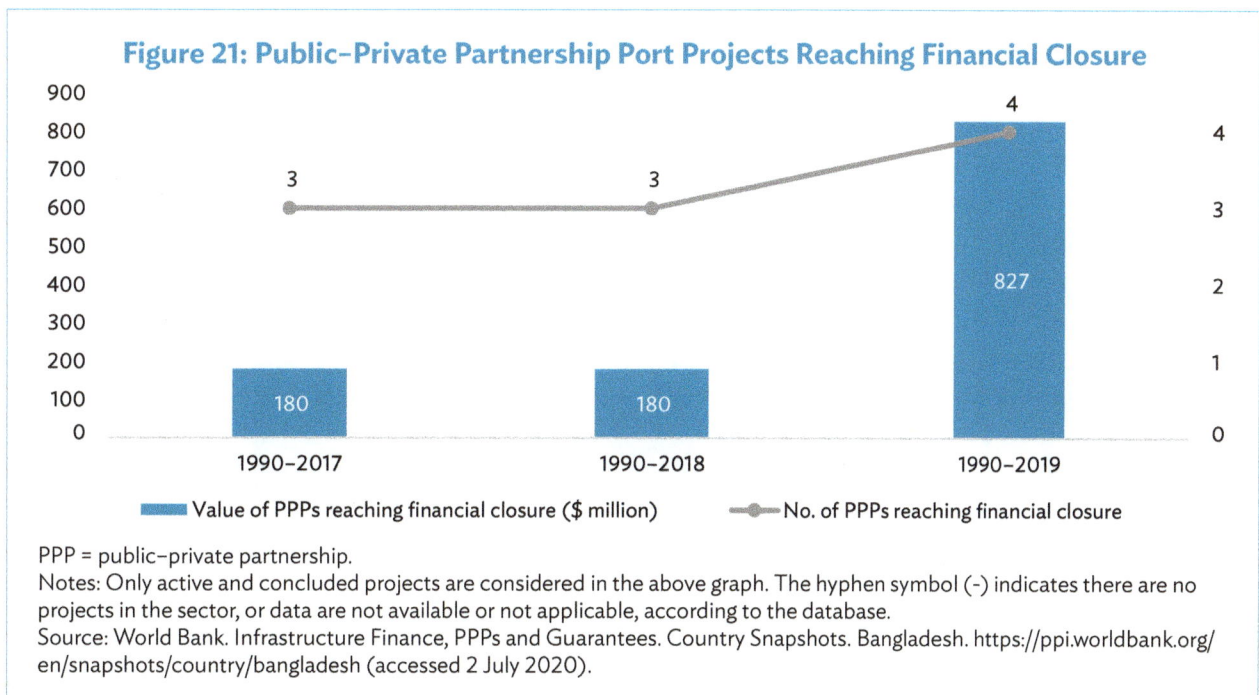

PPP = public–private partnership.
Notes: Only active and concluded projects are considered in the above graph. The hyphen symbol (-) indicates there are no projects in the sector, or data are not available or not applicable, according to the database.
Source: World Bank. Infrastructure Finance, PPPs and Guarantees. Country Snapshots. Bangladesh. https://ppi.worldbank.org/en/snapshots/country/bangladesh (accessed 2 July 2020).

The first Chittagong Container Terminal contract, a management and lease contract that was awarded in 2006, was concluded before 2019 and, hence, does not get reflected in the active projects shown above.

Figure 22 shows the number of PPP projects that have received foreign sponsor participation in Bangladesh's port sector.

Figure 22: Public–Private Partnership Port Projects with Foreign Sponsor Participation

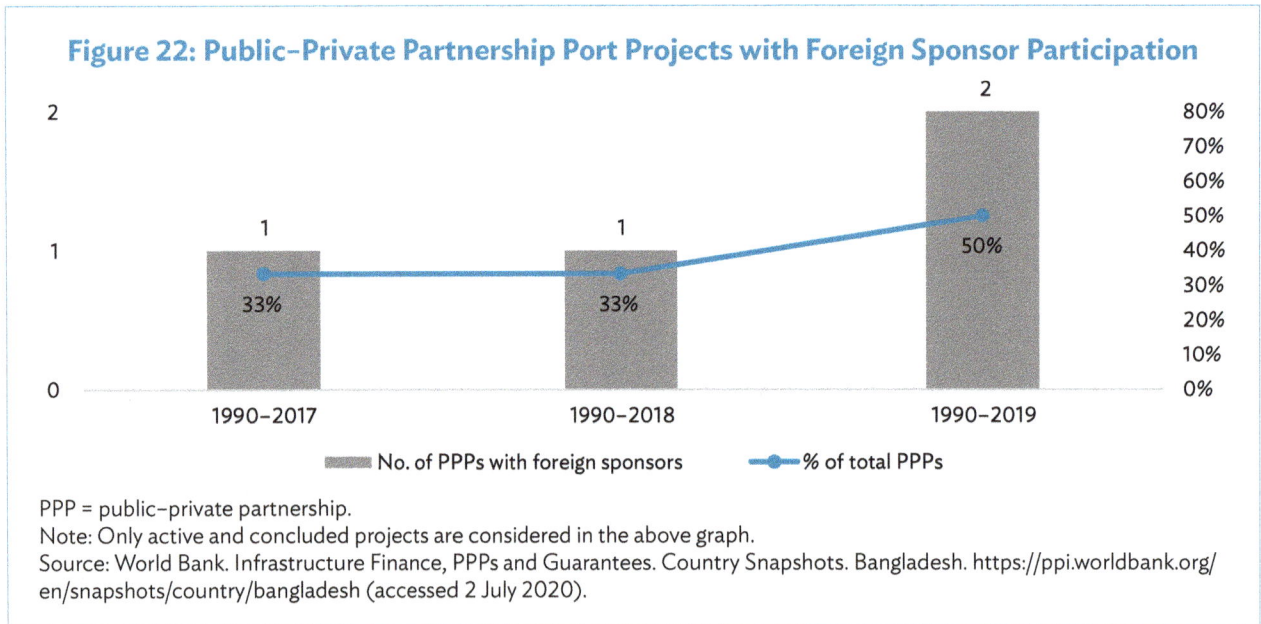

PPP = public–private partnership.
Note: Only active and concluded projects are considered in the above graph.
Source: World Bank. Infrastructure Finance, PPPs and Guarantees. Country Snapshots. Bangladesh. https://ppi.worldbank.org/en/snapshots/country/bangladesh (accessed 2 July 2020).

"As per the World Bank PPI database, no ports sector projects in Bangladesh received government support, including viability gap funding mechanism, government guarantees, and availability or performance payment."

Figure 23 shows the number of PPP projects that have received payment in the form of user charges and government pay (offtake) in Bangladesh's ports sector.

Figure 23: Payment Mechanism for Public–Private Partnership Port Projects

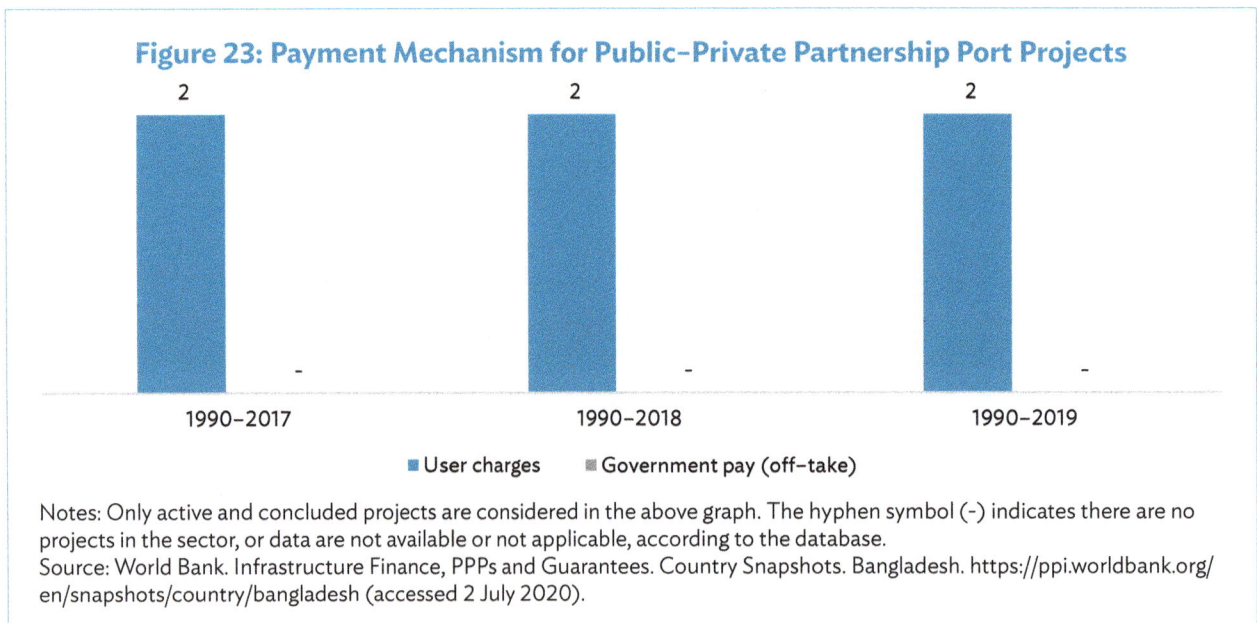

Notes: Only active and concluded projects are considered in the above graph. The hyphen symbol (-) indicates there are no projects in the sector, or data are not available or not applicable, according to the database.
Source: World Bank. Infrastructure Finance, PPPs and Guarantees. Country Snapshots. Bangladesh. https://ppi.worldbank.org/en/snapshots/country/bangladesh (accessed 2 July 2020).

4.1 Tariffs in the Ports Sector

The government regulates tariffs. Terminal handling charges are charges made by the terminal operators for container movement services performed at a terminal. For container terminals, terminal handling charges cover the movement of a container between the ship's hold to the exit–entry gate via the container terminal yard.

4.2 Typical Risk Allocation for Public–Private Partnership Port Projects

The risk allocation for PPP projects in the ports sector is unavailable.

4.3 Financing Details of Public–Private Partnership Projects in the Ports Sector

Parameter	1990–2017	1990–2018	1990–2019
Public–private partnership (PPP) projects with foreign lending participation	1	1	2
PPP projects that received export credit agency/international financing institution support[a]	1	1	1
Typical debt-to-equity ratio		70:30	
Time for financial close		UA	
Typical concession period		UA	
Typical financial internal rate of return		UA	

✓ = Yes, ✗ = No, NA = Not Applicable, UA = Unavailable
[a] Includes both foreign bank lending and international financial institution support.
Source: World Bank. Infrastructure Finance, PPPs and Guarantees. Country Snapshots. Bangladesh. https://ppi.worldbank.org/en/snapshots/country/bangladesh (accessed 2 July 2020).

5. Challenges in the Ports Sector

- Involvement of the private sector in infrastructure development is one of the most effective ways of reducing the financing gap faced by the government. However, due to the lack of a PPP framework specific to the ports sector, private sector developers have shown less interest toward development of projects in this sector (footnote 26).

- Specific tariff mechanisms and policies for private sector players are inexistent.

- Rail and road connectivity to the ports is lacking, making it difficult for ports to offload and receive cargo.

- The ports in Bangladesh suffer from infrastructure issues such as lack of adequate warehouse space, inadequate parking for trucks waiting for cargo, and absence of banking facilities at the ports for submission of challan (footnote 26).

- Existing maritime ports are not sufficient to accommodate projected container throughput in the coming years. The Chittagong Port throughput has reached maximum capacity and new ports are still under development stage. As a result, this capacity constraint leads to congestion at the port and affects turnaround time of vessels (footnote 26).

D. AIRPORTS

Parameter	Value	Unit
Number of airports	16	no.
Total passenger capacity	5.98	million passengers
Quality of air transport infrastructure	3.8	1 (low) – 7 (high)
Total number of projects with cumulative lending, grant, and technical assistance commitments in the transport sector	117	no.
Total amount of cumulative lending, grant, and technical assistance commitments in the transport sector	5,076	$ million

Sources: Airports Authority. Airports. https://airport-authority.com/browse; Asian Development Bank. Cumulative Lending, Grant, and Technical Assistance Commitments. https://data.adb.org/dataset/cumulative-lending-grant-and-technical-assistance-commitments; The Global Economy. Compare Countries. https://www.theglobaleconomy.com/compare-countries/; and World Bank. Air Transport, Passengers Carried. https://data.worldbank.org/indicator/is.air.psgr?locations=bd-kh-ge-kz-mm-pk-pg-lk-uz-vn-cn-in-id-ph-th.

1. Contracting Agencies in the Airport Sector

The Civil Aviation Authority of Bangladesh (CAAB) is responsible for developing and regulating aviation facilities in the country.

2. Airport Sector Laws and Regulations

The Civil Aviation Ordinance, 1960 (XXXII of 1960) aims to make better provisions for the control of manufacture, possessions, use, operation, sale, import, and export of aircraft; the control and regulation of air transport services; and the control and development of aerodromes in the country.[35]

The Civil Aviation Rules, 1984 was made and promulgated by the government in exercise of the powers conferred by sections 4, 5, 7, and 8 of the Civil Aviation Ordinance, 1960 (XXXII of 1960); section 10 of the Aircraft (Removal of Danger to Safety) Ordinance, 1965 (XII of 1965); and section 4 of the Telegraph Act, 1885 (XIII of 1885). The 1984 Rules have replaced the Aircraft Rules, 1937 and the Airport Obstruction Clearance Rules, 1981 (footnote 35).

This set of rules elaborately dealt with personnel (e.g., pilot, flight engineer, air traffic controller, aircraft maintenance engineer), licensing, airworthiness requirements, operation of aircraft, rules of the air, and air transport services, among others. Much of today's operational responsibilities and functions of the CAAB has been defined and formulated based on these rules (footnote 35).

The President of Bangladesh made and promulgated the Civil Aviation Authority Ordinance, 1985 in pursuance of the Proclamation of 24 March 1982, and in exercise of all powers enabling him in that behalf (footnote 35).

The current active pieces of legislation are the Civil Aviation Act, 2017 and the Civil Aviation Authority Act, 2017.[36]

---

[35] Civil Aviation Authority of Bangladesh. Flight Safety Regulations. http://caab.portal.gov.bd/site/page/c49efdae-7d58-4a91-9895-aea173abacb0/-.
[36] Civil Aviation Authority of Bangladesh. Primary Aviation Legislation. http://caab.portal.gov.bd/site/page/c22eb144-f662-46fd-bb67-6bf6d26ef630/-.

2.1 Foreign Investment Restrictions in the Airport Sector

Parameter	2017	2018	2019
Maximum allowed foreign ownership of equity in greenfield projects	100%	100%	100%

The above may be reviewed against the restrictions and limitations held by the government, as explained in Chapter II Section 8.

2.2 Standard Contracts in the Airport Sector

Type of Contract	Availability
Public–private partnership/concession agreement	UA
Performance-based operations and maintenance contract	UA
Engineering, procurement, and construction contract	UA

✓ = Yes, ✗ = No, NA = Not Applicable, UA = Unavailable

3. Airport Sector Master Plan

The CAAB has envisaged construction of a new airport to cater to future demands. The Public–Private Partnership Authority is in the planning stages for the development of an airport expansion project and the construction of a new airport on a public–private partnership (PPP) model. To attract funds from the global market, the Government of Bangladesh has recently allowed 100% ownership of equity in greenfield projects for foreign investors (footnote 26).

The government has planned to execute several projects, which include construction of four airports, under the Seventh Five-Year Plan. Details of the airport projects are mentioned in Table 21.

Table 21: Projects Planned in the Airport Sector in Bangladesh

Airport	Project Description	Funding Structure
Hazrat Shahjalal International Airport	Construction of a new passenger terminal and other facilities at an estimated cost of $1,776.3 million	Government of Bangladesh and Japan International Cooperation Agency— PPP
Bangabandhu Sheikh Mujib International Airport	Construction of a new airport at an estimated cost of $6,552.6 million	PPP
Khan Jahan Ali Airport	Construction of a new airport at an estimated cost of $64.4 million	PPP
Cox's Bazar Airport	Development of the first phase at an estimated cost of $32.8 million	CAAB (public funding)

CAAB = Civil Aviation Authority of Bangladesh, PPP = public–private partnership.
Note: Based on the comments provided by the PPP Authority, construction of a new passenger terminal at Hazrat Shahjalal International Airport had a groundbreaking ceremony in December 2019 and is now in the development stage.
Source: Private Infrastructure Development Group, GuarantCo, and Technical Assistance Facility. 2019. *Study of Bangladesh Bond Market*. Dhaka. https://guarantco.com/gco/wp-content/uploads/2019/Documents/news/Study-of-Bangladesh-Bond-Market.pdf.

3.1 Projects under Preparation and Procurement in the Airport Sector

Figure 24 indicates the number of projects in the airport sector that are under preparation and procurement.

Figure 24: Public–Private Partnership Airport Projects under Preparation and Procurement

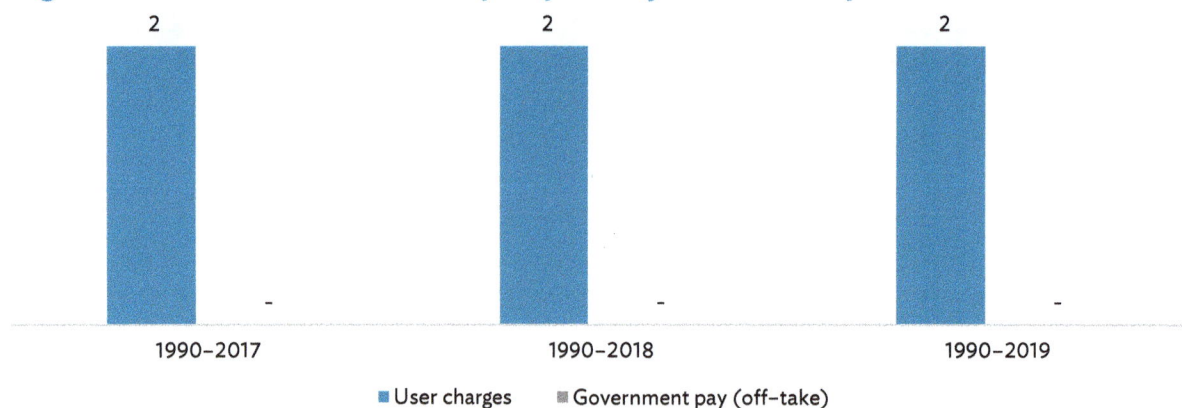

| | 1990–2017 | 1990–2018 | 1990–2019 |

■ User charges   ■ Government pay (off-take)

Note: The hyphen symbol (-) indicates there are no projects in the sector or data are not available.
Source: Government of Bangladesh, Public Private Partnership Authority. PPP Projects. http://www.pppo.gov.bd/projects.php (accessed 15 June 2020).

A feasibility study has been completed for the development of Khan Jahan Ali Airport and the special tourism zone in Khulna under the PPP mode. To date, no other projects are at preparatory or procurement stages.

4. Features of Past Public–Private Partnership Projects in the Airport Sector

"The information on features of past PPP projects in Bangladesh's airport sector is not available."

4.1 Tariffs in the Airport Sector

Tariff-related details in the airport sector are unavailable.

4.2 Typical Risk Allocation for Public–Private Partnership Airport Projects

The risk allocation for PPP projects in the airport sector is not available.

4.3 Financing Details of Public–Private Partnerships in the Airport Sector

Parameter	1990–2017	1990–2018	1990–2018
Public–private partnership (PPP) projects with foreign lending participation	NA	NA	NA
PPP projects that received export credit agency/international financing institution support	NA	NA	NA
Typical debt-to-equity ratio		NA	
Time for financial close		NA	
Typical concession period		NA	
Typical financial internal rate of return		NA	

✓ = Yes, ✗ = No, NA = Not Applicable, UA = Unavailable

5. Challenges in the Airport Sector

- Regulatory challenges. The CAAB is the sole regulator who operates the airports and determines tariffs. This leads to a lack of operational efficiency, accountability, and probable monetization opportunities (footnote 26).

- Demand risks. The passenger movement and transportation of cargo traffic are concentrated at Hazrat Shah Jalal International Airport, when compared to the country's other airports. That leads to demand risk for the new airports, which could substantially affect the developer's revenues (footnote 26).

- Exchange rate fluctuations. The aviation sector faces currency fluctuation risks due to revenues being collected in local currency; operating expenses (fuel) and servicing of debt/equity involves foreign currency payments (footnote 26).

- Lack of government support. Government support and new incentives are essential in achieving sustained level of growth of the aviation industry. Moreover, the pressing need for modernization and effective planning to execute various projects must be immediately addressed (footnote 26).

E. ENERGY

Parameter	Value	Unit
Electric power consumption	310.40	kilowatt-hour per capita
Share of clean energy	34.75	% of total energy use
Access to electricity	85.16	% of population
Getting electricity (score out of 100)	34.90	no.
Energy imports	16.84	% of total energy use
Investment in energy with private participation	170	current $ million
Total number of projects with cumulative lending, grant, and technical assistance commitments in the energy sector	115	no.
Total amount of cumulative lending, grant, and technical assistance commitments in the energy sector	5,823	$ million

✓ = Yes, ✗ = No, NA = Not Applicable, UA = Unavailable
Sources: Asian Development Bank. Cumulative Lending, Grant, and Technical Assistance Commitments. https://data.adb.org/dataset/cumulative-lending-grant-and-technical-assistance-commitments; Doing Business. Getting Electricity. https://www.doingbusiness.org/en/data/doing-business-score?topic=getting-electricity; The Economist Intelligence Unit. Bangladesh. https://infrascope.eiu.com/; The Global Economy. Energy Imports. https://www.theglobaleconomy.com/rankings/energy_imports/; The Global Economy. Share of Clean Energy—Country Rankings. https://www.theglobaleconomy.com/rankings/share_of_clean_energy/; and World Bank. Access to Electricity. https://data.worldbank.org/indicator/EG.ELC.ACCS.ZS?locations=BD.

1. Contracting Agencies in the Energy Sector

The Bangladesh Power Development Board is the contracting authority for entering into power purchase agreements (PPAs) from power-generating private players.

There are no instances of private sector participation in transmission and distribution.

2. Energy Sector Laws and Regulations

The Ministry of Power, Energy, and Mineral Resources has two main divisions (footnote 1):

- The Power Cell was created to implement power sector reform and to manage the electricity business.
- The Energy and Mineral Resources Division manages the energy sector and has two corporations:
    (i)   Bangladesh Oil, Gas and Mineral Corporation (PetroBangla), responsible for mining, developing, producing, and transporting natural gas and mineral resources; and
    (ii) Bangladesh Petroleum Corporation, responsible for import, refining, marketing, transportation, and storage of oil.

The Bangladesh Power Development Board (BPDB) operates most of the publicly owned generators and urban distributors (except in Dhaka and West Zone); it acts as a single buyer, purchasing from public and private generators and selling to distributors. In addition, it conducts procurement processes for independent power producers (IPPs) (footnote 1).

The Sustainable and Renewable Energy Development Agency is mandated to promote renewable energy. It acts as the state nodal agency for all renewable energy programs and projects in Bangladesh. It is responsible for promoting and approving all renewable energy projects, developing an energy audit, and administering activities related to energy efficiency and conservation (footnote 1).

To create flexibility in the energy sector, the Government of Bangladesh has adopted various models specific to the energy sector (footnote 1):

- The government created a special status for IPPs—these public–private partnership (PPP) plants have been particularly successful in providing new generation capacity. Usually, IPPs sell energy to utilities under a PPA with one of the public companies, either the BPDB or the Power Grid Company of Bangladesh. As per the policies, such contracts benefit from sovereign guarantees (footnote 1).
- To meet Bangladesh's energy needs, a special type of project was also developed—quick rental power plants, or "rentals." These are typically small, oil-fired power plants established as an emergency measure to cope with power shortages in the short term and to be used during peak demand periods in the long term. With the exception of several rentals whose contracts last for a relatively long term of 15 years, most of the contracts are short (i.e., 3–5 years). Power generated from rentals is purchased by the BPDB under government initiatives. The BPDB usually purchases the rental power at high cost (due to the short term of the rental contracts) and sells the power at the regulated bulk tariff, with the negative margin incurred at the BPDB being the cost of the policy implementation (footnote 1).

There is a good level of activity in the power sector in Bangladesh and willingness to consider different delivery methods and incentives for the private sector to deliver a step change in energy supply. However, rentals are not considered to be the type of projects currently developing as typical PPPs as they lack long-term performance obligations. However, for the purpose of this report, and because this type of project represents a significant aspect of the local context, it has been decided to keep track of it. Rental projects, therefore, are counted in the assessment of the energy sector (footnote 1).

In general, a license is required for any power generation and energy transmission, distribution, supply, and storage project. Licenses are issued by the Bangladesh Energy Regulatory Commission.

The key government agencies associated with the energy sector are shown in Table 22.

Table 22: Key Institutions in the Energy Sector

Agency	Function
Bangladesh Energy Regulatory Commission (BERC)	The commission has the mandate to regulate electricity, gas, and petroleum products for the whole country. Among others, the BERC has authority over consumer protection, approval of tariffs and pricing, issuance of generation and distribution licenses, and promotion of competition. The BERC Act, 2003 gives the commission a legal mandate for liberalization of the sector, which makes it a quasi-judicial authority.
Ministry of Power, Energy and Mineral Resources	The government is responsible for overall planning and development of the energy sector, through the issuance of policy directives relating to energy. It functions through the Energy and Mineral Resources Division and Power Division. The Power Division, in turn, functions through the Office of the Electrical Advisor and Chief Electric Inspector and the Energy Monitoring Unit and Power Cell.
Sustainable and Renewable Energy Development Authority	Responsible for all renewable energy sector regulation.
Power Division	The Power Division, under the Ministry of Power, Energy and Mineral Resources, helps develop power projects. As a critical arm of the ministry, it handles the following functions: • All activities related to power generation, transmission, and distribution; • Manage all matters and policies related to the power sector; • Expand, rehabilitate, and modernize power generation, transmission, and distribution services in line with the increasing national demand, and prepare action plans and programs accordingly; • Encourage private and joint venture investment in the power sector in addition to the government investment; • Improve the standard of living of the rural poor through rural electrification and the introduction of renewable energy; • Monitor revenue earnings and commercial activities of the utilities; and • Promote renewable energy and energy efficiency through formulation of policy or regulation, incentive mechanisms, and research and development.

Sources: Asian Development Bank. 2019. *Public–Private Partnership Monitor.* Second Edition. Manila. https://www.adb.org/sites/default/files/publication/509426/ppp-monitor-second-edition.pdf; and Government of Bangladesh, Department of Power. Work Plan of the Power Department. https://powerdivision.gov.bd/site/page/5abb0723-5119-410a-9036-9eb99c91a0c7/Major-Functiion.

Other key players in the energy sector

The Power Grid Company of Bangladesh, a wholly owned subsidiary of the BPDB, operates the national transmission grid, schedules grid operations, and wheels energy to distributors (footnote 1).

The Dhaka Electric Supply Company Limited is a public company that provides power supply services (footnote 1).

The Bangladesh Rural Electrification Board was established in 1977 to monitor electrification projects and facilitate socioeconomic development and improve agriculture in the rural areas of Bangladesh (footnote 1).

The Infrastructure Development Company Limited is a state-owned nonbanking financial institution that administers financing for rural energy and renewable energy development projects (mainly solar home systems and biogas) with 15 participating national nongovernment organizations (NGOs). The company has a long list of projects financed by development partners such as Japan International Cooperation Agency, World Bank, and ADB, among others (footnote 1).

The various regulations and laws related to the energy sector are listed below:[37]

- The Electricity Act, 1910;
- The Electricity Rules, 1937;
- The Electricity Regulations, 1961;
- National Energy Policy, 1996;
- Private Sector Power Generation Policy of Bangladesh, 1996;
- Policy Guidelines for Small Power Plant in the Private Sector, 2000;
- The Bangladesh Energy Regulatory Commission Act, 2003;
- Policy Guidelines for Power Purchase from Captive Power Plant, 2007;
- Private Sector Power Generation Policy of Bangladesh, 1996;
- Guidelines for Remote Area Power Supply System, 2008;
- Policy Guidelines for Enhancement of Private Participation in the Power Sector, 2008;
- Renewable Energy Policy of Bangladesh, 2008;
- The Bangladesh Private Sector Infrastructure Guidelines;
- The Sustainable and Renewable Energy Development Authority Act, 2012;
- Energy Efficiency and Conservation Rules, 2015; and
- Power and Energy Fast Supply Enhancement (Special Provision) Act.

2.1 Foreign Investment Restrictions in the Energy Sector

Business Activity	Maximum % of FDI Allowed
Power generation	100%
Power transmission	100%
Power distribution	100%
Oil and gas	100%

FDI = foreign direct investment.

The above may be reviewed against the restrictions and limitations held by the government, as explained in Chapter II Section 8.

---

[37]   Sustainable and Renewable Energy Development Authority. SREDA at a Glance. http://www.sreda.gov.bd/index.php/site/page/14eb-6e9e-27c2-bd05-9e73-9ed4-4137-8a1e-9432-6e41.

2.2 Standard Contracts in the Energy Sector

Type of Contract	Availability
Public–private partnership/power purchase agreement	✓
Capacity take-or-pay contract	UA
Fuel supply agreement	✓
Implementation agreement (government guarantee)	✓
Transmission and use of system agreement	UA
Engineering, procurement, and construction contract	UA

✓ = Yes, ✗ = No, NA = Not Applicable, UA = Unavailable

3. Energy Sector Master Plan

The Power System Master Plan (PSMP) 2016, sponsored by the Japan International Cooperation Agency, seeks to assist Bangladesh in formulating an extensive energy and power development plan up to 2041, covering energy balance, power balance, and tariff strategies. The PSMP 2016 is a key document detailing the road map of the power sector of Bangladesh.[38]

Based on the projections of supply made under the PSMP, the dependence on gas-based plants is likely to shift toward balancing it with coal and partly by nuclear power. The outlook for energy mix is shown in Table 23.

Table 23: Outlook on Energy Mix in Bangladesh

Primary Energy Sources	2014		2041	
	ktoe	Share	ktoe	Share
Natural gas	20,726	56%	50,149	38%
Oil (crude oil + refined products)	6,263	17%	32,153	25%
Coal	1,361	4%	26,273	20%
Nuclear power	...	...	11,942	9%
Hydro, solar, wind power and others	36	0%	197	0%
Biofuel and waste	8,449	23%	4,086	3%
Power (import)	377	1%	6,027	5%
Total	**37,212**	**100%**	**130,827**	**100%**

... = not available, ktoe = kiloton of oil equivalent.
Note: Percentages may not total 100% because of rounding.
Source: Ministry of Power, Energy and Mineral Resources. 2016. *Power System Master Plan 2016*. Dhaka. https://mpemr.gov.bd/assets/media/pdffiles/FR_PSMP_revised.pdf.

The Government of Bangladesh aims to increase the installed capacity from 20 gigawatts (GW) in January 2019 to 24 GW by 2021, 40 GW by 2030, and 60 GW by 2041. For renewable energy, the government has extended policy support for the proliferation of alternative energy sector in the country, targeting 2,470 megawatts (MW) by 2021 and 3,864 MW by 2041 as per the PSMP 2016. According to renewable energy development targets

---

[38]   Ministry of Power, Energy and Mineral Resources. 2016. *Power System Master Plan 2016*. Dhaka. https://mpemr.gov.bd/assets/media/pdffiles/FR_PSMP_revised.pdf.

set by the Sustainable and Renewable Energy Development Agency, a total of 1,270 MW of solar plants and 1,150 MW of wind energy projects will be developed over 2017–2021. Along with this, 40 MW power will be generated from waste-to-energy, 30 MW from biomass, 2 MW from biogas, and 6 MW from hydro by 2021. IPPs are developing power projects in the renewable energy sector totaling 1,416 MW, which include 1,345 MW of solar power plants (footnote 26).

The government has set targets for saving energy: 15% of total energy consumption by 2021, and 20% by 2030. The year-by-year targeted plan for renewable energy is indicated in Table 24.

Table 24: Renewable Energy Plan in Bangladesh
(megawatt)

Technology	Achievement up to 2016	2017	2018	2019	2020	2021	Total
Solar	200.0	120.0	350.0	250.0	300.0	250.0	1,470.0
Wind	2.9	50.0	150.0	350.0	300.0	300.0	1,152.9
Biomass	0.0	6.0	6.0	6.0	6.0	6.0	30.0
Biogas	5.0	0.0	0.5	0.5	0.5	0.5	7.0
Hydro	230.0	0.0	1.0	1.0	2.0	2.0	236.0
Total	**437.9**	**176.0**	**507.5**	**607.5**	**608.5**	**558.5**	**2,895.9**

Source: Sustainable and Renewable Energy Development Authority. http://www.sreda.gov.bd/index.php/site/page/14eb-6e9e-27c2-bd05-9e73-9ed4-4137-8a1e-9432-6e41.

The Power Cell has also notified the coal-based megaprojects that are expected to be developed or under development. The list is provided in Table 25.

Table 25: Coal-Based Megaprojects in Bangladesh

Name	Capacity (MW)	Executing Agency	Completion Date
Matarbari Coal-Based Power Plant	1,200	CPGCBL	June 2022
Paira Coal-Based Power Plant	1,320	NWPGCL–PRC JV	June 2022
G2G Coal-Based Power Plant	1,320	Bangladesh–ROK JV	June 2023
Moheshkhali Coal-Based Power Plant	1,200	BPDB	June 2021
Moheshkhali Coal-Based Power Plant	1,320	Bangladesh–Malaysia JV	June 2022
Ashuganj 2 x 660 MW Power Plant	1,320	APSCL	UA
Maheshkhali Coal-Based Power Plant	1,320	BPDB–CHDHK, PRC JV	June 2021

APSCL = Ashuganj Power Station Company Ltd., BPDB = Bangladesh Power Development Board, CHDHK = China Huadian Hong Kong Co. Ltd., CPGCBL = Coal Power Generation Company Bangladesh Limited, G2G = government-to-government, JV = joint venture, MW = megawatt, NWPGCL = North–West Power Generation Co. Ltd., PRC = People's Republic of China, ROK = Republic of Korea, UA = Unavailable.
Source: Power Cell. Coal Based Megaproject. https://powercell.portal.gov.bd/site/page/e35bd93a-c1ba-45b3-b7c2-21a0e035df30/- (accessed 29 June 2020).

The country also has a Gas Sector Master Plan 2017, which envisages gas-based developments up to 2041.

There has not been any private sector involvement in the transmission and distribution infrastructure or operations in Bangladesh. In the transmission sector, projects have been partly funded by the Government of Bangladesh and the Power Grid Corporation of Bangladesh. Apart from these government entities, multiple funding agencies such as ADB, Economic Development Cooperation Fund Korea, German development cooperation through KfW, Japan International Cooperation Agency, Swedish International Development Cooperation Agency, World Bank's International Development Association, People's Republic of China (bilateral agreement), and Indian lines of credit have provided funds for the completed projects. In the distribution sector, 75% to 80% of the funds for the Bangladesh Rural Electrification Board's ongoing projects are provided by the Government of Bangladesh, whereas ADB and the International Development Association have provided approximately 10% each. The Dhaka Power Distribution Company, on the other hand, plans to implement projects with funds through internal accruals, Government of Bangladesh, ADB, KfW, and concessional loans from the Government of the People's Republic of China (footnote 26).

3.1 Projects under Preparation and Procurement in the Energy Sector

Figure 25 indicates the number of projects under preparation and procurement in the energy sector in Bangladesh.

Figure 25: Public–Private Partnership Energy Projects under Preparation and Procurement

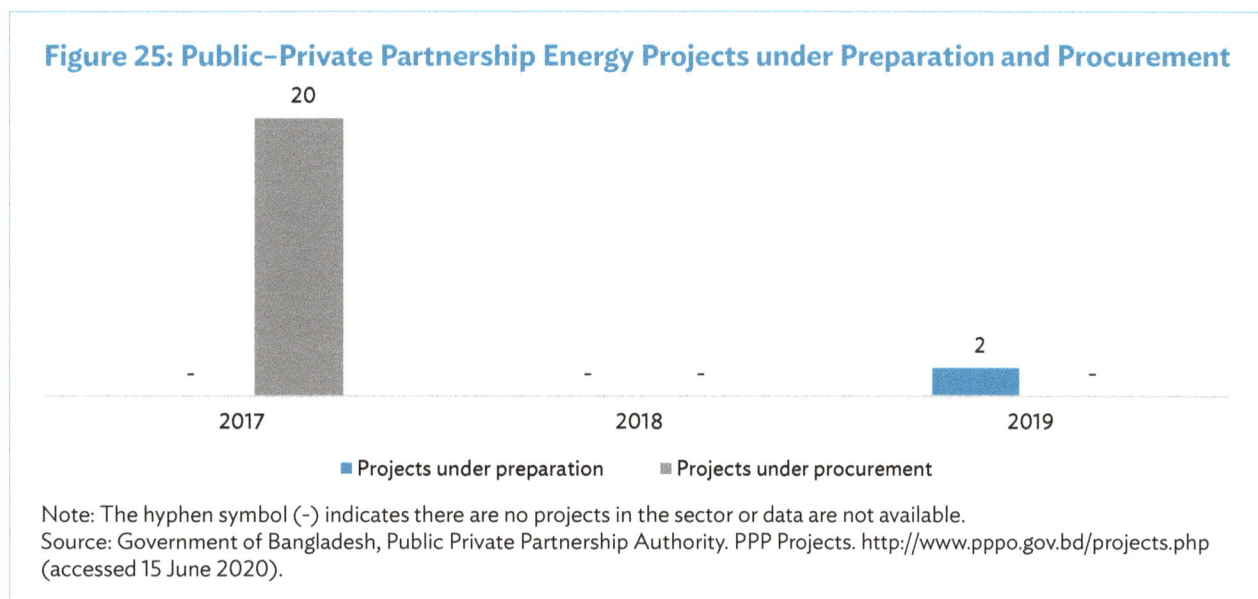

Note: The hyphen symbol (-) indicates there are no projects in the sector or data are not available.
Source: Government of Bangladesh, Public Private Partnership Authority. PPP Projects. http://www.pppo.gov.bd/projects.php (accessed 15 June 2020).

Currently, two projects have received (in-principle) approval from the Cabinet Committee on Economic Affairs (CCEA) and are at preparatory stages for the next steps of feasibility studies:

(i)   Construction of liquefied petroleum gas import, storage, and bottling plant at Kumira or any suitable place at Chittagong, including import facilities of liquefied petroleum gas, jetty, pipeline, and storage tanks under PPP; and

(ii) Construction of Matarbari–Banshkhali–Madunaghat 400-kilovolt (kV) transmission.

4. Features of Past Public–Private Partnership Projects in the Energy Sector

Figure 26 shows the number of PPP projects procured through various modes, including direct appointment, unsolicited bids, and competitive bids in Bangladesh's energy sector.

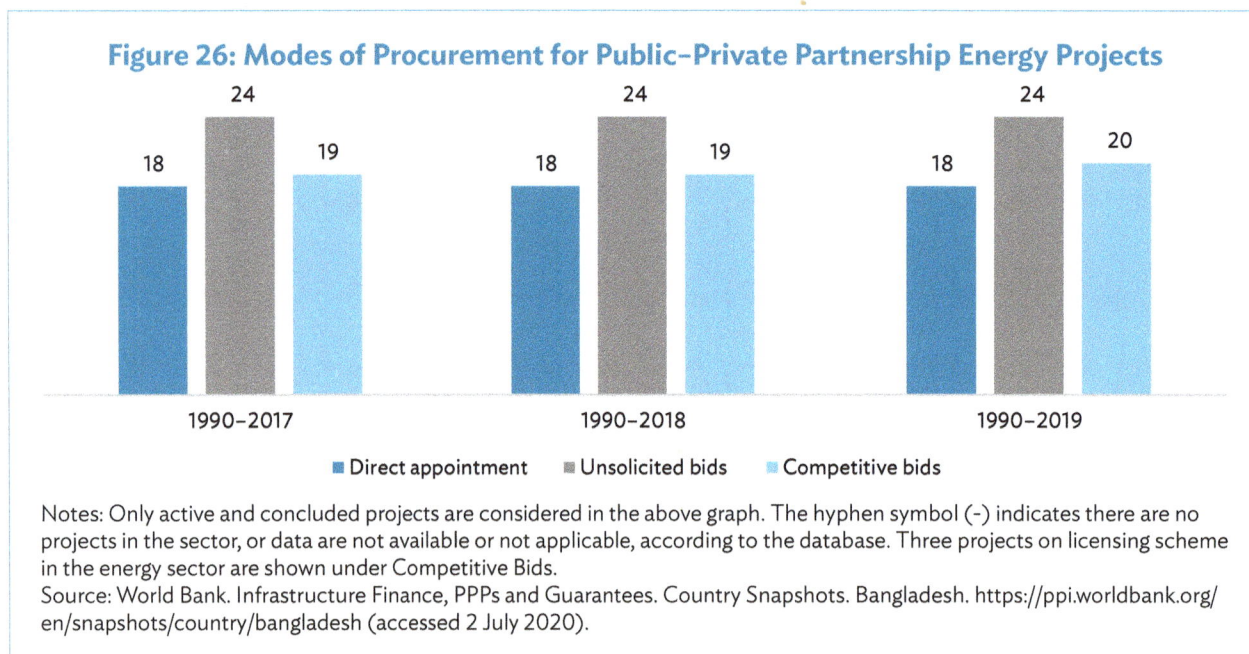

Figure 26: Modes of Procurement for Public–Private Partnership Energy Projects

Mode	1990–2017	1990–2018	1990–2019
Direct appointment	18	18	18
Unsolicited bids	24	24	24
Competitive bids	19	19	20

Notes: Only active and concluded projects are considered in the above graph. The hyphen symbol (-) indicates there are no projects in the sector, or data are not available or not applicable, according to the database. Three projects on licensing scheme in the energy sector are shown under Competitive Bids.
Source: World Bank. Infrastructure Finance, PPPs and Guarantees. Country Snapshots. Bangladesh. https://ppi.worldbank.org/en/snapshots/country/bangladesh (accessed 2 July 2020).

Figure 27 shows the number of PPP projects that have reached financial closure and the total value of those projects in Bangladesh's energy sector.

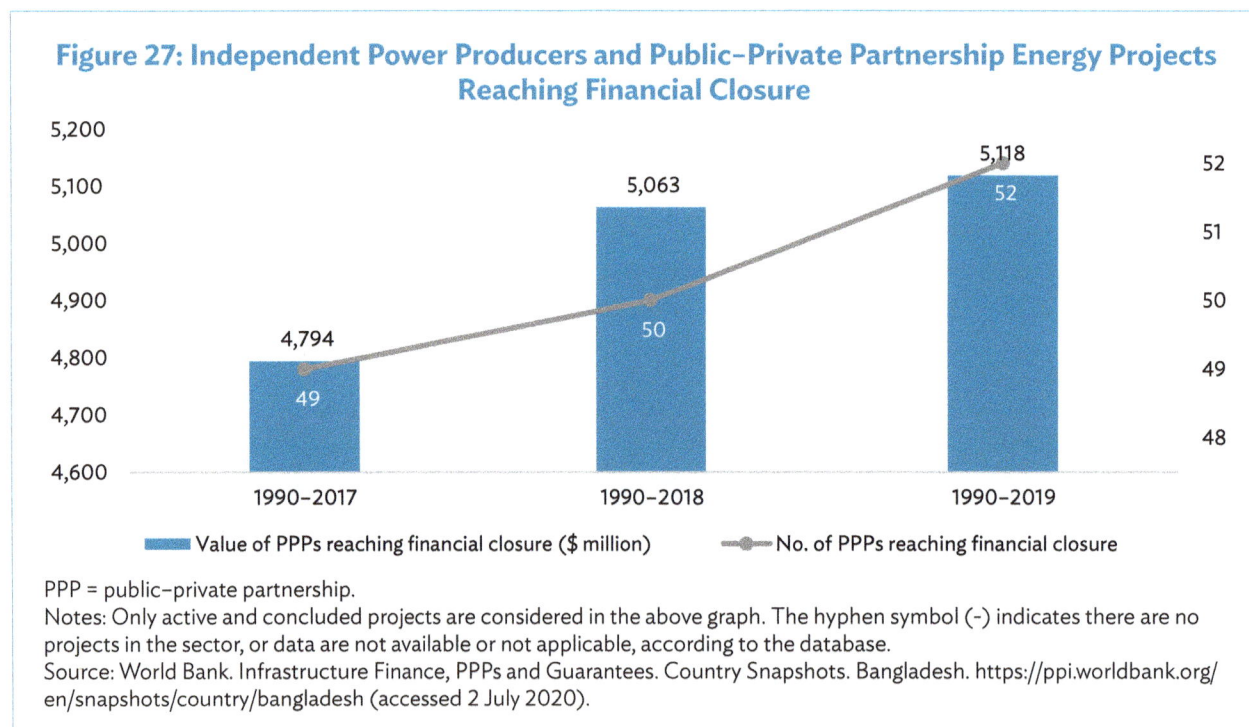

Figure 27: Independent Power Producers and Public–Private Partnership Energy Projects Reaching Financial Closure

	1990–2017	1990–2018	1990–2019
Value of PPPs reaching financial closure ($ million)	4,794	5,063	5,118
No. of PPPs reaching financial closure	49	50	52

PPP = public–private partnership.
Notes: Only active and concluded projects are considered in the above graph. The hyphen symbol (-) indicates there are no projects in the sector, or data are not available or not applicable, according to the database.
Source: World Bank. Infrastructure Finance, PPPs and Guarantees. Country Snapshots. Bangladesh. https://ppi.worldbank.org/en/snapshots/country/bangladesh (accessed 2 July 2020).

Figure 28 presents the number of PPP projects that have received foreign sponsor participation in Bangladesh's energy sector.

Figure 28: Independent Power Producers and Public–Private Partnership Energy Projects with Foreign Sponsor Participation

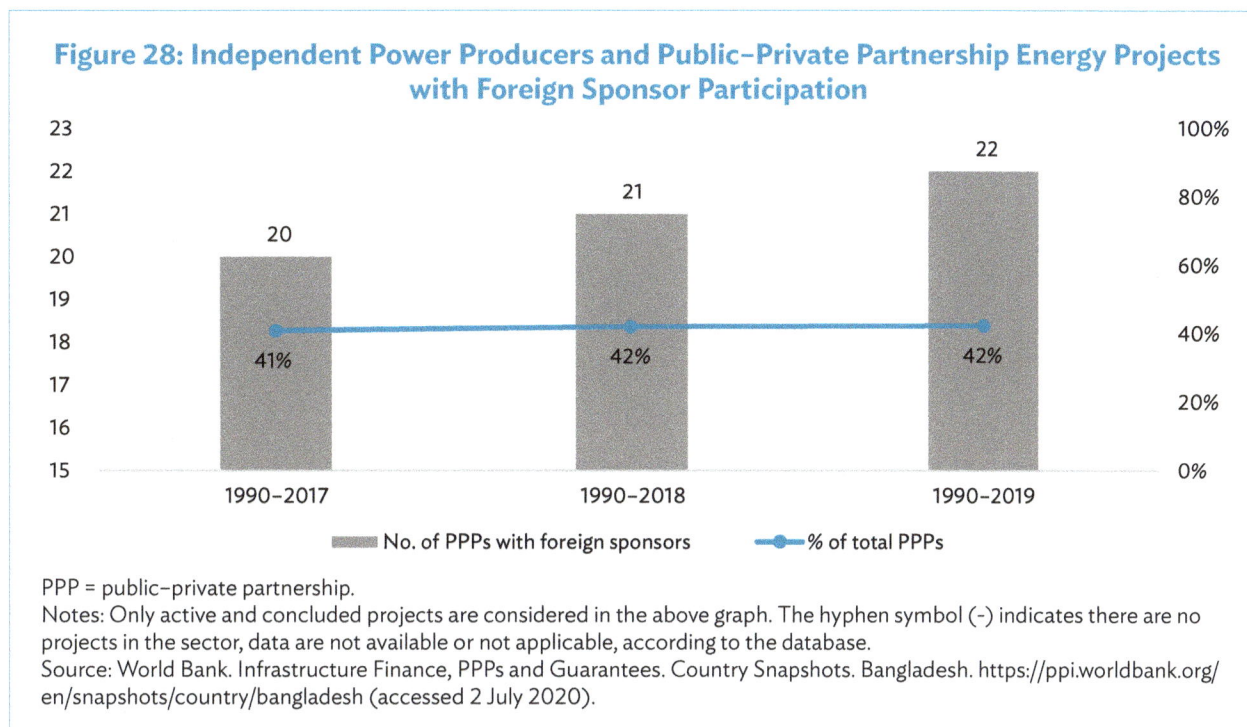

PPP = public–private partnership.
Notes: Only active and concluded projects are considered in the above graph. The hyphen symbol (-) indicates there are no projects in the sector, data are not available or not applicable, according to the database.
Source: World Bank. Infrastructure Finance, PPPs and Guarantees. Country Snapshots. Bangladesh. https://ppi.worldbank.org/en/snapshots/country/bangladesh (accessed 2 July 2020).

Figure 29 shows the number of PPP projects that have received government support, including viability gap funding, government guarantees, and availability/performance payment in the energy sector.

Figure 29: Government Support for Independent Power Producers and Public–Private Partnership Energy Projects

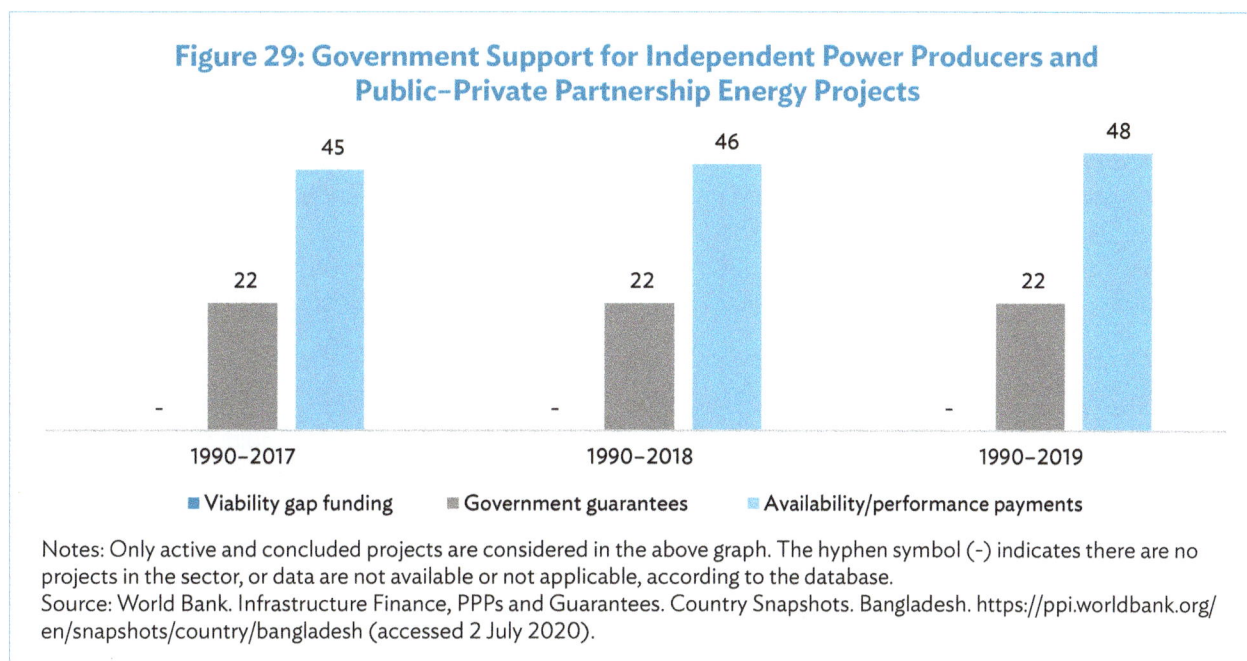

Notes: Only active and concluded projects are considered in the above graph. The hyphen symbol (-) indicates there are no projects in the sector, or data are not available or not applicable, according to the database.
Source: World Bank. Infrastructure Finance, PPPs and Guarantees. Country Snapshots. Bangladesh. https://ppi.worldbank.org/en/snapshots/country/bangladesh (accessed 2 July 2020).

Figure 30 shows the number of PPP projects that have received payment in the form of user charges and government pay (offtake) in Bangladesh's energy sector.

Figure 30: Payment Mechanisms for Public–Private Partnership Energy Projects

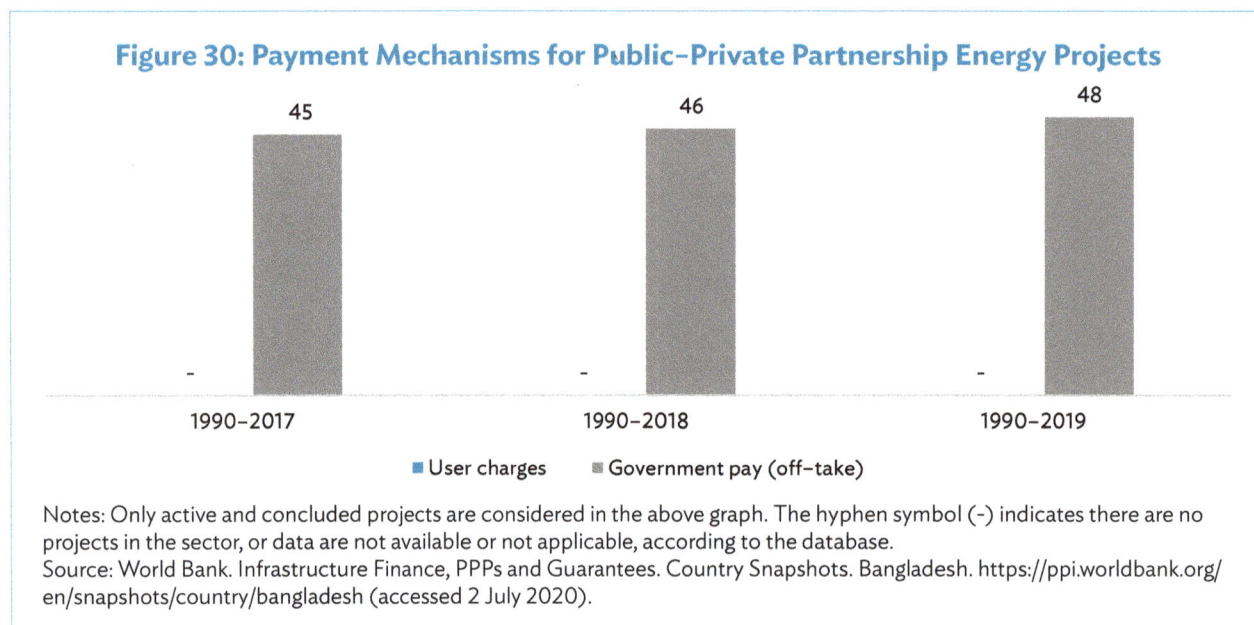

Notes: Only active and concluded projects are considered in the above graph. The hyphen symbol (-) indicates there are no projects in the sector, or data are not available or not applicable, according to the database.
Source: World Bank. Infrastructure Finance, PPPs and Guarantees. Country Snapshots. Bangladesh. https://ppi.worldbank.org/en/snapshots/country/bangladesh (accessed 2 July 2020).

4.1 Tariffs in the Energy Sector

Prices of electricity, gas, and petroleum in bulk and in retail are determined by the Bangladesh Energy Regulatory Commission. The commission published the Power Pricing Framework in 2004 and tariff regulations. To date, however, Bangladesh has not yet introduced a feed-in-tariff scheme. The policy tool is not yet in effect, although the draft document has been completed (footnote 1).

The charges applicable to the end consumers are divided into two parts: per unit charge (taka/kilowatt-hour) and demand charges (taka/kilowatt/month). Further, the electricity consumers are divided into 10 categories: residential, agricultural pumping, small industries, nonresidential, commercial and office, medium voltage for generation purpose (11 kV), extra-high voltage for general purpose (132 kV), high voltage for general purpose (33 kV), streetlights, and water pumps. The tariff rates vary based on (i) electricity supply (low tension, medium tension, high tension, and extra-high tension) and (ii) unit slab—flat rate consumption during off-peak and peak time (except for category residential consumers who are charged based on six-step slab basis). The tariff rate is determined based on the Bangladesh Energy Regulatory Commission (Electricity Generation Tariff) Regulation, 2008 (footnote 26).

As of now, the tariff for IPPs is fixed under direct negotiation between the offtaker and the project company and its sponsors, which in turn requires offtaker line ministry approval and approval from the Cabinet Committee on Government Purchase. Also, there is no separate regime for tariff for energy from renewable IPPs. However, the Renewable Energy Policy of Bangladesh, 2008 provides for a premium for tariff for renewable powers over nonrenewable powers.

4.2 Typical Risk Allocation for Public–Private Partnership Energy Projects

A typical risk allocation based on a sample power purchase agreement (PPA) signed by the BPDB is shown in Table 26.

Table 26: Typical Risk Allocation for Public–Private Partnership Energy Projects

Risk Category	Private	Public	Shared	Comment
Demand risk		✓		The Bangladesh Power Development Board (BPDB) agrees to accept and purchase from the special-purpose vehicle the power produced on a no-electricity, no-payment basis.
Revenue collection risk		✓		The private sector directly gets payment from the BPDB and is not exposed to revenue collection risk.
Tariff risk		✓		
Government payment risk		✓		Secured by letter of credit.
Environmental and social risks	✓			In the power purchase agreement (PPA) reviewed, the land was owned by the private player; else, the risk is generally borne by the contracting authority.
Land acquisition risk	✓			In the PPA reviewed, the land was owned by the private player; else, the risk generally is borne by the contracting authority.
Permits			✓	
Handover risk				UA
Political risk		✓		
Regulatory risk		✓		
Interconnection risk		✓		
Brownfield risk: asset condition				NA
Grid performance risk		✓		
Hydrology risk				UA
Exploration and drilling risk				UA

✓ = Yes, ✗ = No, NA = Not Applicable, UA = Unavailable

4.3 Financing Details of Public–Private Partnership Projects in the Energy Sector

Parameter	1990–2017	1990–2018	1990–2019
Public–private partnership (PPP) projects with foreign lending participation	16	17	19
PPP projects that received export credit agency/international financing institution support[a]	14	15	16
Typical debt-to-equity ratio	(60:40); (70:30)		
Time for financial close	UA		
Typical concession period	15		
Typical financial internal rate of return	UA		

✓ = Yes, ✗ = No, NA = Not Applicable, UA = Unavailable
[a] Includes both foreign bank lending and international financial institution support.
Source: World Bank. Infrastructure Finance, PPPs and Guarantees. Country Snapshots. Bangladesh. https://ppi.worldbank.org/en/snapshots/country/bangladesh (accessed 2 July 2020).

ADB and the International Finance Corporation (IFC) have been the most active in terms of providing guarantees and loans. In 2019, of the 16 projects that attracted multilateral support, 11 have been supported by ADB and IFC.

5. Challenges in the Energy Sector

- Inadequate tariff levels and insufficient regulation. However, the Bangladesh Energy Regulatory Commission has been receiving assistance from multilateral agencies to carry out its mandate. The government is focusing on reforming the regulatory framework to facilitate development of new projects (footnote 1).

- Institutional weakness. This is being addressed through reform measures. Reform of energy sector institutions is starting to show results, with corporatization of state-owned operating entities such as the Dhaka Electric Supply Company Limited and the Electricity Generation Company of Bangladesh, and by empowering the BPDB (footnote 1).

- Human resources and skill issues. Due to the absence of sector-specific skills development programs, there is a lack of skilled human resources to work in power plants. Hence, extensive training and exposure are required to build up a suitable workforce within the country (footnote 26).

- Despite the government's commitment, there have been utility-scale solar photovoltaic projects delivered in Bangladesh. A number of unsolicited proposals for grid-tied solar power totaling around 500 MW were received by the power division over the past few years. But none of the projects awarded are expected to become operational anytime soon, due to difficulties experienced by the private sector in obtaining land and the inexperience of some of the companies involved (footnote 26).

F. WATER AND WASTEWATER

Parameter	Value	Unit
Improved water source access	87	% of population with access
Improved sanitation facilities access	61	% of population with access
Investment in water and sanitation with private participation	UA	$ million
Total number of projects with cumulative lending, grant, and technical assistance commitments in water and other urban infrastructure and services	64	no.
Total amount of cumulative lending, grant, and technical assistance commitments in water and other urban infrastructure and services	2,015	$ million

✓ = Yes, ✗ = No, NA = Not Applicable, UA = Unavailable
Sources: Asian Development Bank (ADB). 2016. *Country Partnership Strategy: Bangladesh, 2016–2020*. Manila. https://www.adb.org/sites/default/files/institutional-document/198831/cps-ban-2016-2020.pdf; ADB. Cumulative Lending, Grant, and Technical Assistance Commitments. https://data.adb.org/dataset/cumulative-lending-grant-and-technical-assistance-commitments; and The Economist Intelligence Unit. Bangladesh. https://infrascope.eiu.com/.

1. Contracting Agencies in Water and Wastewater Sector

The government operates through its various institutional setups at the central level (ministries, divisions, departments, and agencies), different tiers of local governments—*upazila* (a subunit of a district) and union parishads, *pourashavas* (municipalities), and city corporations—and the semigovernment organizations (e.g., the Dhaka, Chittagong, and Khulna Water Supply and Sewerage Authorities). According to the National Policy for Safe Water Supply and Sanitation, the Department of Public Health and Engineering (DPHE) is the lead sector agency.[39]

---

[39]   Ministry of Local Government, Rural Development and Cooperatives, Local Government Division. 2011. *Sector Development Plan (FY 2011-25), Water Supply and Sanitation Sector in Bangladesh*. Dhaka. http://psb.gov.bd/policies/sdpwsssbe.pdf.

2. Water and Wastewater Sector Laws and Regulations

The application process for raw water extraction is provided by the Ministry of Water Resources as per the Bangladesh Water Rules, 2015 under the Bangladesh Water Act, 2013.

At the national level, the Local Government Division (LGD) of the Ministry of Local Government, Rural Development and Co-operatives is responsible for local governance matters such as financing, regulation, and inspection of authorities established for local government and village administration. The DPHE is responsible for implementing water supply and sanitation (WSS) projects of the public sector in rural and urban areas—outside the areas covered by the Water Supply and Sewerage Authority (WASA). In addition to the DPHE, the Local Government Engineering Department, also under the LGD, implements water and drainage projects in urban areas as part of the urban infrastructure development projects. National-level coordination among sector stakeholders, such as government agencies, NGOs, development partners, and the private sector, is done by the National Forum for Water Supply and Sanitation (NFWSS), which is established within the LGD and with the Secretary of the LGD as its chairperson. In rural areas, the coordination of WSS service provisions is the responsibility of local government institutions. The WSS committees of the *upazila* parishads and the union parishads coordinate the activities of the DPHE, the NGOs, and other stakeholders. The district-level local government institution, the Zila Parishad, is functioning; however, election is yet to take place. In urban areas, the DPHE was originally responsible for the WSS service, but gradually the *pourashavas* and the city corporations are becoming more involved in planning, implementing, and managing the water systems.

WASAs were established in 1963 in Dhaka and Chittagong cities as special-purpose institutions, responsible for water supply, sewerage, and drainage. Since 1990, Dhaka WASA's coverage has extended to Narayanganj Town. In 2008, Khulna WASA was created to develop the WSS sector. The DPHE and the WASAs function under the administrative control of the LGD (footnote 39).

Wastewater treated effluent discharge regulations are detailed in Schedule 9 and Schedule 10 of the Environmental Conservation Rules. Table 27 lists the key institutions in water and wastewater sector in Bangladesh.

Table 27: Key Institutions in Water and Wastewater Sector in Bangladesh

Agency	Function

Water Supply and Sewerage Authority (WASA)	• The key public authorities responsible for managing and providing water and sewage services are Dhaka WASA and Chittagong WASA. In other conurbations, this responsibility is delegated to the local municipality office and includes:
	  – construction, operation, improvement, and maintenance of the necessary infrastructure for collecting, treating, preserving, and supplying potable water to the public, industries, and commercial concerns; and
	  – construction, operation, improvement, and maintenance of the necessary infrastructure for collecting, treating, and disposing domestic sewage.

National Water Resource Council	• Responsible for coordinating all aspects of water management and issues directives through its executive committee
Water Resources Planning Organization	• Responsible for preparing the National Waste Management Plan, providing subsequent updates, and monitoring the plan's implementation
Department of Environment	• Enforcement of environmental legislation including wastewater discharge
Bangladesh Water Development Board	• Development of knowledge and capability that will enable the country to design future water resources management plans

Source: Asian Development Bank. 2019. *Public–Private Partnership Monitor.* Second Edition. Manila. https://www.adb.org/sites/default/files/publication/509426/ppp-monitor-second-edition.pdf.

Regulations related to water supply and wastewater (sanitation) sector are as follows:

- Bangladesh Water Act
- The Rules of Business, 1996 allocates responsibilities to government departments and ministries. It also allocates WSS provision in rural and urban areas not declared as municipalities to the DPHE.
- Local Government Acts
  - Local Government (Pourashava) Act, 2009;
  - Local Government (City Corporations) Act, 2009;
  - Upazila Parishad Act, 2009; and
  - Union Parishad Act, 2009.
- The WASA Act, 1996 gives the government power to establish WASAs in any area. It permits WASAs to carry out works related to water supply, sewerage systems, solid waste collection, and drainage. It also describes the composition of the WASA board and delineates responsibilities between the board and the managing director. Presently, WASAs work in Dhaka, Chittagong, and Khulna cities (footnote 39).
- The Environmental Conservancy Act, 1995 and the Environmental Conservation Rules, 1997 established a framework for environmental management and set environmental quality standards, including water quality standards (footnote 39).

2.1 Foreign Investment Restrictions in Water and Wastewater Sector

Parameter	2017	2018	2019
Maximum allowed foreign ownership of equity in greenfield projects	100%	100%	100%

The above may be reviewed against the restrictions and limitations held by the government, as explained in Chapter II Section 8.

2.2 Standard Contracts in Water and Wastewater Sector

Type of Contract	
Public–private partnership/concession agreement	✗
Performance-based operations and maintenance contract	✗
Engineering, procurement, and construction contract	✗

✓ = Yes, ✗ = No, NA = Not Applicable, UA = Unavailable

3. Water and Wastewater Sector Master Plan

A master plan for the water and wastewater sector has been developed in the form of the Water Supply and Sanitation Sector Development Plan (2011–2025) (footnote 39) and the National Strategy for Water Supply and Sanitation 2014.[40] The National Environmental Management Action Plan also covers some aspects of wastewater management.

---

[40]   Ministry of Local Government, Rural Development and Cooperatives, Local Government Division. 2014. *National Strategy for Water Supply and Sanitation 2014.* Dhaka. https://www.who.int/globalchange/resources/wash-toolkit/national-strategy-for-water-supply-and-sanitation-bangladesh.pdf?ua=1.

The Water Supply and Sanitation Sector Development Plan provides various contours of water supply and sanitation sector development, including identification of specific areas to be developed to attract private sector involvement. The plan provides a sector investment plan that determines the investment required to achieve the objectives in accordance with the policies and strategies set therein. Investment requirements are calculated for the short (FY2011–FY2015), medium (FY2016–FY2020), and long term (FY2021–FY2025). The plan focuses on areas that require investments and estimates the total investment requirements. Three scenarios are provided that are based on varying levels of service level indicators across the water supply and sanitation sectors (footnote 39).

Table 28 provides an example of the investment costs required for Scenario 2 for different categories of the urban subsector and rural subsector.[41]

Table 28: Expected Investments in Water and Wastewater Sector in Bangladesh

Category	Short Term 2010–2015 (Tk billion)	Medium Term 2016–2020 (Tk billion)	Long Term 2021–2025 (Tk billion)	Total (Tk billion)	Total ($ billion)
Urban water supply	165.22	280.47	269.26	714.95	8.43
Urban sanitation	93.51	107.56	134.82	335.89	3.96
Urban drainage	40.49	65.45	74.54	180.47	2.13
Rural water supply	44.69	42.82	55.11	142.62	1.68
Rural sanitation	36.50	27.73	27.36	91.59	1.08
Total	380.41	524.02	561.09	1,465.52	17.28

Note: Numbers may not sum precisely because of rounding.
Source: Ministry of Local Government, Local Government Division. 2011. *Sector Development Plan (FY 2011–2025), Water Supply and Sanitation Sector in Bangladesh*. Dhaka. http://psb.gov.bd/policies/sdpwsssbe.pdf.

More than 18% of the expected investments in water and wastewater sector are expected to be generated from various forms of private sector involvement. The sector's estimated sources of financing are presented in Table 29.

Table 29: Estimated Sources of Financing in Water and Wastewater Sector in Bangladesh

Source of Fund	FY2011–FY2015	FY2016–FY2020	FY2021–FY2025	Total FY2011–FY2025
1. Public Sector				
Public sector investment (Tk billion)	210.46	288.30	232.38	731.13
Revenue from WSS utilities (Tk billion)	88.96	144.47	209.53	442.95
2. Private Sector				
Community contribution as cost sharing (Tk billion)	2.11	0.11	0.07	2.28
Private household investment (Tk billion)	69.68	70.19	85.39	225.25
Private entrepreneur (Tk billion)	0.00	14.78	28.47	43.24

continued on next page

[41] The WSS sector development plan of Bangladesh (FY2021–FY2025) defines various scenarios related to the development of the WSS sector based on service levels and operating efficiencies. The scenarios are base case (Scenario 1), moderate (Scenario 2), and high (Scenario 3). Each scenario is described in terms of two parameters: (i) service level, indicating the quality of WSS facilities and user convenience; and (ii) operating efficiency, indicating the level of operating performance of the technology options or the service providers. The outputs under Scenario 2 are presented here as an example.

Table 29 *continued*

Source of Fund	FY2011–FY2015	FY2016–FY2020	FY2021–FY2025	Total FY2011–FY2025
3. NGOs (Tk billion)	9.21	6.18	5.26	20.66
Total (Tk billion)	380.41	524.02	561.09	1,465.52
Total ($ billion)	5.43	7.49	8.02	20.94

FY = fiscal year, NGO = nongovernment organization, Tk = taka, WSS = water supply and sanitation.
Note: Numbers may not sum precisely because of rounding.
Source: Ministry of Local Government, Local Government Division. 2011. *Sector Development Plan (FY 2011–2025), Water Supply and Sanitation Sector in Bangladesh*. Dhaka. http://psb.gov.bd/policies/sdpwsssbe.pdf.

3.1 Projects under Preparation and Procurement in Water and Wastewater Sector

Figure 31 presents the number of public–private partnership (PPP) projects that are under preparation and procurement in Bangladesh's water and wastewater sector.

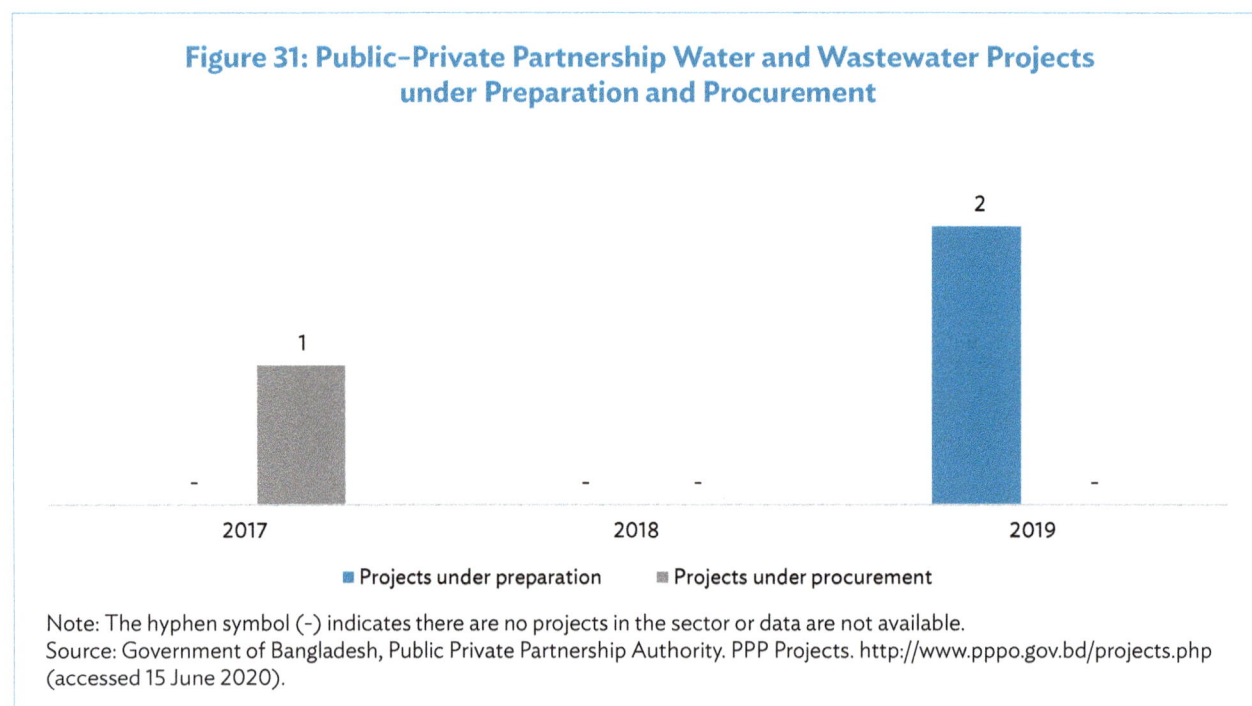

Figure 31: Public–Private Partnership Water and Wastewater Projects under Preparation and Procurement

■ Projects under preparation   ■ Projects under procurement

Note: The hyphen symbol (-) indicates there are no projects in the sector or data are not available.
Source: Government of Bangladesh, Public Private Partnership Authority. PPP Projects. http://www.pppo.gov.bd/projects.php (accessed 15 June 2020).

There are two projects that are in the procurement stage, as indicated in Table 30.

Table 30: Projects under Procurement in Water and Wastewater Sector in Bangladesh

Project Name	Status
Central Effluent Treatment Plant	Technical feasibility complete, Tender to be launched
Development of Integrated Wastewater Management System for Gazipur City Corporation	Technical feasibility ongoing

Source: Government of Bangladesh, Public Private Partnership Authority. PPP Projects. http://www.pppo.gov.bd/projects.php (accessed 15 June 2020).

4. Features of Past Public–Private Partnership Projects in Water and Wastewater Sector

Figure 32 shows the number of PPP projects procured through various modes, including direct appointment, unsolicited bids, and competitive bids, in Bangladesh's water and wastewater sector.

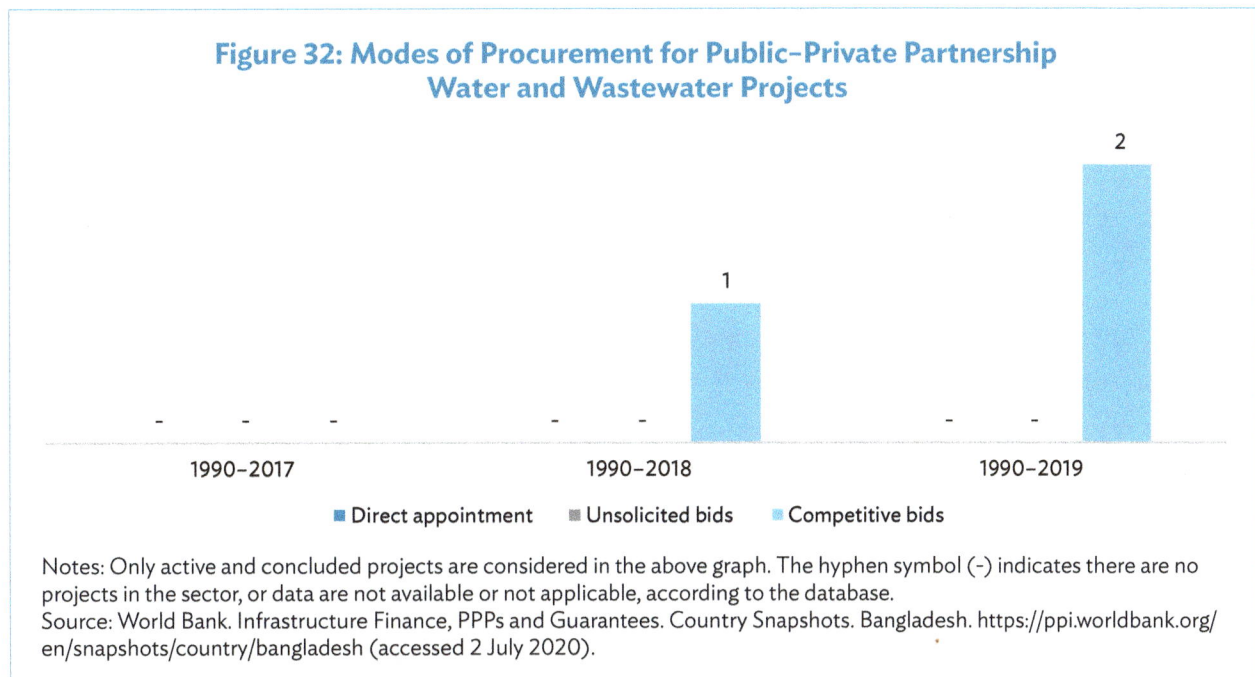

Figure 32: Modes of Procurement for Public–Private Partnership Water and Wastewater Projects

Notes: Only active and concluded projects are considered in the above graph. The hyphen symbol (-) indicates there are no projects in the sector, or data are not available or not applicable, according to the database.
Source: World Bank. Infrastructure Finance, PPPs and Guarantees. Country Snapshots. Bangladesh. https://ppi.worldbank.org/en/snapshots/country/bangladesh (accessed 2 July 2020).

Figure 33 presents the number of PPP projects that have reached financial closure and the total value of those projects in Bangladesh's water and wastewater sector.

Figure 34 shows the number of PPP projects that have received foreign sponsor participation in Bangladesh's water and wastewater sector.

Figure 33: Public–Private Partnership Water and Wastewater Projects Reaching Financial Closure

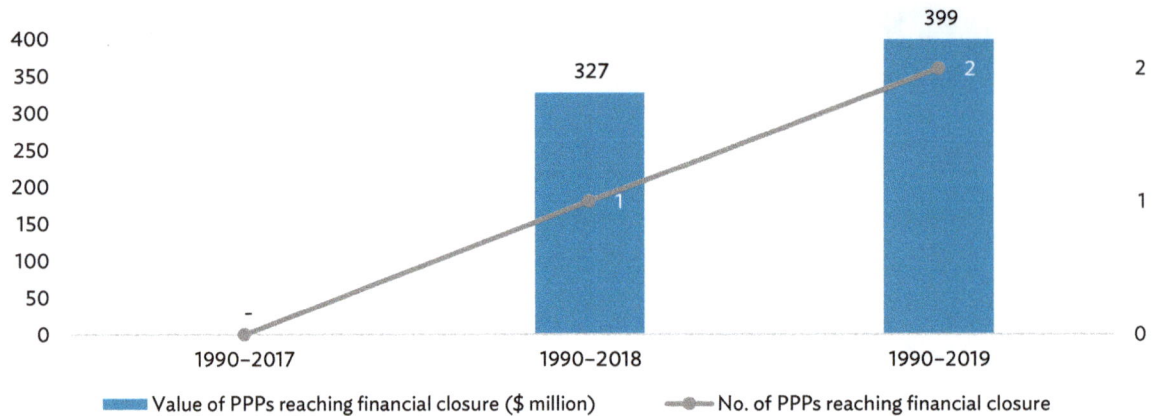

PPP = public–private partnership.
Notes: Only active and concluded projects are considered in the above graph. The hyphen symbol (-) indicates there are no projects in the sector, or data are not available or not applicable, according to the database.
Source: World Bank. Infrastructure Finance, PPPs and Guarantees. Country Snapshots. Bangladesh. https://ppi.worldbank.org/en/snapshots/country/bangladesh (accessed 2 July 2020).

Figure 34: Public–Private Partnership Water and Wastewater Projects with Foreign Sponsor Participation

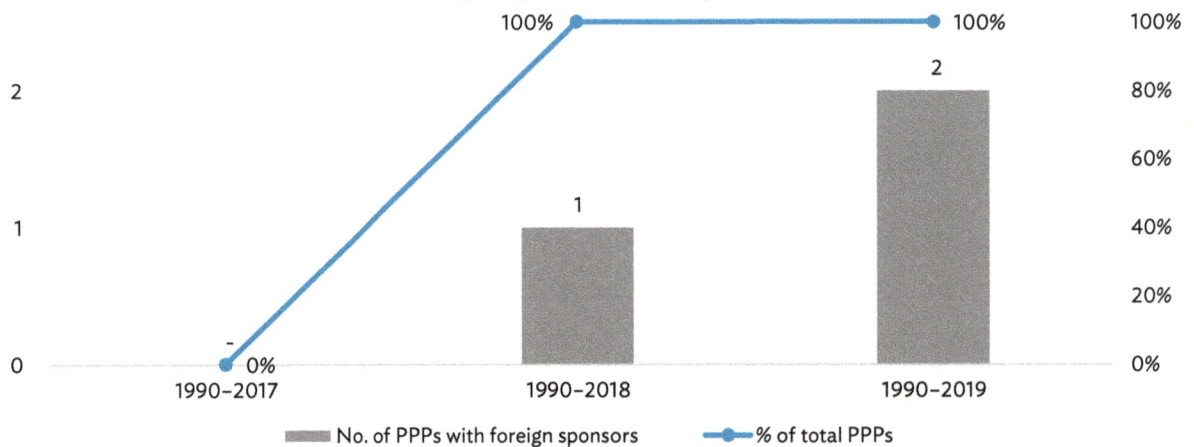

PPP = public–private partnership.
Notes: Only active and concluded projects are considered in the above graph. The hyphen symbol (-) indicates there are no projects in the sector, or data are not available or not applicable, according to the database.
Source: World Bank. Infrastructure Finance, PPPs and Guarantees. Country Snapshots. Bangladesh. https://ppi.worldbank.org/en/snapshots/country/bangladesh (accessed 2 July 2020).

Figure 35 presents the number of PPP projects that have received government support, including viability gap funding, government guarantees, and availability/performance payment in Bangladesh's water and wastewater sector.

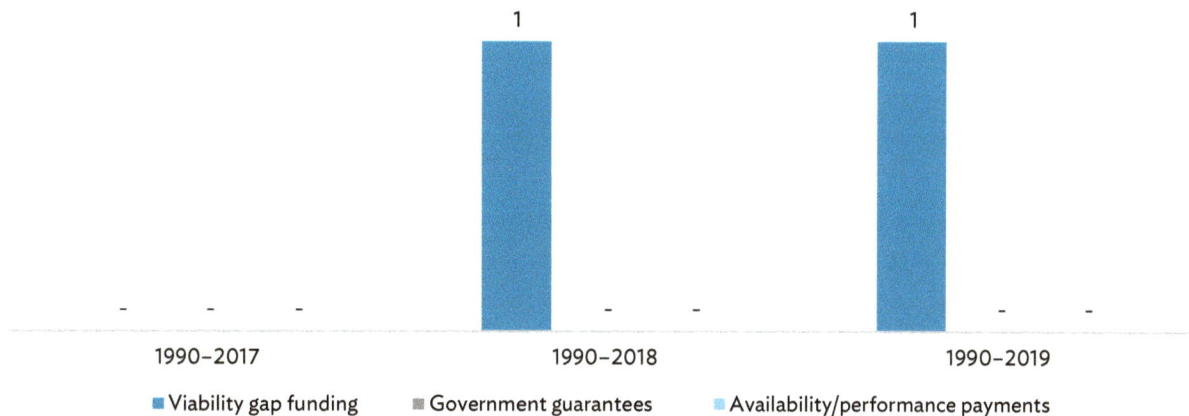

Figure 35: Government Support for Public–Private Partnership Water and Wastewater Projects

Notes: Only active and concluded projects are considered in the above graph. The hyphen symbol (-) indicates there are no projects in the sector, or data are not available or not applicable, according to the database.
Source: World Bank. Infrastructure Finance, PPPs and Guarantees. Country Snapshots. Bangladesh. https://ppi.worldbank.org/en/snapshots/country/bangladesh (accessed 2 July 2020).

Figure 36 presents the number of PPP projects that have received payment in the form of user charges and government pay (offtake) in Bangladesh's water and wastewater sector.

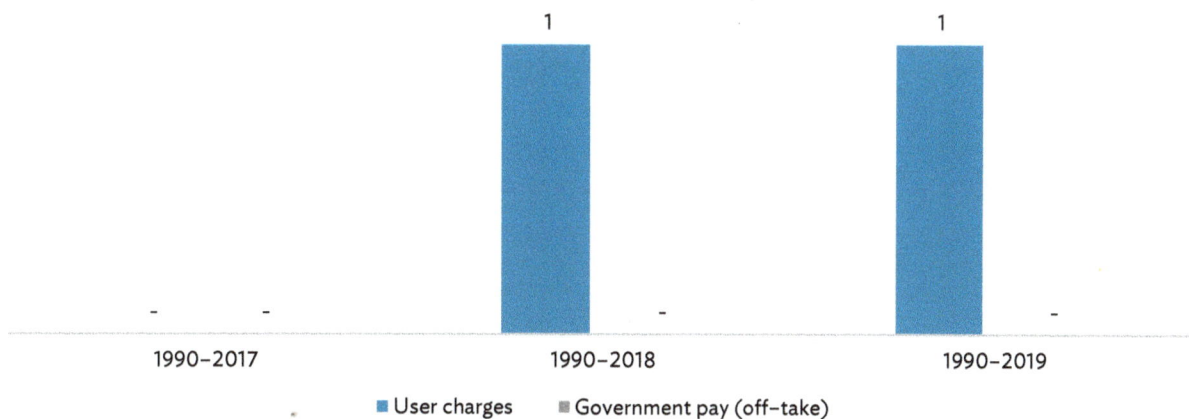

Figure 36: Payment Mechanisms for Public–Private Partnership Water and Wastewater Projects

Notes: Only active and concluded projects are considered in the above graph. The hyphen symbol (-) indicates there are no projects in the sector, or data are not available or not applicable, according to the database.
Source: World Bank. Infrastructure Finance, PPPs and Guarantees. Country Snapshots. Bangladesh. https://ppi.worldbank.org/en/snapshots/country/bangladesh (accessed 2 July 2020).

4.1 Tariffs in Water and Wastewater Sector

The applicable tariffs at Chattogram Water Supply and Sewerage Authority are indicated in Table 31.

Table 31: Tariffs at Chattogram Water Supply and Sewerage Authority

User Type	Amount (Taka)
Domestic	
Per 1,000 gallons	56.56
Per cubic meter	12.40
Nondomestic	
Per 1,000 gallons	137.72
Per cubic meter	30.30

Source: Chattogram Water Supply and Sewerage Authority. Bangladesh. Water Tariff. http://ctg-wasa.org.bd/site/page/69b086be-cf2d-48b4-96f4-49e7790cb664/- (accessed 16 July 2020).

Any revision to the tariff rates generally requires prior approval of the government. However, Clause 22 of the Water Supply and Sewerage Authority Act, 1996 permits water supply and sewerage authorities to increase the tariff at a rate of 5% per fiscal year, in certain circumstances.

4.2 Typical Risk Allocation for Public–Private Partnership Projects in Water and Wastewater Sector

The risk allocation for PPP projects in water and wastewater sector is not available.

4.3 Financing Details of Public–Private Partnership Projects in Water and Wastewater Sector

Parameter	1990–2017	1990–2018	1990–2019
Public–private partnership (PPP) projects with foreign lending participation	0	1	1
PPP projects that received export credit agency/international financing institution support[a]	0	1	1
Typical debt-to-equity ratio	UA	UA	UA
Time for financial close		UA	
Typical concession period		20 years	

✓ = Yes, ✗ = No, NA = Not Applicable, UA = Unavailable
[a] Includes both foreign bank lending and international financial institution support.
Source: World Bank. Infrastructure Finance, PPPs and Guarantees. Country Snapshots. Bangladesh. https://ppi.worldbank.org/en/snapshots/country/bangladesh (accessed 2 July 2020).

5. Challenges in Water and Wastewater Sector

- Dhaka WASA and Chittagong WASA have both financial and human resource constraints arising from ongoing services and projects, thus limiting their capacity to engage in PPP project development (footnote 1).

- Despite the relative abundance of water throughout Bangladesh and its conurbations, the abnormally high population densities result in severe stress on water resources from pollution and overabstraction. Consequently, identifying water resources suitable for abstraction has been very challenging (footnote 1).

- There are more than 40 different agencies, organizations, and categories of organizations involved in the water sector, which means that the private sector is required to manage multiple stakeholders (footnote 1).

- Investor returns may be constrained from managing the significant raw water pollution risks (including groundwater pollution with arsenic and surface water polluted with sewage and industrial pollution), which result in affordability issues arising from more expensive treatment requirements, as well as the high risk of standards not being achieved, having only basic treatment (footnote 1).

G. INFORMATION AND COMMUNICATION TECHNOLOGY

Parameter	Value	Unit
Telephone subscribers	0.90	per 100 inhabitants
Cellular phone subscribers	100.24	per 100 inhabitants
Cellular network coverage	99.00	% of population covered
Internet subscribers	6.34	per 100 inhabitants
Internet bandwidth per internet user	6.64	kilobits per second
Total number of projects with cumulative lending, grant, and technical assistance commitments in the information and communication technology (ICT) sector	1.00	no.
Total amount of cumulative lending, grant, and technical assistance commitments in the ICT sector	2.86	$ million

✓ = Yes, ✗ = No, NA = Not Applicable, UA = Unavailable
Sources: Trading Economics. Bangladesh—Mobile and Fixed Line Telephone Subscribers. https://tradingeconomics.com/bangladesh/mobile-and-fixed-line-telephone-subscribers-wb-data.html; World Bank. Cell Phone Subscribers. https://data.worldbank.org/indicator/IT.CEL.SETS.P2?locations=BD; and World Bank. Internet Subscribers. https://data.worldbank.org/indicator/IT.NET.USER.ZS?locations=BD.

1. Contracting Agencies in the Information and Communication Technology Sector

The Information and Communication Technology Division under the Ministry of Posts, Telecommunications and Information Technology is the key contracting authority for the sector.

2. Information and Communication Technology Sector Laws and Regulations

The Bangladesh Telecommunication Regulatory Commission is an independent commission founded under the Bangladesh Telecommunication Act, 2001 (Act No. 18 of 2001). The commission is responsible for regulating all matters related to telecommunications of Bangladesh (wire, cellular, satellite, and cable). Table 32 indicates the key institutions in the information and communication technology (ICT) sector in Bangladesh.

Table 32: Key Institutions in the Information and Communication Technology Sector in Bangladesh

Agency	Function
ICT Division	• Formulate and modernize national policies and regulations on ICT and provide assistance to ICT-related activities of ministries/divisions and agencies. • Implement the recommendations of the National Task Force on ICT. • Conduct research, development, and dissemination in various ICT sectors. • Increase integrity with various countries and international organizations related to ICT, and implement agreements and cooperation activities in relevant field. • Assist and coordinate the adoption of integrated action plans for e-governance, e-infrastructure, e-health, and e-commerce of various ministries/agencies. Formulate the necessary policies and guidelines for making ICT services accessible to people through commercialization, creation of skilled human resources, and raising public awareness. Monitor implementation of such policies and guidelines. • Through the Software Technology Park, Hi-Tech Park, and ICT, attract domestic and foreign investment in the ICT sector by developing infrastructures, including installation of incubators, to make local companies competitive and to increase employment and exports; and ensure and enforce the legal validity and security of electronic records related to ICT, the identity of the recipient and sender, and the preservation of all data repositories.
Department of ICT	The Department of ICT was formed on 31 July 2013 to ensure the provision of e-services in remote areas of the country by controlling expansion standards and enhancing the skills of computer professionals. Among other things, the department is responsible for • creating a high-speed electronic connection system into the country's peripheries; • preparing laws, policies, guidelines, and standards related to ICT; and • developing appropriate infrastructure to provide ICT-related services throughout the country.
Bangladesh Hi-Tech Park Authority	Functioning under the ICT Division, the Bangladesh Hi-Tech Park Authority aims to establish an international standard infrastructure; create a congenial and sustainable business environment; develop an IT/ITES-based industrial ecosystem; and ensure services are provided for IT/ITES businesses and industries through a one-stop platform.
Bangladesh Computer Council	The Bangladesh Computer Council is a statutory body under the Ministry of Posts, Telecommunications and Information Technology. It was established by Act No. IX of 1990, passed by the Parliament. The main activities are (not limited to) encouraging and providing support for ICT-related activities, formulating national ICT strategy and policy, creating standards and specifications of ICT tools for government organizations according to their necessity, and working for human resources development in the ICT sector.
Digital Security Agency	According to Section 5 of the Digital Security Act, 2016, the Department of ICT has set up a Digital Security Agency on 5 December 2016 to ensure digital security in the country. A Digital Security Council has been formed under Section 12 of the Digital Security Act, 2016. The agency's purpose is to establish a secure digital state and to coordinate with and provide support and guidance to all relevant organizations.

ICT = information and communication technology, IT = information technology, ITES = information technology enabled services.
Sources: Bangladesh Computer Council. Welcome to BCC. https://bcc.gov.bd/site/page/01cbf22a-b9f5-4a67-829e-55c27ab216f6/-; Bangladesh Hi-Tech Park Authority. About Us. http://bhtpa.gov.bd/site/page/b75f7889-05c8-446e-9a7b-8e5d1e2f339a/-; Digital Security Agency. About DSA. http://dsa.gov.bd/; and Government of Bangladesh, Department of ICT. History and Functions. https://ictd.gov.bd/site/page/ab439356-145f-4759-942d-39ea506ff144/History-&-Main-Function.

Key regulations in the ICT sector are as follows:[42]

- ICT Act, 2006 and amendments of 2009 and 2013;
- Bangladesh Hi-Tech Park Authority (Amendment) Act, 2014;
- Digital Security Act, 2018 and Digital Security Rules, 2020;
- One Stop Service Act, 2018;
- The Bangladesh Hi-Tech Park Authority (Amendment) Act, 2014; and
- Other strategy papers and policy-related documents drafted by the ICT Division toward encouraging investments into the ICT such as
  - National ICT Policy, 2018;
  - National Blockchain Strategy: Bangladesh, 2020;
  - Strategy to Promote Microprocessor Design Capacity in Bangladesh, 2020;
  - National Strategy for Artificial Intelligence Bangladesh, 2020;
  - National Internet of Things Strategy Bangladesh, 2020; and
  - Bangladesh National Digital Architecture Guidelines, 2019.

2.1 Foreign Investment Restrictions in the Information and Communication Technology Sector

Parameter	2017	2018	2019
Maximum allowed foreign ownership of equity in greenfield projects	UA	UA	UA

✓ = Yes, ✗ = No, NA = Not Applicable, UA = Unavailable

The above may be reviewed against the restrictions and limitations held by the government, as explained in Chapter II Section 8. However, it is noted that there are regulations in telecommunication infrastructure that currently include provisions for 60% foreign ownership, and 70% for tower sharing (footnote 18).

2.2 Standard Contracts in the Information and Communication Technology Sector

Type of Contract	Availability
Public–private partnership/concession agreement	UA
Performance-based operations and maintenance contract	UA
Engineering, procurement, and construction contract	UA

✓ = Yes, ✗ = No, NA = Not Applicable, UA = Unavailable

---

42   Government of Bangladesh, Department of ICT. Laws and Regulations. https://ictd.gov.bd/site/view/law/Acts-.

3. Information and Communication Technology Sector Master Plan

The National ICT Policy 2018 is a key document providing guidance on the focus and investment areas for the ICT sector in Bangladesh. The policy provides an action plan for the sector with short-term (2021), medium-term (2030), and long-term (2041) visions. The action plan identifies specific projects and programs for focus in these periods and provides targets for public–private partnership (PPP) participation in the identified segments.[43]

The action plan focuses on the following key themes for ICT:

- digital government/governance;
- digital security;
- social equity and universal access for ICT;
- education, research, and innovation in ICT;
- skills development and employment generation in ICT;
- strengthening domestic capacity for ICT;
- application of ICT in environment, climate, and disaster management; and
- enhancing productivity through use of ICT (footnote 18).

In addition, the Department of Information and Communication Technology provides a list of projects that are planned to be undertaken along with timelines (Table 33).

Table 33: Planned Projects in the Information and Communication Technology Sector in Bangladesh

No.	Project Name	Implementation Timeframe	Estimated Cost	
			($ million)	(Tk billion)
1	Establishing Digital Connectivity Project	February 2020–January 2024	705.83	59.86
2	Digitalization of Islands along Bay of Bengal, Haor, and Beel area	July 2020–July 2023	141.51	12.00
3	Establishment of LED Display Board in 492 *Upazilas*	February 2020–January 2023	36.02	3.05
4	Establishment of Sheikh Russel Digital Labs	July 2020–June 2023	110.72	9.39
5	She Power Project: Sustainable Development for Women through ICT (Phase-2)	July 2020–June 2023	36.60	3.10
6	Accelerating Digital Content Industry	July 2020–June 2023	106.99	9.07
7	Digital Opportunity for Youth	April 2020–March 2022	5.85	0.50
8	Digital Transformation of Textbooks	July 2020–June 2023	42.89	3.64
9	Capacity Building of ICT Officials through Strengthening their ICT Skill	July 2020–June 2023	5.56	0.47

ICT = information and communication technology, LED = light-emitting diode, Tk = taka.
Source: Government of Bangladesh, Department of Information and Communication Technology. Proposed Projects. http://doict.portal.gov.bd/site/page/443a0f0a-168a-482a-9376-85a5045668d2/-.

---

[43]   Government of Bangladesh, Department of ICT. 2018. *National ICT Policy 2018*. Dhaka. https://ictd.gov.bd/site/view/policies/Policy-.

3.1 Projects under Preparation and Procurement in the Information and Communication Technology Sector

Figure 37 presents the number of PPP projects that are under preparation and procurement in Bangladesh's ICT sector.

Figure 37: Public–Private Partnership Information and Communication Technology Projects under Preparation and Procurement

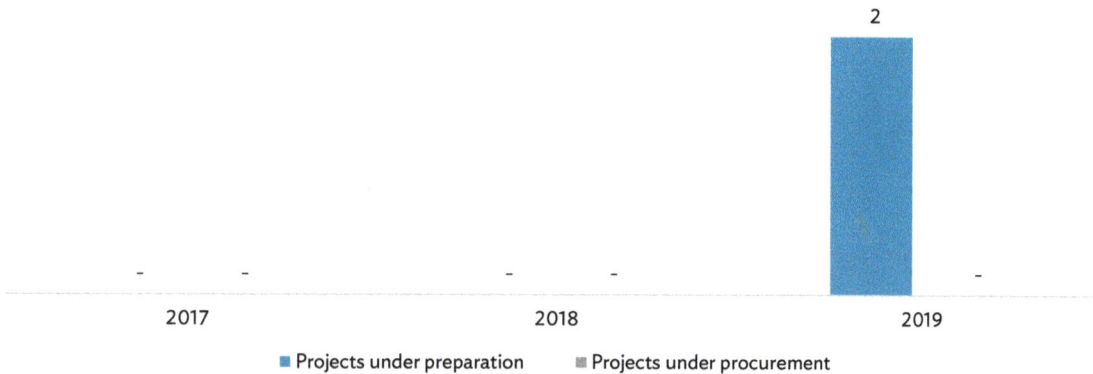

Note: The hyphen symbol (-) indicates there are no projects in the sector or data are not available.
Source: Government of Bangladesh, Public Private Partnership Authority. PPP Projects. http://www.pppo.gov.bd/projects.php (accessed 15 June 2020).

4. Features of Past Public–Private Partnership Projects in the Information and Communication Technology Sector

Figure 38 shows the number of PPP projects procured through various modes, including direct appointment, unsolicited bids, and competitive bids, in Bangladesh's ICT sector.

Figure 38: Modes of Procurement for Public–Private Partnership Information and Communication Technology Projects

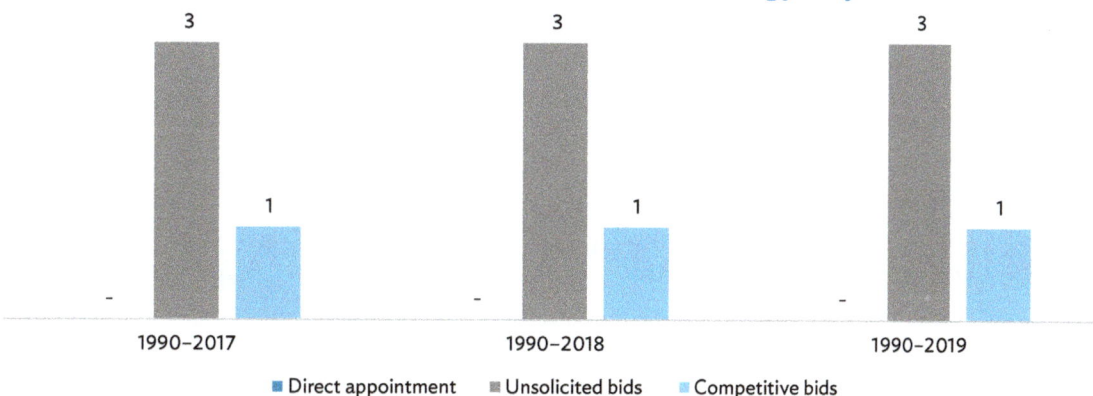

Notes: Only active and concluded projects are considered in the above graph. The hyphen symbol (-) indicates there are no projects in the sector, or data are not available or not applicable, according to the database.
Source: World Bank. Infrastructure Finance, PPPs and Guarantees. Country Snapshots. Bangladesh. https://ppi.worldbank.org/en/snapshots/country/bangladesh (accessed 2 July 2020).

Figure 39 presents the number of PPP projects that have reached financial closure and the total value of those projects in Bangladesh's ICT sector.

Figure 39: Public–Private Partnership Information and Communication Technology Projects Reaching Financial Closure

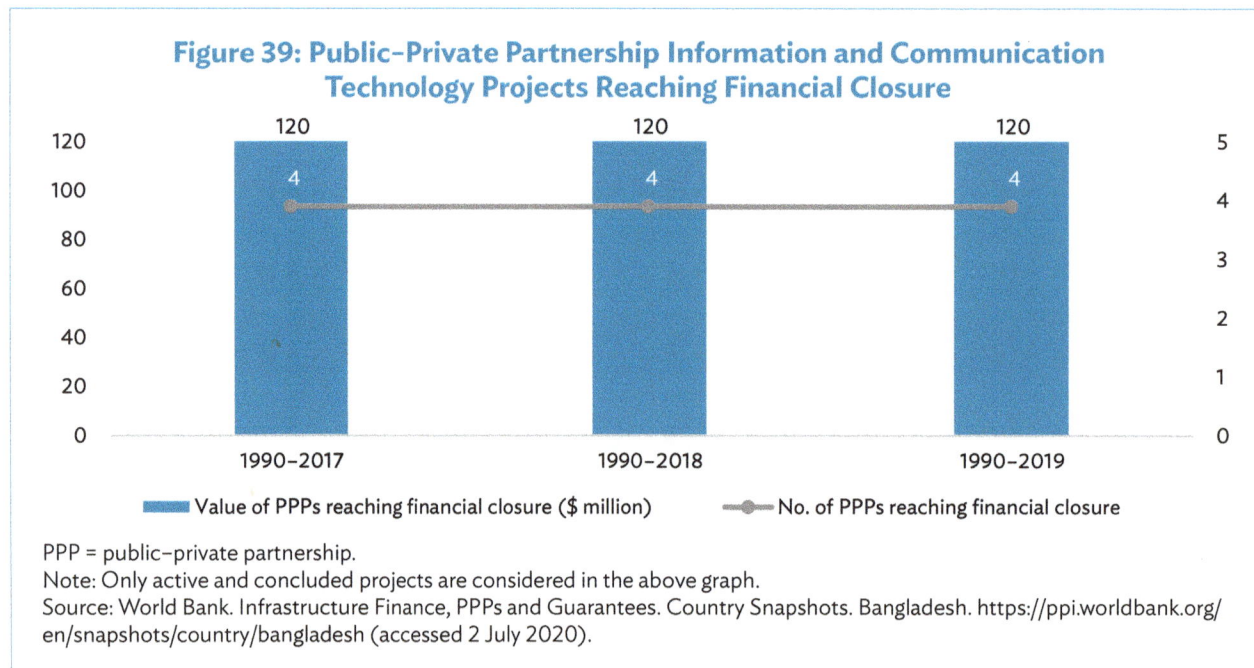

PPP = public–private partnership.
Note: Only active and concluded projects are considered in the above graph.
Source: World Bank. Infrastructure Finance, PPPs and Guarantees. Country Snapshots. Bangladesh. https://ppi.worldbank.org/en/snapshots/country/bangladesh (accessed 2 July 2020).

Figure 40 shows the number of PPP projects that have received foreign sponsor participation in Bangladesh's ICT sector.

Figure 40: Public–Private Partnership Information and Communication Technology Projects with Foreign Sponsor Participation

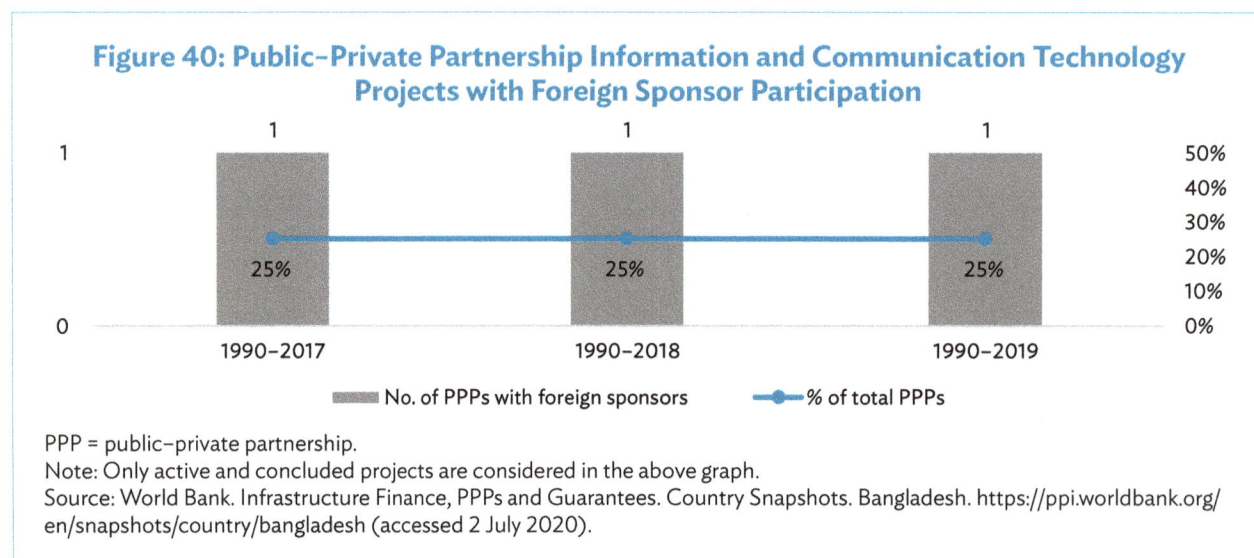

PPP = public–private partnership.
Note: Only active and concluded projects are considered in the above graph.
Source: World Bank. Infrastructure Finance, PPPs and Guarantees. Country Snapshots. Bangladesh. https://ppi.worldbank.org/en/snapshots/country/bangladesh (accessed 2 July 2020).

"As per the World Bank PPI database, no Information and Communication Technology sector projects in Bangladesh received government support, including viability gap funding mechanism, government guarantees, and availability or performance payment."

Figure 41 presents the number of PPP projects that have received payment in the form of user charges and government pay (offtake) in Bangladesh's ICT sector.

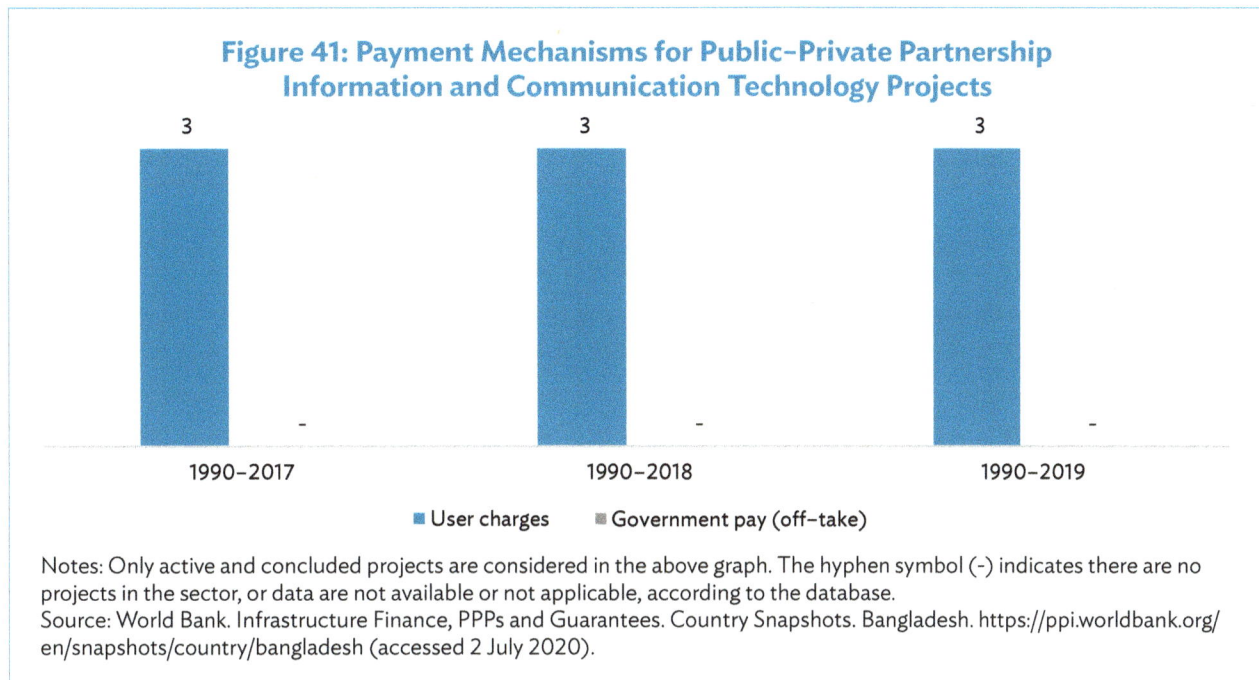

Figure 41: Payment Mechanisms for Public–Private Partnership Information and Communication Technology Projects

Notes: Only active and concluded projects are considered in the above graph. The hyphen symbol (-) indicates there are no projects in the sector, or data are not available or not applicable, according to the database.
Source: World Bank. Infrastructure Finance, PPPs and Guarantees. Country Snapshots. Bangladesh. https://ppi.worldbank.org/en/snapshots/country/bangladesh (accessed 2 July 2020).

4.1 Tariffs in the Information and Communication Technology Sector

Tariff details for the ICT sector are unavailable.

4.2 Typical Risk Allocation for Public–Private Partnership Projects in the Information and Communication Technology Sector

Information on the risk allocation for PPP projects in the ICT sector is not available.

4.3 Financing Details of Public–Private Partnership Projects in the Information and Communication Technology Sector

Parameter	1990–2017	1990–2018	1990–2019
Public–private partnership (PPP) projects with foreign lending participation	0	1	1
PPP projects that received export credit agency/international financing institution support[a]	0	1	1
Typical debt-to-equity ratio	UA	UA	UA
Time for financial close		UA	

✓ = Yes, ✗ = No, NA = Not Applicable, UA = Unavailable
[a] Includes both foreign bank lending and international financial institution support.
Source: World Bank. Infrastructure Finance, PPPs and Guarantees. Country Snapshots. Bangladesh. https://ppi.worldbank.org/en/snapshots/country/bangladesh (accessed 2 July 2020).

5. Challenges in the Information and Communication Technology Sector

Challenges related to the ICT sector are not available.

H. SOCIAL INFRASTRUCTURE

Parameter	Value	Unit
Government expenditure on education	1.9	% of gross domestic product (GDP)
Education spending as % of government spending	18.39	%
Primary school gross enrollment	108.6	%
Adult literacy rate	64.6	%
Total number of projects with cumulative lending, grant, and technical assistance commitments in the education sector	76	no.
Total amount of cumulative lending, grant, and technical assistance commitments in the education sector	3,117.65	$ million
Total health expenditure	2.8	% of GDP
Health spending per capita	36.28	$
Maternal mortality ratio (modelled estimates)	176.0	per 100,000 live births
Infant mortality rate	29.0	below 1 year old, per 1,000 live births
Life expectancy at birth	70.9	years
Child malnutrition	32.6	% below 5 years old
Total number of projects with cumulative lending, grant, and technical assistance commitments in the health sector	31	no.
Total amount of cumulative lending, grant, and technical assistance commitments in the health sector	389.00	$ million
Existing number of affordable housing units	UA	no.
Affordable housing gap	UA	

✓ = Yes, ✗ = No, NA = Not Applicable, UA = Unavailable
Sources: Asian Development Bank (ADB). 2016. *Country Partnership Strategy: Bangladesh, 2016–2020*. Manila. https://www.adb. org/sites/default/files/institutional-document/198831/cps-ban-2016-2020.pdf; ADB. Cumulative Lending, Grant, and Technical Assistance Commitments. https://data.adb.org/dataset/cumulative-lending-grant-and-technical-assistance-commitments; The Economist Intelligence Unit. Bangladesh. https://infrascope.eiu.com/; The Global Economy. Education Spending, Percent of Government Spending—Country Rankings. https://www.theglobaleconomy.com/rankings/Education_spending_percent_of_government_spending/; The Global Economy. Health Spending per Capita—Country Rankings. https://www.theglobaleconomy.com/rankings/Health_spending_per_capita/; and World Bank. Bangladesh Government Expenditure on Education. https://data.worldbank.org/indicator/SE.XPD.TOTL.GD.ZS?locations=BD.

1. Contracting Agencies in the Social Infrastructure Sector

The Ministry of Education is the relevant ministry for the education sector.

The Ministry of Health and Family Welfare is the ministry concerned with health-care-related activities. Depending on the project, various divisions such as the Directorate General of Health Services, under the ministry, become implementing agencies.

The Ministry of Housing and Public Works is the relevant ministry for social housing and related projects. However, local government authorities develop and implement projects based on the approvals from the ministry.

2. Social Infrastructure Sector Laws and Regulations

2.1 Education Sector Regulations

The Ministry of Primary and Mass Education is responsible for primary education (grades 1–5), and the Ministry of Education oversees secondary and postsecondary education. Table 34 indicates the key institutions in the education sector in Bangladesh.

Table 34: Key Institutions in the Education Sector in Bangladesh

Agency	Function
Ministry of Education	Formulates policies and programs for the development of post-primary to higher education, including *madrasah* (religious system of education), and technical and vocational education. Formulates laws, rules, and regulations for the management and administration of the post-primary education sector and its institutions in the country.
Ministry of Primary and Mass Education	Formulates policies and programs for the development of primary education.

Source: Asian Development Bank. 2019. *Public–Private Partnership Monitor.* Second Edition. Manila. https://www.adb.org/sites/default/files/publication/509426/ppp-monitor-second-edition.pdf.

2.2 Health Care Sector Regulations

For the health care sector, the government or public sector is the first key actor which, by the constitution, is responsible for policy and regulation, and for the provision of comprehensive health services, including financing and employment of health staff. The Ministry of Health and Family Welfare, through the Directorate General of Health Services and the Directorate General of Family Planning, manages a dual system of general health and family planning services through district hospitals (footnote 1).

The Ministry of Local Government, Rural Development and Cooperatives manages the provision of urban primary care services. Although the Ministry of Health is the lead agency for institution-based health care delivery at the national level and in rural areas, primary health care in urban areas is the responsibility of respective local government institutions (municipalities and city corporations), which are under the Ministry of Local Government, Rural Development, and Cooperatives. The quality of services at these facilities, however, is quite low, mainly because of insufficient resources, institutional limitations, and absenteeism or negligence of providers (footnote 1).

The key institutions in the health care sector are shown in Table 35.

Table 35: Key Institutions in the Health Care Sector in Bangladesh

Agency	Function
Ministry of Health and Family Welfare	Sets standards and regulations for the sector.
Directorate General of Health Services	Licenses health facilities to function. Licenses the administration of controlled medicines. Approves nonmedical and non-nursing health care training institutions. Sets standard operating procedures for the operation of laboratory and diagnostic centers.
Directorate General of Family Planning	Licenses the administration of controlled family planning methods.

Source: Asian Development Bank. 2019. *Public–Private Partnership Monitor.* Second Edition. Manila. https://www.adb.org/sites/default/files/publication/509426/ppp-monitor-second-edition.pdf.

2.3 Social Housing Sector Regulations

The National Housing Authority is the relevant regulatory authority for planning of social housing and related topics. The National Housing Policy of 2016 establishes priorities and focuses on affordable housing offered by the government.[44]

The Ministry of Housing and Public Works is the key ministry for the sector. Among other functions, it provides support to low-cost housing plans, while RAJUK (Rajdhani Unnayan Kartripakkha), a public sector land development agency, develops plots of land to facilitate urban housing. Under Bangladesh's Seventh Five-Year Plan, the government has proposed approximately $345 million (about 18% increase year-on-year) to the Ministry of Housing and Public Works (footnote 26).

2.4 Foreign Investment Restrictions in the Social Infrastructure Sector

Parameter	2017	2018	2019
Maximum allowed foreign ownership of equity in greenfield projects			
– Health care	100%	100%	100%
– Education	100%	100%	100%
– Government buildings	100%	100%	100%
– Social housing	100%	100%	100%
– Prisons and correctional centers	100%	100%	100%

There is no limitation on foreign equity participation in social infrastructure. The country has not been able to attract much public–private partnership (PPP) investment in social infrastructure. However, two hemodialysis centers at Chittagong Medical College Hospital and at the National Institute of Kidney Diseases and Urology are being operated by Sandor.

The above may be reviewed against the restrictions and limitations held by the government, as explained in Chapter II Section 8.

2.5 Standard Contracts in the Social Infrastructure Sector

Parameter	
Public–private partnership/concession agreement	UA
Performance-based operations and maintenance contract	UA
Engineering, procurement, and construction contract	UA

✓ = Yes, ✗ = No, NA = Not Applicable, UA = Unavailable

3. Social Infrastructure Sector Master Plan

Education Sector

In 2010, the Government of Bangladesh issued the National Education Policy to set the sector priorities. However, even though the size of the government budget has gradually increased over the years, the share of education in the

---

[44]   Government of Bangladesh, National Housing Authority. History and Responsibilities. http://www.nha.gov.bd/site/page/f2616672-9261-4b18-8571-4cfde9ae85e4/.-.

overall budget has decreased. While the United Nations Educational, Scientific and Cultural Organization stipulates that the budgetary allocation for education should constitute at least 6% of gross domestic product (GDP) or 20% of the total budget, the government spends only 2% of GDP for education (footnote 1).

However, the government has begun a major initiative in its Master Plan for ICT in Education 2012–2021, with select programs seeking to improve the quality and reach of education.

Health Care Sector

The master plan for the health care sector is inaccessible and unavailable.

Parallel to the National Five-Year Plan, the Ministry of Health and Family Welfare has prepared a strategic investment plan, which sets out the sector's strategic priorities and defines an overall strategic framework to guide investments in the health sector. The plan is intended to outline and implement health sector investments over the next 5 years (footnote 1).

Social Housing Sector

Through the National Housing Authority, the government has been actively undertaking initiatives to address the demand for more housing units. Those initiatives include the Pro-Poor Slum Integration Project, which has been initiated by the Government of Bangladesh with the World Bank to improve the quality of living conditions for those residing in slum areas. The project aims to provide 7,000 residential flats and 5,000 residential plots to people living in slum areas by 2021 (footnote 26).

The National Housing Policy, established in 2016, sets a direction for the proper implementation of projects in the affordable housing sector. The government has provisioned incentives to private sector developers for keeping a reasonable share of units in their projects as affordable housing units by means of cross-subsidization. The developers can avail of these incentives in the form of low-cost financing and low-cost building materials (footnote 26).

3.1 Projects under Preparation and Procurement in the Social Infrastructure Sector

The Public–Private Partnership Authority project pipeline lists the projects that were under preparation and under procurement as of March 2020 in the social infrastructure sector (Table 36).

Table 36: Projects under Preparation and Procurement in the Social Infrastructure Sector

Sector	Project Name	Status
Civil accommodation	Mirpur Integrated Township Development	Under construction
Civil accommodation	Construction of high-rise apartment at Purbachal New Town project	CCEA-approved (in principle)
Civil accommodation	Construction of multistory commercial/residential apartment complex with modern amenities at Nasirabad, Chittagong under PPP	To be re-tendered
Education	Innovation and Innovator Cell development under PPP	Project development stage, advisor appointment to be initiated

continued on next page

Table 36 *continued*

Sector	Project Name	Status
Health	New medical college and 250-bed hospital in Khulna	Project development stage, advisor appointment to be initiated
Health	Medical college and modernization of Railway Hospital at Paksey in Pabna	Transaction advisor mobilized
Health	Medical college and modernization of Railway Hospital at Saidpur, Nilphamari	Transaction advisor mobilized
Health	Medical college and nursing institute and modernization of Railway Hospital in Kamlapur	Tender launched
Health	Medical college and modernization of Railway Hospital at central railway building in Chittagong	Procurement stage, CCEA final approval to be obtained
Health	Development of occupational diseases hospital, labor welfare center, and commercial complexes at Tongi, Gazipur under PPP	Procurement stage, tender unsuccessful

CCEA = Cabinet Committee on Economic Affairs, PPP = public–private partnership.
Source: Government of Bangladesh, Public Private Partnership Authority. PPP Projects. http://www.pppo.gov.bd/projects.php (accessed 15 June 2020).

Figure 42 shows the number of PPP projects that are under preparation and procurement in Bangladesh's social infrastructure sector.

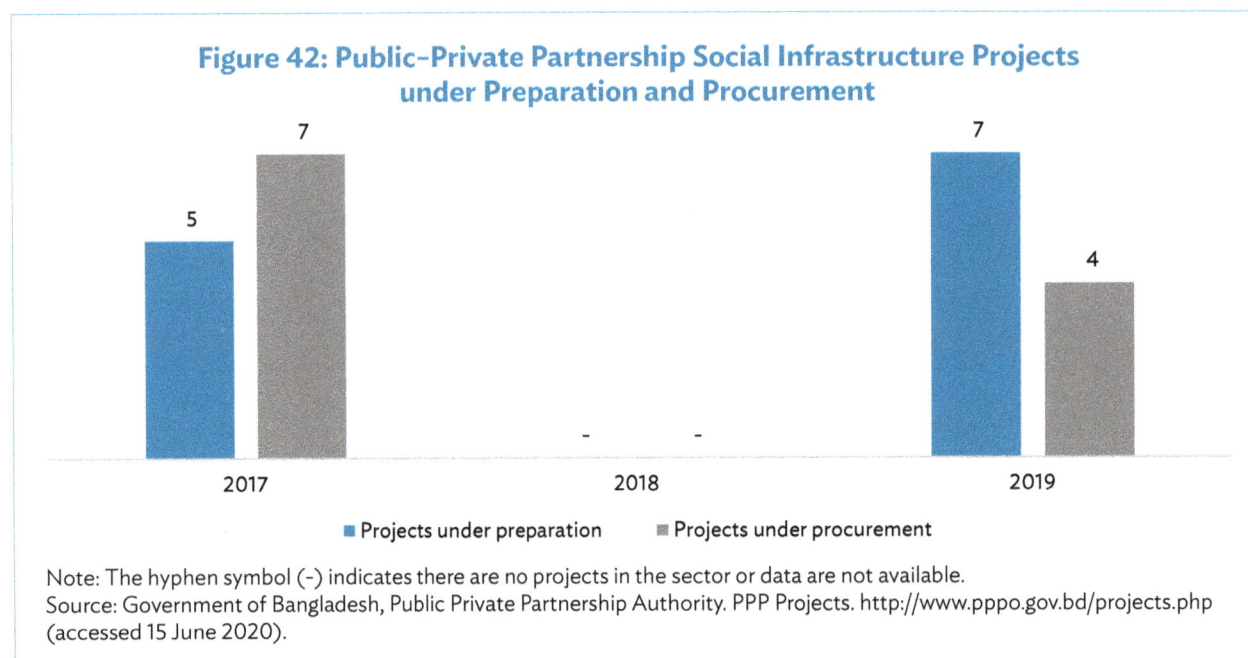

Figure 42: Public–Private Partnership Social Infrastructure Projects under Preparation and Procurement

Note: The hyphen symbol (-) indicates there are no projects in the sector or data are not available.
Source: Government of Bangladesh, Public Private Partnership Authority. PPP Projects. http://www.pppo.gov.bd/projects.php (accessed 15 June 2020).

4. Features of Past Public–Private Partnership Projects in the Social Infrastructure Sector

"The information on features of past PPP projects in Bangladesh's social infrastructure sector is not available."

4.1 Tariffs in the Social Infrastructure Sector

Tariff details for the social infrastructure sector are unavailable.

4.2 Typical Risk Allocation for Public–Private Partnership Projects in the Social Infrastructure Sector

Information on the risk allocation for PPP projects in the social infrastructure sector is not available.

4.3 Financing Details of Public–Private Partnership Projects in the Social Infrastructure Sector

Parameter	1990–2017	1990–2018	1990–2019
Public–private partnership (PPP) projects with foreign lending participation	NA	NA	NA
PPP projects that received export credit agency/international financing institution support	NA	NA	NA
Typical debt-to-equity ratio	NA	NA	NA
Time for financial close		NA	

✓ = Yes, ✗ = No, NA = Not Applicable, UA = Unavailable

5. Challenges in the Social Infrastructure Sector

Social Housing

- Scarcity of land is one of the major reasons for escalation in land prices, which substantially increases the overall project cost of affordable housing projects. The unfavorable location of projects for low-income housing limits the mobility and livelihood opportunities for residents (footnote 26).

- Concentrated growth with lack of initiatives for directing real estate development toward existing urban agglomerations outside the core city of Dhaka (footnote 26).

- Absence of strong legislation on affordable housing for all, urban planning, and development. There is no real estate legislation to protect homebuyers or to help boost investments in the real estate industry (footnote 26).

- Lack of access to cheap financing for a large portion of the population and a lack of information on access to loan products for low-income groups (footnote 26).

- Complex and lengthy processes for pre-implementation activities, such as land registration and building plan scrutiny and approval. Receiving No Objection Certificate from multiple departments turns out to be a major hindrance for private sector developers (footnote 26).

Health Care and Education

- Lack of efficiency control in health services. The Bangladesh public health system remains highly centralized, with planning undertaken by the Ministry of Health and Family Welfare and little authority delegated to local levels. This leads to a lack of focus on local levels, slow decision-making processes, and inefficiency in program implementation (footnote 26).

- Low government spending on health care and education as a share of the GDP. Government spending on health care and education is around 3% of GDP, the second lowest in South Asia. This results in potential inability to provide adequate services to residents (footnote 26).

- Lack of robust performance standards for institutions. This paves the way for large variations in performance levels across schools. Incentives for good performance are nonexistent or minimal, rendering good policies ineffective (footnote 26).

I. OTHER SECTORS

The project pipeline of the PPP Authority in Bangladesh lists several projects separate from traditional PPP sectors discussed in earlier sections of this report. The list also covers industry projects that are not traditionally classified as PPPs but are being undertaken as PPPs by the PPP Authority (Table 37).

Table 37: List of Public–Private Partnership Projects in Other Sectors

Sector	Project Name	Status	Implementing Agency	Estimated Investment Range ($ million)
Zone	IT Village at Mohakhali	CCEA-approved (in principle)	Bangladesh Hi-tech Park Authority, Ministry of Information Communication and Technology	NA
Industry	Development of BTMC Textile Mills: Afsar Cotton Mills Limited	Project development stage – Detailed feasibility study ongoing	BTMC, MOTJ	30–80
Industry	Development of BTMC Textile Mills: Darwani Textile Limited	Project development stage – Detailed feasibility study ongoing	BTMC, MOTJ	30–80
Industry	Development of BTMC Textile Mills: Dinajpur Textile Mills Limited	Project development stage – Detailed feasibility study ongoing	BTMC, MOTJ	30–80
Industry	Development of BTMC Textile Mills: Rajshahi Textile Mills Limited	Project development stage – Detailed feasibility study ongoing	BTMC, MOTJ	30–80
Industry	Development of BTMC Textile Mills: Magura Textile Mills Limited	Project development stage – Detailed feasibility study ongoing	BTMC, MOTJ	30–80

continued on next page

Table 37 *continued*

Sector	Project Name	Status	Implementing Agency	Estimated Investment Range ($ million)
Industry	Development of BTMC Textile Mills: Sundarbon Textile Mills Limited	Project development stage – Detailed feasibility study ongoing	BTMC, MOTJ	30–80
Industry	Development of BTMC Textile Mills: Bengal Textile Limited	Project development stage – Detailed feasibility study ongoing	BTMC, MOTJ	30–80
Industry	Development of BTMC Textile Mills: Jalil Textile Limited	Project development stage – Detailed feasibility study ongoing	BTMC, MOTJ	30–80
Industry	Development of BTMC Textile Mills: The Asiatic Cotton Miles Limited	Project development stage – Detailed feasibility study ongoing	BTMC, MOTJ	30–80
Industry	Development of BTMC Textile Mills: Rangamati Textile Miles Limited	Project development stage – Detailed feasibility study ongoing	BTMC, MOTJ	30–80
Industry	Development of BTMC Textile Mills: Dost Textile Limited	Project development stage – Detailed feasibility study ongoing	BTMC, MOTJ	30–80
Industry	Development of BTMC Textile Mills: Amin Textile Limited	Project development stage – Detailed feasibility study ongoing	BTMC, MOTJ	30–80
Industry	Development of BTMC Textile Mills: RR Textile Miles Limited	Project development stage – Detailed feasibility study ongoing	BTMC, MOTJ	30–80
Zone	Development of Economic Zone at Jamalpur with private sector participation	Project development stage – Detailed feasibility study completed	BEZA, PMO	210–250
Urban	Shopping mall with hotel-cum-guest house on the unused railway land in Khulna	Project development stage – Detailed feasibility study completed	Bangladesh Railway, MOR	<6
Industry	Development of Cotton Mills project in Tangail	Procurement stage – Retender to be started	BTMC, MOTJ	NA
Tourism	Development of a five-star hotel in Chittagong.	Procurement stage – No bid received	Bangladesh Railway, MOR	80–200
Tourism	Development of a five-star standard hotel along with an application hotel and training center on existing land of BPC at Muzgunni, Khulna.	Procurement stage – No bid received	BPC, MOCAT	6–30
Tourism	Establishment of international standard tourism complex at existing Motel Upal Compound of BPC at Cox's Bazar.	Procurement stage – IFB evaluation ongoing	BPC, MOCAT	30–80

continued on next page

Table 37 *continued*

Sector	Project Name	Status	Implementing Agency	Estimated Investment Range ($ million)
Tourism	Establishment of international standard hotel-cum-resort with other facilities at existing Parjatan Motel Sylhet Compound of BPC, Sylhet through public–private partnership	Procurement stage – IFB evaluation ongoing	BPC, MOCAT	6–30
Tourism	Establishment of three-star standard hotel and other facilities of existing Hotel Pashur Compound of BPC at Mongla Bagerhat	Procurement stage – IFB to be issued	BPC, MOCAT	11–15

BEZA = Bangladesh Economic Zone Authority, BPC = Bangladesh Parjatan Corporation, BTMC = Bangladesh Textile Mills Corporation, CCEA = Cabinet Committee on Economic Affairs, IFB = invitation for bids, MOCAT = Ministry of Civil Aviation and Tourism, MOR = Ministry of Railways, MOTJ = Ministry of Textiles and Jute, PMO = Prime Minister's Office.
Source: Government of Bangladesh, Public Private Partnership Authority. PPP Projects. http://www.pppo.gov.bd/projects.php (accessed 15 June 2020).

While there are a few projects in these categories that have been awarded or are in the process of an award, the current World Bank Private Participation in Infrastructure (PPI) database does not include these. Therefore, no further details on these projects are available.

IV. Local Government Public–Private Partnership Landscape

Parameter	Value	Unit
Number of Subnational Governments (SNGs)		
– Municipal level	UA	no.
– Intermediate level	UA	no.
– Regional or state level	UA	no.
Total number of SNGs	UA	no.
SNG Expenditure Profile		
Total SNG expenditure as % of gross domestic product (GDP)	UA	%
– SNG current expenditure as % of GDP	UA	%
– SNG staff expenditure as % of GDP	UA	%
– SNG investment as % of GDP	UA	%
Total SNG expenditure as % of the total general government (% of total public expenditure)	UA	%
– SNG current expenditure as a % of total current expenditure of the general government	UA	%
– SNG staff expenditure as a % of total staff expenditure of the general government	UA	%
– SNG investment as a % of total investment of the general government	UA	%
Current expenditure of SNG as a % of total SNG expenditure	UA	%
Staff expenditure of SNG as a % of total SNG expenditure	UA	%
Investments of SNG as a % of total SNG expenditure	UA	%
SNG Expenditure by Function		
– General public services	UA	%
– Defense	UA	%
– Security and public order	UA	%
– Economic affairs	UA	%
– Environmental protection	UA	%
– Housing and community amenities	UA	%
– Health	UA	%
– Recreation, culture, and religion	UA	%
– Education	UA	%
– Social protection	UA	%

continued on next page

continued from previous page

Parameter	Value	Unit
SNG Revenue Profile		
Total SNG revenue as a % of GDP	UA	%
– SNG tax revenue as a % of GDP	UA	%
– SNG grants and subsidies as a % of GDP	UA	%
– SNG other revenues as a % of GDP	UA	%
Total SNG revenue as % of total general government revenue	UA	%
– SNG tax revenue as a % of total general government tax revenue	UA	%
– SNG grants and subsidies as a % of total general government grants and subsidies	UA	%
– SNG other revenues as a % of total other revenues	UA	%
SNG tax revenue as a % of total SNG revenue	UA	%
SNG grants and subsidies as a % of total SNG revenue	UA	%
SNG other revenues as a % of total SNG revenue	UA	%
SNG Debt Profile		
Outstanding SNG debt as % of GDP	UA	%
Outstanding SNG debt as % of total outstanding debt of general government	UA	%
Parameters for Transfers to SNGs from National Government		
Score on transfers to SNGs	C+	
– Score on system for allocating transfers	C	
– Score on timeliness of information on transfers	D	
– Score on extent of collection and reporting of consolidated fiscal data for general government	N/A	
Value of central government transfers to SNGs	UA	% of GDP
Value of actual budgetary allocation to SNGs from national government[a]	7	% of total expenditure
Value of deviation of actual against budgeted transfers to SNGs	UA	% of budgeted transfers

✓ = Yes, ✗ = No, NA = Not Applicable, UA = Unavailable
[a] Includes transfers to local government and rural development.
Sources: International Monetary Fund. 2015. *Bangladesh Public Expenditure and Financial Accountability Assessment*. Washington, DC. https://www.pefa.org/country/bangladesh; and United Cities and Local Governments. 2016. *Subnational Governments around the World—Structure and Finance*. https://www.uclg.org/sites/default/files/global_observatory_of_local_finance-part_iii.pdf.

LOCAL GOVERNANCE SYSTEM IN BANGLADESH

Bangladesh is a unitary state and has no provincial or state government within the governance structure. Bangladesh has a two-tier government system. The ministries and divisions at the Secretariat constitute the policy tier, while the other tier is general administration (law and order, land administration, and revenue collection). Delivery of public services and implementation of development programs are carried out at the subnational levels—districts and *upazilas* (subdistricts) that represent the ministries and divisions.

There are 7 central government divisions; 11 city corporations; 223 *pourashavas* (municipalities); 64 district councils (zila parishads); 500 *upazila* parishads; and 4,451 union parishads.[45]

The local government has several tiers and includes a large network of institutions: city corporations and *pourashavas* at the urban level; zila parishads headed by a deputy commissioner (a deputy secretary appointed by the government from the Administration Cadre); *upazila* parishads headed by an executive officer; and the lowest tier in the local government subsector, the elected union parishad working at the grassroots level to deliver public services (footnote 45).

The Local Government Division (LGD) within the Ministry of Local Government, Rural Development and Cooperatives is responsible for the development and implementation of legislation regulating local government, with the exception of the Hill District Local Government Parishad Act 1989, which is administered by the Ministry of Hill Tracts Affairs. The LGD is undertaking work and implementing programs to attain Vision 2021, the Seventh Five-Year Plan, and the Sustainable Development Goals.[46]

Most of Bangladesh's local governments are highly dependent on a historically centralized national government system. Most of their funding comes from the central government (largely using development aid), and it is not nearly enough. Less than 1% of Bangladesh's gross domestic product (GDP) funds 85% of local government development expenditures, and local governments generate very little of their own revenue, especially compared to their counterparts in other low-GDP countries (footnote 46).

The responsibilities and functions of *pourashavas* are specified in the Local Government (Pourashava) Act, 2009 (footnote 45).

INFRASTRUCTURE DEVELOPMENT PLAN OF LOCAL GOVERNMENTS

The Local Government (Pourashava) Act, 2009 mandates municipal governments to

- provide all types of urban facilities to citizens of the respective areas in accordance with the Pourashava Act, 2009 and other relevant legislation;
- establish coordination between *pourashava* administration and government officials in undertaking programs; and
- develop infrastructure, and prepare and implement urban development plan, including building control.[47]

In line with the above, local governments are responsible for providing all infrastructure, including water and wastewater, solid waste management, health-care-related infrastructure, local road, footpath, and traffic-management-related infrastructure.

---

[45]   Commonwealth Local Government Forum. 2018. *The Local Government System in Bangladesh, Country Profile 2017-18*. Dhaka. http://www.clgf.org.uk/default/assets/File/Country_profiles/Bangladesh.pdf.

[46]   Ministry of Planning, Planning Commission, Programming Division. 2018. *Local Government and Rural Development: Sector Strategy Paper*. Dhaka. https://plandiv.portal.gov.bd/sites/default/files/files/plandiv.portal.gov.bd/publications/0c526c77_bb8b_42fe_99d7_f6c217986e77/LGRD-SSP.pdf.

[47]   Ministry of Local Government, Rural Development and Cooperatives; Local Government Division. 2018. *Municipal Public Finance Scenario in Bangladesh*. Dhaka. https://www.unescap.org/sites/default/files/BANGLADESH_presentation.pdf.

SECTORS IN WHICH LOCAL GOVERNMENTS CAN IMPLEMENT PUBLIC–PRIVATE PARTNERSHIPS

Services vary across local governments. The main responsibilities of city corporations and municipalities are as follows:

- water, sanitation, and drainage;
- refuse collection and disposal;
- births, deaths, and marriages registration;
- public health, hospitals, health centers, and medical aid;
- bathing places, *dhobi Ghats* (place used for laundry);
- fisheries, milk processing, and markets;
- slaughterhouses;
- animal husbandry, stray animals, farms;
- building control and regulation, development plans, and community development projects;
- public streets and traffic control;
- civil defense, flood and fire services;
- burial and burning places;
- arboriculture, gardens, open spaces, and forests;
- education and libraries;
- culture fairs and shows; and
- social welfare (footnote 45).

The main responsibilities of zila parishads and hill district parishads are as follows:

- implementing development projects;
- public libraries;
- roads, culverts, and bridges not covered by *upazila* parishads, municipalities, or the national government;
- gardens, playgrounds, open places, and trees in public areas;
- ferry ghats not maintained by other levels of government;
- rest houses and inns;
- assisting *upazila* parishads; and
- implementing the development plan assigned by the national government (footnote 45).

Discretionary services include

- education and culture;
- social and financial welfare; and
- public health and public works (footnote 45).

REVENUES FOR LOCAL GOVERNMENTS

All local governments have the power to levy taxes and rates. There are no aggregate figures available, but the main sources of local government revenue are as follows:

- income from taxes, rates, tolls, fees, and other charges;
- rents and profits from property;
- grants made by the national government through annual development plan and special allocations;
- profits from investments; and
- donations and transfers of private or public funds (footnote 45).

According to the Local Government (City Corporation) Act, 2009, there are 26 types of revenue sources for city corporations. For example, the funding sources of the Dhaka North City Corporation are internal revenue collection, central government grants, development grants, project development loans, and other loans.[48]

- Internal revenue collection

  The power to levy and collect revenues is contained in the Dhaka City Corporation Ordinance, 1983. The revenues are in the form of taxes, rates, and fees whose amounts are established in their respective model tax schedules (footnote 48).

- Taxes and rates (collectively known as the holding tax)

  This levy is applicable to all properties (domestic, commercial, industrial, and institutional). It is a major source of municipal revenue and is composed of

  – Land and buildings assessment (property tax with a ceiling of 7% on the balance of the annual rental value);

  – Lighting rate (street lighting, rate set at maximum of 3%); and

  – Conservancy rate (a rate for provision of solid waste collection and disposal services, also with a ceiling of 7%) (footnote 48).

- Service elements of holding tax

  These are charged for all properties in areas where each service is provided, irrespective of whether the individual property owner avails of the service. The service elements include the following:

  – Fixed property transfer tax (levied by the central government, 2% of the declared property value is remitted to the city corporation);

  – Octroi compensation grant (grant from the central government to compensate municipalities for the abolition in 1985 of their powers to levy import and export taxes transmitting their territories);

  – Trades and profession license tax (an annual fixed amount paid by tradespeople and professionals as a license fee to conduct their business activities);

  – Entertainment tax (10%–15% of the entrance ticket value for cinemas, theaters, and exhibitions);

  – Rickshaw license (annual fee);

---

[48] Dhaka North City Corporation. Funding Sources. http://www.dncc.gov.bd/site/page/52fff120-67c2-4f99-bf65-4bf9a4e6d4ff/Funding-Sources (accessed 27 August 2020).

- Income from residential, market, and other properties (from advance payments and annual rentals paid by lessees for a property developed by the municipalities);

- Road excavation fees (charged for utilities that lay pipes and cables under roads); and

- Others (those that generate minimal revenues) (footnote 48).

• Development grants

These are equity contributions from the central government toward capital project implementation costs. Typically, these are made for the funding of no-cost or indirect cost recovery programs such as roads, flood protection, and drainage, whether from internally generated central government revenues or from external loan or grant proceeds (footnote 48).

• Project development loans

For cost-recovery projects, such as land development, sanitation, and solid waste management, the central government extends external loan proceeds under subsidiary loan agreements (footnote 48).

• Other loans

The Dhaka North City Corporation has access to domestic long-term loans from government-owned banks (footnote 48).

BORROWINGS BY LOCAL GOVERNMENTS

The Bangladesh Economic Review 2019 reports the outstanding borrowings of the Local Government Division. Table 38 shows the outstanding position of debt service liabilities of the top 15 local governments as of 31 December 2018.[49]

Table 38: Debt Service Liabilities of the Top 15 Local Governments in Bangladesh

Entity	Not Due (Tk million)	Total Principal Due (Tk million)	Total Interest Due (Tk million)	Total Due (Tk million)	Total Outstanding (Tk million)	Total Outstanding ($ million)
Chittagong WASA	45,106.22	2,889.49	6,162.98	9,052.47	54,158.68	638.64
Dhaka WASA	27,173.03	10,081.69	12,775.24	22,856.92	50,029.95	589.96
Khulna WASA	16,603.64	0.00	0.00	0.00	16,603.64	195.79
Dhaka City Corporation	162.63	1,937.07	2,633.17	4,570.24	4,732.88	55.81
Khulna City Corporation	0.00	1,623.44	1,595.90	3,219.34	3,219.34	37.96
Rajshahi City Corporation	0.00	1,191.18	954.31	2,145.49	2,145.49	25.30
Chittagong City Corporation	0.00	525.45	541.75	1,067.20	1,067.20	12.58
Mathbaria *Pourashava*	98.56	0.00	0.00	0.00	98.56	1.16
Mymensingh *Pourashava*	43.05	11.35	28.91	40.26	83.31	0.98

continued on next page

49   Ministry of Finance, Finance Division. 2019. *Bangladesh Economic Review 2019*. Dhaka. https://mof.portal.gov.bd/sites/default/files/files/mof.portal.gov.bd/page/e8bc0eaa_463d_4cf9_b3be_26ab70a32a47/Banglades%20Economic%20Review%202019%20Eng.zip.

Table 38 *continued*

Entity	Not Due (Tk million)	Total Principal Due (Tk million)	Total Interest Due (Tk million)	Total Due (Tk million)	Total Outstanding (Tk million)	($ million)
Gazipur *Pourashava*	45.08	7.67	29.00	36.67	81.75	0.96
Jessore *Pourashava*	33.75	13.56	32.98	46.55	80.30	0.95
Sirajgonj *Pourashava*	43.64	7.01	18.20	25.21	68.85	0.81
Narsingdi *Pourashava*	18.28	5.57	15.30	20.87	39.15	0.46
Pirojpur *Pourashava*	20.34	3.96	9.63	13.59	33.93	0.40
Madaripur *Pourashava*	13.84	5.56	13.52	19.09	32.92	0.39
Others	306.80	53.42	153.81	207.23	514.03	6.06
Total	**89,668.86**	**18,356.41**	**24,964.70**	**43,321.11**	**132,989.97**	**1,568.23**

Tk = taka, WASA = Water Supply and Sewerage Authority.
Note: Numbers may not sum precisely because of rounding.
Source: Ministry of Finance, Finance Division. 2019. *Bangladesh Economic Review 2019*. Dhaka. https://mof.portal.gov.bd/sites/default/files/files/mof.portal.gov.bd/page/e8bc0eaa_463d_4cf9_b3be_26ab70a32a47/Banglades%20Economic%20Review%202019%20Eng.zip.

BUDGETARY ALLOCATION TO LOCAL GOVERNMENTS

The national budget for the local government and rural development sector was Tk378.86 billion ($4.47 billion) in fiscal year (FY) 2019 to FY2020 and increased to Tk395.73 billion ($4.67 billion) in FY2020–FY2021. An assessment of the country's public financial management system is presented in the box below.

Assessment of Bangladesh's Public Financial Management and Accountability

In the latest assessment of the Public Financial Management System (PFMS) in Bangladesh, based on the Public Expenditure and Financial Accountability (PEFA) framework, 2016, Bangladesh has an **overall rating of D+** for the transparency of intergovernmental fiscal relations. This is based on a four-point rating scale from A (best) to D (worst). The three subindicators used to establish this overall rating include (i) transparent and rule-based systems in the horizontal allocation among subnational governments, having a rating of B; (ii) timeliness and reliability of allocations to subnational governments, having a rating of D; and (iii) extent of consolidation of fiscal data for general government according to sectoral categories, having a rating of D.

The horizontal allocation of most transfers from the central government to subnational governments is determined by transparent, rule-based systems. Formula transfers represent over 51% of all transfers. Local governments can submit development project proposals to the Planning Commission for cofinancing by the central government. Final decisions on qualifying projects are made by the Executive Council of the National Economic Council (Planning Council).

The Local Government Division makes the formal delivery of information regarding transfers to local governments about 2 months into the financial year, coinciding with the release of the first quarterly tranche. The Minister of Local Government makes the final decision on transfer amounts at about this time. Additional transfer decisions are made after the revised budget and may arrive in the final month of the fiscal year.

Source: Public Expenditure and Financial Accountability. 2016. *Bangladesh: Public Expenditure and Financial Accountability, Public Financial Management Performance Report*. Dhaka. https://www.pefa.org/node/506.

Throughout the Sixth Five-Year Plan period, the government increased its allocation for the Local Government Division from Tk80.99 billion in FY2011 to Tk144.30 billion in FY2015—an annual growth rate of 15%. The Local Government Division's Annual Development Program disbursement rates never exceeded the allocation during the Sixth Five-Year Plan period as indicated in Table 39 (footnote 46).

Table 39: Allocation and Disbursements to the Local Government Division under the Sixth Five-Year Plan

| | Local Government Division | | | | Annual Growth Rate of ADP Expenditures (%) | Disbursement Rate (%) |
| | 6th FYP Allocations | | ADP Expenditures | | | |
Year	$ million	Tk billion	$ million	Tk billion		
FY2011	955.04	80.99	892.66	75.70		93.5
FY2012	1,122.49	95.19	942.19	79.90	5.1	84.0
FY2013	1,274.02	108.04	1,229.92	104.30	30.5	96.5
FY2014	1,496.06	126.87	1,273.55	108.00	3.5	85.1
FY2015	1,701.60	144.30	1,471.66	124.80	15.6	86.7

ADP = Annual Development Program, FY = fiscal year, FYP = five-year plan, Tk = taka.
Source: Ministry of Planning, Planning Commission, Programming Division. 2018. *Local Government and Rural Development: Sector Strategy Paper*. Dhaka. https://plandiv.portal.gov.bd/sites/default/files/files/plandiv.portal.gov.bd/publications/0c526c77_bb8b_42fe_99d7_f6c217986e77/LGRD-SSP.pdf.

The allocation for the Local Government Division as per the Annual Development Program of the Seventh Five-Year Plan is presented in Table 40.

Table 40: Allocation for the Local Government Division under the Seventh Five-Year Plan

Ministry/Division	FY2016/17	FY2017/18	FY2018/19	FY2019/20	FY2020/21
Local Government Division (Tk billion)	166.50	20.34	24.21	28.38	33.30
Local Government Division ($ million)	1,963.39	239.85	285.49	334.66	392.68

FY = fiscal year, Tk =taka.
Source: Ministry of Planning, Planning Commission, Programming Division. 2018. *Local Government and Rural Development: Sector Strategy Paper*. Dhaka. https://plandiv.portal.gov.bd/sites/default/files/files/plandiv.portal.gov.bd/publications/0c526c77_bb8b_42fe_99d7_f6c217986e77/LGRD-SSP.pdf.

CREDIT RATING OF LOCAL GOVERNMENTS

No specific details related to credit ratings of local government are available.

CASE STUDY: RAJUK WATER

The contents of the case study are primarily extracted from the Public–Private Partnership (PPP) Stories case study publication by the World Bank Group's International Finance Corporation (IFC) and other news articles.[50]

---

[50]   International Finance Corporation. *PPP Stories: Bangladesh—RAJUK Water*. Washington, DC: World Bank. https://www.ifc.org/wps/wcm/connect/f4c491c6-8f44-41b0-a940-bad27d33629a/Rajuk+Water+PPP+Story.pdf?MOD=AJPERES&CVID=naxbsGL.

Background

Dhaka is one of the most densely populated cities in the world (22,234 people per square kilometer). Decentralizing population and activities away from Dhaka's center to reduce intense congestion is one of the top priorities of the Government of Bangladesh. The development of Purbachal Township, about 8 kilometers from the city's airport in the northeastern suburbs of Dhaka, is a key element of the government's strategy. The publicly managed piped water supply of Bangladesh faces severe challenges—only 10% of the population has access to piped water; and the system has high losses of 25%–30%, limited hours of supply, and poor water quality, particularly in the dry seasons (footnote 50). Rajdhani Unnayan Kartripakkha (RAJUK), the capital development authority of the Government of Bangladesh, has been developing the area as a self-contained township with all modern facilities and opportunities (footnote 50).

Recognizing the need for private sector investment and expertise to mobilize capital and introduce best practice efficiencies, RAJUK chose to develop the 340 million liters per day (MLD) water distribution network and supply facilities for the township through a PPP. Once completed and operational, the project will provide important lessons and experience for the government, as they implement massive investment plans ($20 billion) in the sector over the next 5 years (footnote 50). The Government of Bangladesh, through its PPP Authority, appointed IFC as the lead transaction advisor for RAJUK on the project.

Physical Infrastructure

The project required the development of 340 MLD water distribution network and supply facilities for the township. The proposed project was to be taken up in phases (footnote 50).

Description of the Public–Private Partnership Model

The project developed the water distribution and supply facility under a design–build–finance–operate–maintain–transfer model (footnote 50).

Several project structure innovations were adopted for the successful bidding of the project, including the following:

- Flexibility for phased development of the project to allow for optimal asset utilization;
- Optimal determination of bulk water source through a combination of deep tube wells and a tie-up to another bulk water project, helping RAJUK avoid unnecessary capital expenditure and associated delays;
- Hybrid annuity PPP model to reduce demand risks and incentivize operational efficiencies and the use of high-quality materials. Under this model, about $36 million (almost 50% of the project capital cost) will be reimbursed to the private sector through construction-linked milestone payments, incentivizing quality construction and lowering the fixed annuity payments to the operator over the life of the contract, with payments based on achieving important key performance indicators;
- Bankable structure with provisions for an escrow, an irrevocable letter of credit mechanism, international arbitration, and an independent engineer;
- Fully automated operations and maintenance to ensure an uninterrupted supply of pressurized potable water that meets World Health Organization and national quality standards; and
- Setting of water tariffs remaining with public authorities (RAJUK) to ensure affordability for consumers, with the private partner billing and collecting from consumers (footnote 50).

After a competitive bidding process, the United Water Delcot Limited—a consortium of the United Water Suqian Limited (China) and Delcot Limited (Bangladesh)—won the bid and signed a contract on 11 November 2019 with RAJUK. The project is expected to develop a water distribution network and supply facilities with a capacity to produce 340 MLD of potable water to ensure uninterrupted piped water to the occupants of the new township. The project will be developed in four phases, with the first phase to be commissioned by December 2020 (footnote 50).

Table 41 shows an indicative risk-sharing matrix for the project.

Table 41: Risk-Sharing Matrix for RAJUK Water Project

Risk Category	Private	Public	Shared
Financing			✓
Traffic		✓	
Revenue		✓	
Operations and maintenance	✓		
Approvals		✓	

Project Finance

The government had given its support by way of partial payment of the capital cost (hybrid annuity). The remaining financing was to be arranged by a private sector player. The project was implemented with the financial support of DevCo, a multidonor facility affiliated with the Private Infrastructure Development Group. DevCo provides critical financial support for important infrastructure transactions in the poorest countries, helping boost economic growth and combat poverty. DevCo is funded by the United Kingdom's Department for International Development, the Austrian Development Agency, the Dutch Ministry of Foreign Affairs, Swedish International Development Cooperation Agency, and IFC (footnote 50).

Project Construction

The project construction is in four phases, with the final phase expected to be completed in 2023. Apart from establishing 15 deep tube wells, water pipes will be laid along a 320-kilometer road alignment by the developer.[51] The total construction period is 4 years.

Project Revenues

The project adopted a hybrid annuity model whereby the private sector player is initially supported by providing partial capital cost up front, and the remaining payments are paid in the performance-based annuity payment model during the concession period.

Annuity payments would be for a period of 11 years, with a project timeline of 15 years (concession period).[52]

---

[51]   *Xinhua News.* 2019. China–Bangladesh Joint Venture to Implement Dhaka's Mega Purbachal New Town Water Project. 12 November. http://www.xinhuanet.com/english/2019-11/12/c_138548688.htm.

[52]   *The Daily Star.* 2020. Purbachal's Water Supply to be under Private Sector. 9 January. https://www.thedailystar.net/business/news/purbachals-water-supply-be-under-private-sector-1851550.

Expected Project Outcomes

The project will ensure uninterrupted access to high-quality piped water, impacting the public health of about 250,000 people by 2023 and 1.5 million people over the next 15–20 years when the township reaches full occupation (footnote 50).

The 24/7 clean water supply for township residents will meet World Health Organization quality standards, which exceed national standards, establishing a new benchmark for water projects in Bangladesh (footnote 50).

The project facilitated $36 million of foreign direct investment in Bangladesh (footnote 50).

Key Lessons

The following key lessons have been learned from the project:

- Undertaking strong feasibility studies and understanding the key issues at the ground level help bring successful transactions.

- Each project requires customized project structure depending on several factors such as regulatory framework, appetite of the private sector, and available financing support in the country. The RAJUK water project took several of these factors into consideration in designing a successful project.

- Protections offered for private sector players have largely contributed to ensuring investor confidence. In the case of this project, mechanisms such as provisions for an escrow, an irrevocable letter of credit mechanism, international arbitration, and an independent engineer helped instill investor confidence.

Appendixes

Appendix 1: Critical Macroeconomic and Infrastructure Sector Indicators for Bangladesh

The various macroeconomic and infrastructure sector indicators for Bangladesh are provided in the table below.

Parameter	Value	Unit
Total population	167.37	million
Average annual population growth rate	1.3	%
Population density	1,134	persons per km² of surface area
Urban population	36.6	% of total population
Surface area	147.63	'000 km²
Unemployment rate	4.2	%
Proportion of population below $1.90 purchasing power parity a day	14.8	%
Nominal GDP	302.57	$ billion
Annual growth rate of GDP (2019)	8.2	%
Annual growth rate of GDP (2020 forecast)	4.5	%
Annual growth rate of GDP (2021 forecast)	7.5	%
GDP at purchasing power parity per capita	3,870.00	$ at purchasing power parity
GDP at current market prices	249.10	$ billion
Gross fixed investment at current market prices	30.5	% of GDP
Per capita gross national income, Atlas Method	1,750.00	$
Inflation rate (2019)	5.5	%
Inflation rate (2020 forecast)	5.6	%
Inflation rate (2021 forecast)	5.5	%
Current account (2019)	(1.7)	% of GDP
External trade, goods, value of imports, CIF (2018)	41.20	$ billion
External trade, goods, value of exports, FOB (2018)	30.20	$ billion

continued on next page

continued from previous page

Parameter	Value	Unit
CPI % change in 2018	5.6	%
Real effective exchange rate	84.95	
Investment in energy with private sector participation	170.00	current $ million
Investment in transport with private sector participation	NA	current $ million
Investment in water and sanitation with private sector participation	NA	current $ million
Logistics Performance Index rank (out of 100)	2.58	no.
Logistics Performance Index score (out of 5)	2.58	no.
Customs rank (out of 160)	121	no.
Customs score (out of 5)	2.30	no.
Infrastructure rank (out of 160)	100	no.
Infrastructure score (out of 5)	2.39	no.
International shipments rank (out of 160)	104	no.
International shipments score (out of 5)	2.56	no.
Logistics competence rank (out of 160)	102	no.
Logistics competence score (out of 5)	2.48	no.
Tracking and tracing rank (out of 160)	79	no.
Tracking and tracing score (out of 5)	2.79	no.
Timeliness rank (out of 160)	107	no.
Timeliness score (out of 5)	2.92	no.
Structure of Output (% of GDP at current producer | basic prices)		
Agriculture	13.8	%
Industry	30.2	%
Services	56.0	%
CPI (national)	5.8	% annual change
Producer price index	UA	% annual change
Wholesale price index (national)	UA	% annual change
Retail price index	UA	% annual change
Exchange rates (end of period)	83.90	local currency – $
Asian Development Fund Portfolio		
Total number of loans	65	no.
1. Sovereign	63	no.
2. Nonsovereign	2	no.
Net loan amount	6,231.00	$ million, cumulative
1. Sovereign	6,143.90	$ million, cumulative
2. Nonsovereign	87.10	$ million, cumulative

continued on next page

continued from previous page

Parameter	Value	Unit
Disbursed amount	N/A	$ million, cumulative
1. Sovereign	2,383.40	$ million, cumulative
2. Nonsovereign	75.50	$ million, cumulative
Net foreign direct investment inflows	0.9	% of GDP
Sovereign debt risk rating	45.0	letter rating
Central government debt	27.1	% of GDP
CPIA quality of budgetary and financial management rating	3.0	1=low to 6=high
Ease of Doing Business (rank out of 190 economies)		
Ease of doing business (overall rank)	168	no.
Starting a business	131	no.
Dealing with construction permits	135	no.
Getting electricity	176	no.
Registering property	184	no.
Getting credit	119	no.
Protecting minority investors	72	no.
Paying taxes	151	no.
Trading across borders	176	no.
Enforcing contracts	189	no.
Resolving insolvency	154	no.
Corruption and Sustainable Development Index		
Corruption Perceptions Index rank (out of 180)	146	no.
Corruption Perceptions Index score (out of 100)	26	no.
Sustainable Development Index rank	109	no.
Sustainable Development Index score	63.51	no.
Cumulative Lending, Grant, and Technical Assistance Commitments		
Number of projects	755	no.
Total lending	22,944.68	$ million
GCI infrastructure score (out of 7)	2.9	no.
EIU Infrascope Index Score		
PPP regulations rank (out of 21)	8	no.
PPP regulations score (out of 100)	65	no.
PPP institutions rank (out of 21)	6	no.
PPP institutions score (out of 100)	90	no.
PPP market maturity rank (out of 21)	4	no.
PPP market maturity score (out of 100)	71	no.

continued on next page

continued from previous page

Parameter	Value	Unit
PPP financing rank (out of 21)	9	no.
PPP financing score (out of 100)	47	no.
Investment and business climate rank (out of 21)	17	no.
Investment and business climate score (out of 100)	56	no.

( ) = negative; CIF = cost, insurance, and freight; CPI = consumer price index; CPIA = Country Policy and Institutional Assessment; EIU = Economist Intelligence Unit; FOB = freight on board; GCI = global competitive index; GDP = gross domestic product; km² = square kilometer; NA = not applicable; PPP = public–private partnership; UA = unavailable.

Sources: Asian Development Bank (ADB). 2016. *Country Partnership Strategy: Bangladesh, 2016–2020*. Manila. https://www.adb.org/sites/default/files/institutional-document/198831/cps-ban-2016-2020.pdf; ADB. 2019. *Key Indicators for Asia and Pacific 2019*. Manila. https://www.adb.org/publications/key-indicators-asia-and-pacific-2019; ADB. 2020. *Basic Statistics 2020*. Manila. https://www.adb.org/publications/basic-statistics-2020; ADB. Cumulative Lending, Grant, and Technical Assistance Commitments. https://data.adb.org/dataset/cumulative-lending-grant-and-technical-assistance-commitments; ADB. GDP Growth in Asia and the Pacific, Asian Development Outlook (ADO). https://data.adb.org/dataset/gdp-growth-asia-and-pacific-asian-development-outlook; International Monetary Fund (IMF). Exchange Rate Selected Indicators. https://data.imf.org/regular.aspx?key=61545850 (accessed 21 October 2020); IMF. IMF eLibrary Data by Country. https://data.imf.org/?sk=85b51b5a-b74f-473a-be16-49f1786949b3 (accessed 21 October 2020); PPP Knowledge Lab. Bangladesh. https://pppknowledgelab.org/countries/bangladesh; The Economist Intelligence Unit. Bangladesh. https://infrascope.eiu.com/; Transparency International. Countries. https://www.transparency.org/en/countries/bangladesh#; World Bank. 2020. *Doing Business 2020: Economy Profile–Bangladesh*. Washington, DC. https://www.doingbusiness.org/content/dam/doingBusiness/country/b/bangladesh/BGD.pdf; and World Bank. LPI Rankings 2018. https://lpi.worldbank.org/international/global?sort=asc&order=LPI%20Score#datatable.

Appendix 2: World Bank's Ease of Doing Business Parameters for Bangladesh

Table A2.1: Bangladesh Basic Country Profile

Ease of Doing Business in Bangladesh	Region	South Asia	Doing Business Rank: 168	Doing Business Score: 45
	Income category	Lower-middle income		
	Population	165,443,600[a]		
	Cities covered	Dhaka, Chittagong		

[a] Worldometer. Bangladesh Population. https://www.worldometers.info/world-population/bangladesh-population/ (accessed 13 December 2020).

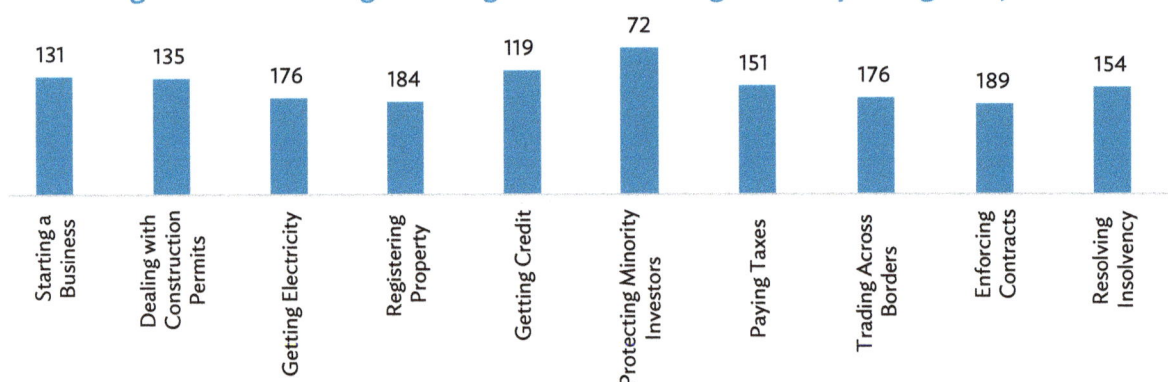

Figure A2.1: Ranking on Doing Business in Bangladesh by Categories, 2020

Notes: The Doing Business project by the World Bank provides objective measures of business regulations and their enforcement across 190 economies and selected cities at the subnational and regional level. The rank represents the ranking of the country on each of these parameters against the 190 economies that are evaluated under the project.
Source: World Bank. 2020. *Doing Business 2020: Economy Profile–Bangladesh*. Washington, DC. https://www.doingbusiness.org/content/dam/doingBusiness/country/b/bangladesh/BGD.pdf.

Figure A2.2: Scoring on Doing Business in Bangladesh by Categories, 2020

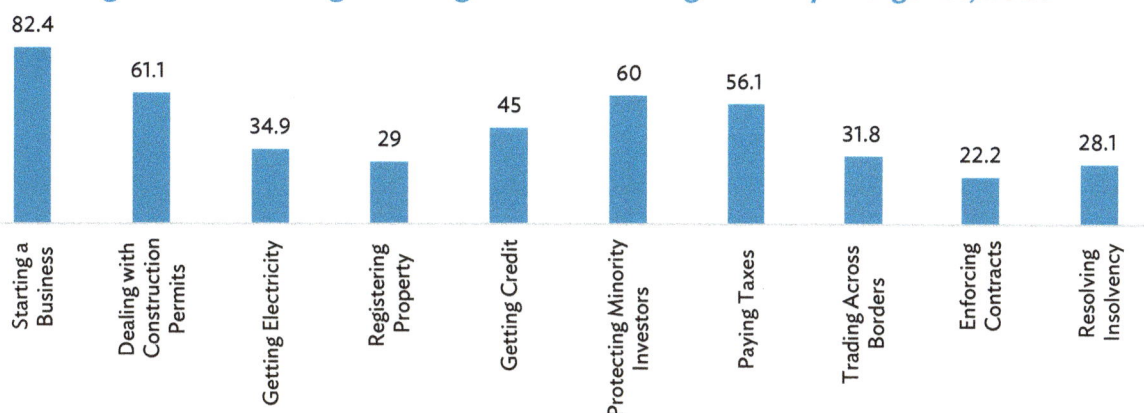

Notes: The World Bank Doing Business scores represent the value assigned to each parameter based on the evaluation done by the World Bank. As noted by the World Bank, the ease of doing business score aids in assessing the absolute level of regulatory performance and how it improves over time. The individual indicator scores show the distance of each economy from the best regulatory performance observed in each of the indicators across all economies in the Doing Business. Scores are against a highest possible score of 100.
Source: World Bank. 2020. *Doing Business 2020: Economy Profile–Bangladesh*. Washington, DC. https://www.doingbusiness.org/content/dam/doingBusiness/country/b/bangladesh/BGD.pdf.

Table A2.2: Scores on Doing Business in Bangladesh, by Categories and Subcategories, 2020

Starting a Business (rank)	131	Dealing with Construction Permits (rank)	135	Getting Electricity (rank)	176	Registering Property (rank)	184
Score of starting a business (0–100)	**82.4**	Score of dealing with construction permits (0–100)	**61.1**	Score of getting electricity (0–100)	**34.9**	Score of registering property (0–100)	**29.0**
Procedures (no.)	9	Procedures (no.)	16	Procedures (no.)	9	Procedures (no.)	8
Time (days)	19.5	Time (days)	274	Time (days)	125	Time (days)	271
Cost (no.)	8.7	Cost (% of warehouse value)	1.6	Cost (% of income per capita)	1745.8	Cost (% of property value)	7.1
Paid-in minimum capital (% of income per capita)	0.0	Building quality control index (0–15)	10	Reliability of supply and transparency of tariff index (0–8)	0	Quality of the land administration index (0–30)	6.5

continued on next page

Table A2.2 *continued*

Getting Credit (rank)	119	Protecting Minority Investors (rank)	72	Paying Taxes (rank)	151
Score of getting credit (0–100)	*45.0*	Score of protecting minority investors (0–100)	*60.0*	Score of paying taxes (0–100)	*56.1*
Strength of legal rights index (0–12)	5	Extent of disclosure index (0–10)	6.0	Payments (no. per year)	33
Depth of credit information index (0–8)	4	Extent of director liability index (0–10)	7.0	Time (hours per year)	435
Credit registry coverage (% of adults)	5.2	Ease of shareholder suits index (0–10)	7.0	Total tax and contribution rate (% of profit)	33.4
Credit bureau coverage (% of adults)	0.0	Extent of shareholder rights index (0–6)	4.0	Post filing index (0–100)	44.4
		Extent of ownership and control index (0–7)	3.0		
		Extent of corporate transparency index (0–7)	3.0		

Trading across Borders (rank)	176	Enforcing Contracts (rank)	189	Resolving Insolvency (rank)	154
Score of trading across borders (0–100)	*31.8*	Score of enforcing contracts (0–100)	*22.2*	Score of resolving insolvency (0–100)	*28.1*
Time to export		Time (days)	1,442	Recovery rate ($ cent)	29.1
Documentary compliance	147	Cost (% of claim value)	66.8	Time (years)	4.0
Border compliance	168	Quality of judicial processes index (0–18)	7.5	Cost (% of estate)	8.0
Cost to export				Outcome (0 as piecemeal sale and 1 as going concern)	0
Documentary compliance	225			Strength of insolvency framework index (0–16)	4.0
Border compliance	408				
*Time to **Import***					
Documentary compliance	144				
Border Compliance	216				
*Cost to **Import***					
Documentary compliance	370				
Border compliance	900				

Source: World Bank. 2020. *Doing Business 2020: Economy Profile–Bangladesh.* Washington, DC. https://www.doingbusiness.org/content/dam/doingBusiness/country/b/bangladesh/BGD.pdf.

Appendix 3: Assessment of the Public Financial Management System in Bangladesh, 2016

In the latest assessment of the Public Financial Management System (PFMS) in Bangladesh, done in 2016 and based on the Public Expenditure and Financial Accountability (PEFA) framework, the country had an **overall rating of C+**, on a four-point rating scale of A (best) to D (worst), for transfers from the national government to the subnational governments.[1]

Parameter / Subparameter	Score	Justification for Score
Transfers to subnational governments	**C+**	**Most of the transfers to subnational governments are based on clearly defined set of rules, procedures, and timing of the information provided to the subnational governments.** In addition to rule-based systems, local governments can submit development project proposals to the Planning Commission; those successful will qualify for cofinancing by the central government. Decisions on qualifying projects are initially made by the Planning Commission, but the final decision rests on the Executive Council of the National Economic Council (Planning Council).
• System for allocating transfers	C	The horizontal allocation of a majority of transfers to subnational governments from the central government is determined by transparent, rule-based systems. Formula transfers represent just over 51% of all transfers.
• Timeliness of information on transfers	D	The bulk of financial transfers are provided alongside the first reliable information on size of the transfer 2 months into the fiscal year.

Notes: The Public Financial Management and Accountability Assessment report, developed by the World Bank and other development partners, comprises scoring of various indicators and rates them from A to D. Ratings of A to D as per criteria stated in the Public Expenditure and Financial Accountability (PEFA) framework are broadly interpreted as follows:
A = represents performance that meets good international practice—the criteria for the indicator are met in a complete, orderly, accurate, timely, and coordinated way.
B = typically represents a level of performance ranging from good to medium by international standards.
C = represents a level of performance ranging from medium to poor.
D = represents either that a process or procedure does not exist at all, or that it is not functioning effectively.
Source: PEFA. 2016. *Bangladesh: Public Expenditure and Financial Accountability, Public Financial Management Performance Report.* Dhaka. https://www.pefa.org/node/506.

As of 2016, the PEFA assessment of the PFMS in Bangladesh is as follows:

Parameter	Value	Unit
Central government transfers to subnational governments	UA	% of the GDP
Actual budgetary allocation to subnational governments from the national government[a]	7	% of total expenditure
Deviation of actual against the budgeted transfers to subnational governments	UA	% of budgeted transfers

GDP = gross domestic product, UA = unavailable.
[a] Includes transfers to local government and rural development.
Source: Public Expenditure and Financial Accountability. 2016. *Bangladesh: Public Expenditure and Financial Accountability, Public Financial Management Performance Report.* Dhaka. https://www.pefa.org/node/506.

[1] PEFA. 2016. *Bangladesh: Public Expenditure and Financial Accountability, Public Financial Management Performance Report.* Dhaka. https://www.pefa.org/node/506.

References

Asian Development Bank (ADB). 2016. *Country Partnership Strategy: Bangladesh, 2016–2020.* Manila. https://www.adb.org/sites/default/files/institutional-document/198831/cps-ban-2016-2020.pdf.

———. 2019. *Key Indicators for Asia and the Pacific 2019.* Manila. https://www.adb.org/publications/key-indicators-asia-and-pacific-2019.

———. 2019. *Public–Private Partnership Monitor.* Second Edition. Manila. https://www.adb.org/sites/default/files/publication/509426/ppp-monitor-second-edition.pdf.

———. 2020. *Basic Statistics 2020.* Manila. https://www.adb.org/publications/basic-statistics-2020.

———. Bangladesh: Strengthening Bangladesh Infrastructure Finance Fund Limited Project. https://www.adb.org/projects/51311-001/main.

———. Cumulative Lending, Grant, and Technical Assistance Commitments. https://data.adb.org/dataset/cumulative-lending-grant-and-technical-assistance-commitments.

———. GDP Growth in Asia and the Pacific, Asian Development Outlook (ADO). https://data.adb.org/dataset/gdp-growth-asia-and-pacific-asian-development-outlook.

Bangladesh Bank. Bangladesh. https://www.bb.org.bd/aboutus/dept/dept_details.

———. *Financial Stability Report 2018.* Issue 9. Dhaka. https://www.bb.org.bd/pub/puball.php.

Bangladesh Bridge Authority. BBA at a Glance. http://www.bba.gov.bd/site/page/d27d493c-4aa1-4ce1-a932-452ec2a5665b/-.

———. Toll Rate Bangabandhu Bridge (last updated 13 March 2017). www.bba.gov.bd/site/page/4093c137-8d48-46db-a1cb-54aaf5924a5c/-.

Bangladesh Computer Council. Welcome to BCC. https://bcc.gov.bd/site/page/01cbf22a-b9f5-4a67-829e-55c27ab216f6/-.

Bangladesh Hi-Tech Park Authority. About Us. http://bhtpa.gov.bd/site/page/b75f7889-05c8-446e-9a7b-8e5d1e2f339a/-.

Bangladesh Infrastructure Finance Fund Limited. About BIFFL. https://biffl.org.bd/.

Bangladesh Inland Water Transport Corporation. Activities of BIWTC. http://www.biwtc.gov.bd/site/page/ee1d42bc-a763-4bc1-b4ce-f2dce4a8c1e0/- .

Bangladesh Inland Waterways Authority. Background and Creation. http://www.biwta.gov.bd/site/page/fe5ad955-65b9-42d0-89a1-e40195261dae/-.

Bangladesh Railway. At a Glance. https://railway.portal.gov.bd/site/page/ce7dd6af-c7c8-4811-86b3-ba871e2e406e/At-a-Glance.

——. Master Plan of Bangladesh Railway. https://railway.portal.gov.bd/site/page/8e5a704d-72e2-4d69-b443-21988229cbbc/Future-Plan.

Bangladesh Securities and Exchange Commission. List of Credit Rating Agencies. https://www.sec.gov.bd/home/cragency.

Bangladesh Shipping Corporation. History. https://bsc.portal.gov.bd/.

Center for Policy Dialogue. 2020. *An Analysis of the National Budget for FY2020-21*. Dhaka. https://cpd.org.bd/wp-content/uploads/2020/06/CPD-Budget-Analysis-FY2021.pdf.

Chattogram Water Supply and Sewerage Authority. Bangladesh. Water Tariff. http://ctg-wasa.org.bd/site/page/69b086be-cf2d-48b4-96f4-49e7790cb664/- (accessed 16 July 2020).

Chittagong Port Authority. Functions of CPA. http://www.cpa.gov.bd/site/page/420f02c4-44a2-42bc-8a53-d747921a7a90/-.

Civil Aviation Authority of Bangladesh (CAAB). Flight Safety Regulations. http://caab.portal.gov.bd/site/page/c49efdae-7d58-4a91-9895-aea173abacb0/-.

——. Primary Aviation Legislation. http://caab.portal.gov.bd/site/page/c22eb144-f662-46fd-bb67-6bf6d26ef630/-.

Commonwealth Local Government Forum. 2018. *The Local Government System in Bangladesh: Country Profile 2017-18*. Dhaka. http://www.clgf.org.uk/default/assets/File/Country_profiles/Bangladesh.pdf.

The Daily Star. 2020. Purbachal's Water Supply to be under Private Sector. 9 January. Dhaka. https://www.thedailystar.net/business/news/purbachals-water-supply-be-under-private-sector-1851550.

DFDL. 2018. *Bangladesh Investment Guide, 2018*. Dhaka. https://www.dfdl.com/resources/publications/investment-guides/bangladesh-investment-guide-2018/.

Dhaka North City Corporation. Funding Sources. http://www.dncc.gov.bd/site/page/52fff120-67c2-4f99-bf65-4bf9a4e6d4ff/Funding-Sources.

Digital Security Agency. About DSA. http://dsa.gov.bd/.

Doing Business. Getting Electricity. https://www.doingbusiness.org/en/data/doing-business-score?topic=getting-electricity.

The Economist Intelligence Unit. 2018. Infrascope: Bangladesh Country Report. https://infrascope.eiu.com.

The Global Economy. Compare Countries. https://www.theglobaleconomy.com/compare-countries/.

——. Education Spending, Percent of Government Spending—Country Rankings. https://www.theglobaleconomy.com/rankings/Education_spending_percent_of_government_spending/.

——. Energy Imports. https://www.theglobaleconomy.com/rankings/Energy_imports/.

——. Health Spending per Capita—Country Rankings. https://www.theglobaleconomy.com/rankings/Health_spending_per_capita/.

———. Internet Bandwidth. https://www.theglobaleconomy.com/rankings/Internet_bandwidth/.

———. Internet Subscribers. https://www.theglobaleconomy.com/rankings/Internet_subscribers_per_100_people/.

———. Mobile Network Coverage. https://www.theglobaleconomy.com/rankings/Mobile_network_coverage/.

———. Mobile Phone Subscribers. https://www.theglobaleconomy.com/rankings/Mobile_phone_subscribers_per_100_people/.

———. Port Traffic—Country Rankings. https://www.theglobaleconomy.com/rankings/Port_traffic/.

———. Railroad Infrastructure Quality—Country Rankings. https://www.theglobaleconomy.com/rankings/railroad_quality/.

———. Railway Passengers—Country Rankings. https://www.theglobaleconomy.com/rankings/railway_passengers/.

———. Railway Transport of Goods—Country Rankings. https://www.theglobaleconomy.com/rankings/Railway_transport_of_goods/.

———. Share of Clean Energy—Country Rankings. https://www.theglobaleconomy.com/rankings/share_of_clean_energy/.

Government of Bangladesh, Department of Information and Communication Technology (ICT). 2018. *National ICT Policy 2018.* Dhaka. https://ictd.gov.bd/site/view/policies/Policy-.

———. History and Functions. https://ictd.gov.bd/site/page/ab439356-145f-4759-942d-39ea506ff144/History-&-Main-Function.

———. Laws and Regulations. https://ictd.gov.bd/site/view/law/Acts-.

———. Proposed Projects. http://doict.portal.gov.bd/site/page/443a0f0a-168a-482a-9376-85a5045668d2/-.

Government of Bangladesh, Department of Power. Work Plan of the Power Department. https://powerdivision.gov.bd/site/page/5abb0723-5119-410a-9036-9eb99c91a0c7/Major-Functiion.

Government of Bangladesh, Department of Shipping. About Us. http://dos.gov.bd/site/page/e847ba4b-8b44-4fa1-8d6f-4d5a8292f5e2/-.

Government of Bangladesh, National Housing Authority. History and Responsibilities. http://www.nha.gov.bd/site/page/f2616672-9261-4b18-8571-4cfde9ae85e4/-.

Government of Bangladesh, Public Private Partnership Authority. 2010. *Policy and Strategy for Public–Private Partnership (PPP), 2010.* Dhaka. http://www.pppo.gov.bd/download/ppp_office/Policy-Strategy-for-PPP-Aug2010.pdf.

———. 2012. *Remarkable Progress Achieved in the Country's PPP Preparation.* Dhaka. http://www.pppo.gov.bd/download/ppp_office/Remarkable-Progress-Achieved-PPP-Preparation.pdf.

———. 2013. *PPP Screening Manual.* Dhaka. http://www.pppo.gov.bd/download/ppp_office/PPP-Screening-Manual_Final-Draft_09April2013.pdf.

———. 2015. *PPP Act 2015.* Dhaka. http://www.pppo.gov.bd/download/ppp_office/PPP-Law-2015.pdf.

———. 2017. *Policy for Implementing PPP Projects through Government to Government (G2G) Partnership, 2017.* Dhaka. http://www.pppo.gov.bd/download/ppp_office/Policy_G2G_Partnership-2017.pdf.

———. 2018. *Guidelines for Unsolicited Proposals, 2018.* Dhaka. http://www.pppo.gov.bd/download/ppp_office/Guidelines-for-Unsolicited-Proposals-2018.pdf.

———. 2018. *Recent Experience of Establishing a PPP Framework to Mitigate Fiscal Risks in Bangladesh.* Presentation for Tokyo Fiscal Forum 2018. 4 June. https://www.mof.go.jp/pri/research/seminar/fy2018/tff2018_s3_03.pdf.

———. 2018. *Procurement Guidelines for PPP Projects.* Dhaka. http://www.pppo.gov.bd/download/ppp_office/Procurement-Guideline-for-PPP-Projects-2018.pdf.

———. 2018. *Rules for Public–Private Partnership Technical Assistance Financing, 2018.* Dhaka. http://www.pppo.gov.bd/download/ppp_office/Rules-for-PPPTAF-2018.pdf.

———. 2018. *Rules for Viability Gap Financing for Public–Private Partnership Projects, 2018.* Dhaka. http://www.pppo.gov.bd/download/ppp_office/Rules-for-VGF-for-PPP-Projects-2018.pdf.

———. Annual Report 2018-19. http://www.pppo.gov.bd/annual_report.php.

———. Government Policy. http://www.pppo.gov.bd/government_policy.php.

———. MOF PPP Unit. http://www.pppo.gov.bd/mof_ppp_unit.php#:~:text=Public%20Private%20Partnership%20Authority%20Bangladesh&text=The%20Finance%20Division%20of%20the,for%20their%20development%20and%20financing.

———. *Policy and Strategy for Public–Private Partnership, 2010.* Dhaka. http://www.pppo.gov.bd/download/ppp_office/Policy-Strategy-for-PPP-Aug2010.pdf.

———. PPP Projects. http://www.pppo.gov.bd/projects.php.

———. Your Guide to PPP in Bangladesh. https://www.pppo.gov.bd/download/ppp_office/Your-Guide-to-PPP-in-Bangladesh.pdf.

Government of Bangladesh, Roads and Highways Department. Overview of RHD. https://rhd.portal.gov.bd/site/page/b34dca5c-5352-4fd2-9533-715058f45951/-.

M. H. Habib. 2021. The International Arbitration Review: Bangladesh. *The Law Reviews.* 4 July. https://thelawreviews.co.uk/title/the-internationalarbitration-review/bangladesh.

Inframation Group. Country Factbook—Bangladesh. https://www.inframationnews.com/country-factbook/3747026/bangladesh.thtml.

Infrastructure Development Company Limited. About IDCOL. https://idcol.org/home/about.

International Finance Corporation. *PPP Stories: Bangladesh—RAJUK Water.* Washington, DC: World Bank. https://www.ifc.org/wps/wcm/connect/f4c491c6-8f44-41b0-a940-bad27d33629a/Rajuk+Water+PPP+Story.pdf?MOD=AJPERES&CVID=naxbsGL.

International Monetary Fund (IMF). Exchange Rate Selected Indicators. https://data.imf.org/regular.aspx?key=61545850.

————. IMF Data Access to Macroeconomic and Financial Data. https://data.imf.org/?sk=85b51b5a-b74f-473a-be16-49f1786949b3.

Ministry of Finance, Finance Division. 2019. *Bangladesh Economic Review 2019*. Dhaka. https://mof.portal.gov.bd/sites/default/files/files/mof.portal.gov.bd/page/e8bc0eaa_463d_4cf9_b3be_26ab70a32a47/Banglades%20Economic%20Review%202019%20Eng.zip.

Ministry of Law, Justice and Parliamentary Affairs, Bangladesh. 1851. *The Tolls Act, 1851*. https://rthd.portal.gov.bd/sites/default/files/files/rthd.portal.gov.bd/law/b777dc03_adef_4c24_8383_38220da8d009/1.%20Toll_Act.pdf.

Ministry of Local Government, Rural Development and Cooperatives; Local Government Division. 2011. *Sector Development Plan (FY 2011-2025): Water Supply and Sanitation Sector in Bangladesh*. Dhaka. http://psb.gov.bd/policies/sdpwsssbe.pdf.

————. 2014. *National Strategy for Water Supply and Sanitation, 2014*. Dhaka. https://www.who.int/globalchange/resources/wash-toolkit/national-strategy-for-water-supply-and-sanitation-bangladesh.pdf?ua=1.

————. 2018. *Municipal Public Finance Scenario in Bangladesh*. Dhaka. https://www.unescap.org/sites/default/files/BANGLADESH_presentation.pdf.

Ministry of Planning, Planning Commission, Programming Division. 2018. *Local Government and Rural Development: Sector Strategy Paper*. Dhaka. https://plandiv.portal.gov.bd/sites/default/files/files/plandiv.portal.gov.bd/publications/0c526c77_bb8b_42fe_99d7_f6c217986e77/LGRD-SSP.pdf.

Ministry of Power, Energy and Mineral Resources. 2016. *Power System Master Plan 2016*. Dhaka. https://mpemr.gov.bd/assets/media/pdffiles/FR_PSMP_revised.pdf.

Ministry of Railways. Organization. https://mor.gov.bd/site/page/e063678a-4897-4e07-b9c8-85b6e956ed27/Department-of-inspections-of-Railway.

Ministry of Road Transport and Bridges, Road Transport and Highways Division. Megaprojects. http://103.48.18.161/mega_project.php.

————. Projects. https://rthd.portal.gov.bd/.

Ministry of Shipping. Acts. https://mos.portal.gov.bd/site/view/law/Acts-&-Ordinance.

————. Background. https://mos.portal.gov.bd/site/page/3c024802-0fbf-4479-a977-b169d3d3cb9a/Background.

Power Cell. Coal Based Megaproject. https://powercell.portal.gov.bd/site/page/e35bd93a-c1ba-45b3-b7c2-21a0e035df30/-.

PPP Knowledge Lab. Bangladesh. https://pppknowledgelab.org/countries/bangladesh.

Private Infrastructure Development Group, GuarantCo, and Technical Assistance Facility. 2019. *Study of Bangladesh Bond Market*. Dhaka. https://guarantco.com/gco/wp-content/uploads/2019/Documents/news/Study-of-Bangladesh-Bond-Market.pdf.

Public Expenditure and Financial Accountability. 2016. *Bangladesh: Public Expenditure and Financial Accountability, Public Financial Management Performance Report*. Dhaka. https://www.pefa.org/node/506.

Sustainable and Renewable Energy Development Authority. SREDA at a Glance. http://www.sreda.gov.bd/index. php/site/page/14eb-6e9e-27c2-bd05-9e73-9ed4-4137-8a1e-9432-6e41.

Thomson Reuters, Practical Law. Project Finance in Bangladesh: Overview. https://uk.practicallaw.thomsonreuters. com/Document/I4a320d6517c111e89bf099c0ee06c731/View/FullText.html?transitionType=SearchItem& contextData=(sc.Search).

Trading Economics. Bangladesh—Mobile and Fixed Line Telephone Subscribers. https://tradingeconomics.com/ bangladesh/mobile-and-fixed-line-telephone-subscribers-wb-data.html.

———. Bangladesh—Roads Total Network. https://tradingeconomics.com/bangladesh/roads-total-network-km-wb-data.html.

Transparency International. Countries. https://www.transparency.org/en/countries/bangladesh#.

United Cities and Local Governments. 2016. *Subnational Governments around the World—Structure and Finance.* https://www.uclg.org/sites/default/files/global_observatory_of_local_finance-part_iii.pdf.

US Department of State. 2020. 2020 Investment Climate Statements: Bangladesh. https://www.state.gov/ reports/2020-investment-climate-statements/bangladesh/.

World Bank. 2020. *Doing Business 2020: Economy Profile–Bangladesh.* Washington, DC. https://www. doingbusiness.org/content/dam/doingBusiness/country/b/bangladesh/BGD.pdf.

———. Access to Electricity. https://data.worldbank.org/indicator/EG.ELC.ACCS.ZS?locations=BD.

———. Air Transport, Passengers Carried. https://data.worldbank.org/indicator/is.air.psgr?locations=bd-kh-ge-kz-mm-pk-pg-lk-uz-vn-cn-in-id-ph-th.

———. Bangladesh Government Expenditure on Education. https://data.worldbank.org/indicator/SE.XPD.TOTL. GD.ZS?locations=BD.

———. Cell Phone Subscribers. https://data.worldbank.org/indicator/IT.CEL.SETS.P2?locations=BD.

———. Infrastructure Finance, PPPs and Guarantees. Country Snapshots. Bangladesh. https://ppi.worldbank.org/ en/snapshots/country/bangladesh.

———. Internet Subscribers. https://data.worldbank.org/indicator/IT.NET.USER.ZS?locations=BD.

———. Procuring Infrastructure Public–Private Partnerships 2018 in Bangladesh.

World Port Source. Ports. http://www.worldportsource.com/countries.php.

Xinhua News. 2019. China–Bangladesh Joint Venture to Implement Dhaka's Mega Purbachal New Town Water Project. 12 November. http://www.xinhuanet.com/english/2019-11/12/c_138548688.htm.

www.ingramcontent.com/pod-product-compliance
Lightning Source LLC
Chambersburg PA
CBHW050043220326
41599CB00045B/7267